ORGANIZING VULNERABILITY

Melissa Tyler

First published in Great Britain in 2026 by

Bristol University Press
University of Bristol
1–9 Old Park Hill
Bristol
BS2 8BB
UK
t: +44 (0)117 374 6645
e: bup-info@bristol.ac.uk

Details of international sales and distribution partners are available at bristoluniversitypress.co.uk

© Bristol University Press 2026

DOI: 10.51952/9781529238983

British Library Cataloguing in Publication Data
A catalogue record for this book is available from the British Library

ISBN 978-1-5292-3895-2 hardcover
ISBN 978-1-5292-3896-9 paperback
ISBN 978-1-5292-3897-6 ePub
ISBN 978-1-5292-3898-3 ePdf

The right of Melissa Tyler to be identified as author of this work has been asserted by her in accordance with the Copyright, Designs and Patents Act 1988.

All rights reserved: no part of this publication may be reproduced, stored in a retrieval system, or transmitted in any form or by any means, electronic, mechanical, photocopying, recording, or otherwise without the prior permission of Bristol University Press.

Every reasonable effort has been made to obtain permission to reproduce copyrighted material. If, however, anyone knows of an oversight, please contact the publisher.

The statements and opinions contained within this publication are solely those of the author and not of the University of Bristol or Bristol University Press. The University of Bristol and Bristol University Press disclaim responsibility for any injury to persons or property resulting from any material published in this publication.

Bristol University Press works to counter discrimination on grounds of gender, race, disability, age and sexuality.

Cover design: Lyn Davies Design
Front cover image: iStock/DNY59

Contents

Acknowledgements		iv
Introduction: Being Vulnerable in Relation to One Another		1
1	Vulnerability and/as Organization	16
2	Existing: The Social Relations of Breathing	49
3	Enduring: The Social Relations of Grieving	70
4	Enacting: The Social Relations of Appearing	90
5	Towards a Radical Vulnerability: Organizing for Workable Lives	115
Notes		150
References		166
Index		176

Acknowledgements

While working on this book, I was invited to give seminars at various universities and research centres in the United Kingdom and Europe and I am very grateful to everyone involved for giving me the opportunity to share emerging ideas, and to be able to develop these with the benefit of their thoughtful and critical questions and suggestions. I am especially grateful to members of the Judith Butler network and reading group. Our regular meetings have provided nourishment and encouragement and have given me so much to think and read about.

In 2024 and 2025, I was very lucky to hold a visiting scholarship at the University of Verona. While there, I was able to spend time with academics in several research centres, including the Hannah Arendt Centre for Political Studies and PoliTeSse, the Research Centre on Politics and Theories of Sexuality, who provided invaluable insight, especially into feminist writing on ethics and vulnerability. Special thanks go to Daniela Pianezzi at the University of Verona for her generosity in sharing her time, insights and ideas, as well as her knowledge and understanding of Butler, Cavarero and Arendt's writing. Some material in Chapter 3 is based on work we co-authored, and I am very grateful to Daniela for allowing me to draw from it here.

While in Verona, and as I was finishing work on the first draft of the book, I was very fortunate to be able to spend time with Judith Butler and Adriana Cavarero, along with Lynne Segal, Nela Smolović Jones, Owain Smolović Jones, Kate Kenny and Daniela Pianezzi. I learnt so much from their intellectual generosity and openness to discussing how their thinking might help us to reimagine organizations, and organizing, through the lens of feminist writing on ethics and vulnerability. They all kindly took time to provide feedback on draft chapters, as did Kat Riach, Moya Lloyd and Sheena Vachhani. For this, and for their work that I draw on throughout this book, I am very grateful.

I would like to express my thanks to colleagues at Bristol University Press, especially Ellen Pearce, Izzie Green, Alexandra Gregory and Lucy Lanyon for their enthusiasm for the proposal, and for their unfailing support and patience throughout the whole process of preparing the book for publication. I am indebted to the two anonymous reviewers of the first draft of the manuscript, to J.B. Priestley's Estate for granting permission for me to quote from *An Inspector Calls* in the epigraph to Chapter 1, and to Alison Lapper and Marc Quinn, for allowing me to include a photograph of 'Alison Lapper Pregnant', in Chapter 4.

As always, I am so grateful to Philip, Ellis and William for their love, and their company.

Introduction: Being Vulnerable in Relation to One Another

> We are never simply vulnerable, but always vulnerable to a situation, a person, a social structure, something upon which we rely and in relation to which we are exposed.
> Judith Butler, *The Force of Nonviolence*, 2020: 36

In a context in which there are unprecedented numbers of displaced and dispossessed people across the world, in which rights and resources are becoming more and more inaccessible to those who need them most, and in which the obligations that we have to one another are being increasingly undermined, or violated, this book asks the following questions: What is vulnerability, when understood through the lens of organization and organizing? How might vulnerability be rethought beyond its traditional associations with dependency, and as a weakness or limitation to be 'overcome'? What ethical and political scope could vulnerability open up, enabling us to think about how – and why – we might organize our lives differently, in ways orientated more towards relationality and solidarity, now and for the future?

This book is written, it feels, in an environment in which our social, political and economic landscapes have ceased to allow for any notion of weakness in our vocabularies, or ways of relating to ourselves and one another, except in so far as such weakness is framed as an aberration to be pitied or disdained, or a constraint to be surmounted. And tragically, but perhaps not surprisingly, through a series of interrelated crises and catastrophes, this false and futile notion of human (and planetary) inviolability is taking us to the brink of destruction. Against this backdrop, the book sets out to consider how vulnerability might be understood, and organized, in ways that affirm our mutual, but socially situated, interdependency in ways that counter the dangerous but persistent myth of invulnerability as the ideal, even 'normal' scenario.

Bringing an organizational perspective to vulnerability, my hope is to show how our desire for recognition comes to be organized in ways that both accentuate and exploit the shared independency that is constitutive of what Hannah Arendt (1998 [1958]) called the 'human condition', at the same time as opening up scope for a recognition-based understanding of our shared, but always socially situated, mutual exposure to one another. Each chapter foregrounds a reflexive awareness that we are 'always vulnerable ... in relation' to one another, and to the world in which we live, as Judith Butler puts it in the lines cited above. With this in mind, the book's central concern is to understand – and advocate for – a radical vulnerability as a reflexive form of openness to one another, one that might serve as the ontological basis of an ethics of relationality, and a politics of solidarity,[1] as a counter to the more widespread borderization (Mbembe, 2019), disinclination,[2] and disavowal of interdependency that currently dominates our social and political landscape.

The book takes as its starting point the idea that human life is conditioned, albeit in ways that are socially situated, structured and contoured, by a shared, existential vulnerability. By virtue of our embodied ways of being, human beings have physical and material needs; we are exposed to illness, injury, impairment and death; and depend upon the care of others (in different ways, of course, and to varying degrees) throughout our lives. As Mark Devenney (2021: 131) has put it, in this sense, vulnerability is 'a dependency in which the biological and the political overlap'. As social creatures, we are emotionally and psychologically vulnerable to others in a whole range of ways: to loss and grief; to neglect, abuse and lack of care; to rejection, ostracism, humiliation, and so on. We are vulnerable to manipulation, oppression, political violence and exploitation. And we are exposed to the natural world, and to its impact on our individual and collective actions and experiences, including to the kind of access we might have to food and water, shelter, and a safe environment in which to live, work and organize our lives, and to co-exist with others.

Deriving from the Latin word *vulnus* ('wound'), a significance that we return to later, vulnerability is generally taken to refer to the capacity to suffer, or to be exposed to violation: 'to be vulnerable is to be fragile, to be susceptible to wounding' (Mackenzie et al, 2013: 4). Being vulnerable means to be exposed to the risk of the other's violence, or indifference to our suffering. Within critical social theory and philosophy, this susceptibility is understood to be an ontological condition of our humanity, 'a universal, inevitable, enduring aspect of the human condition', as legal theorist Martha Fineman (2008: 8) has put it. In feminist writing, vulnerability is taken to refer to our capacity to be both open to the other, and vulnerable to the wounds that such openness can potentially inflict. As our embodied way of being, vulnerability is therefore a precondition of our capacity to connect to others, and to be open to others connecting to us, *at the same time* as being the basis on which that openness can be violated. The relational nature of this mutual exposure means that we must each trust the other not to harm us, and without the recognition of our shared humanity that this requires, we cannot live ethical lives, whether 'we' are individuals, social goups or communities, or entire populations whose right to exist depends upon recognition of our shared exposure to, and reliance upon, one another.

Further, the embodied nature of this relationship creates an intercorporeality, in which our bodies act as the media through we encounter one another, so that vulnerability is an always already embodied phenomenon on which interconnectedness depends; it is therefore also the site on which ethical relations (might) emerge. The latter, as feminist writing has emphasized, depends upon circumstances and social relations capable of '*cultivating vulnerability* and embodied openness toward others' (Johansson and Wickström, 2023: 329, emphasis added), rather than seeking to somehow 'overcome' vulnerability as a weakness or limitation, and as a deviation from a normative position of inviolability.

An approach that acknowledges openness to being 'wounded' as inherent to the human condition, while understanding the situated nature of that condition, is vital to grasping vulnerability as both ontological (as *vital* to the human condition, in all senses of that term) and sociological (socially situated and structured within the context of social relations). It is imperative to apprehending the circumstances of and obligations owed to those who, in any given scenario, are most vulnerable. It is also crucial for devising and acting (including critically) in response to interventions designed to mitigate against the various effects of different aspects and experiences of vulnerability (Segal, 2023). Mackenzie et al refer to those forms of vulnerability that are intrinsic to the human condition as 'inherent vulnerability':

> These vulnerabilities arise from our corporeality, our neediness, our dependence on others, and our affective and social natures. We are all inherently vulnerable to hunger, thirst, sleep deprivation, physical harm, emotional hostility, social isolation, and so forth. Some of these vulnerabilities are constant: we all suffer hunger and thirst if we lack food and fluids for more than a few hours. Others vary depending on a range of factors, such as age, gender, health status, and disability: ill health creates specific vulnerabilities related to the illness in question; extremes of age exaggerate the everyday vulnerabilities of embodiment in proportion to the capacity of the individual to meet her everyday physical needs. (Mackenzie et al, 2013: 7)

What they call 'situational vulnerability' is context-specific, by which they mean vulnerability that is 'caused or exacerbated by the personal, social, political, economic, or environmental situations of individuals or social groups', and which may be short-term, intermittent or enduring (Mackenzie et al, 2013: 8).[3] Of course, these two forms of vulnerability – the 'inherent', or ontological, and the 'situational', or sociological – are only conceptually distinct; all forms of vulnerability are embodied, and interrelated, as Mackenzie et al (2013) emphasize. And both forms of vulnerability necessitate a series of obligations shaped by the ethical relationality they give rise to. Further, as well as the specific harms that inherent and situational vulnerability can bring about, 'being vulnerable can engender a troubling sense of powerlessness, loss of control, or loss of agency' (Mackenzie, 2013: 9), so that a related ethical-political obligation is that of restoring agency to those who are situationally vulnerable, and of (reflexively) engaging with the question of what form that agency might take, from the point of view of those rendered most, or 'unacceptably', vulnerable.

What Mackenzie et al (2013: 9) call 'pathogenic vulnerabilities' are generated by a variety of sources including '[m]orally dysfunctional or abusive interpersonal and social relationships and socio-political oppression or injustice. Pathogenic vulnerabilities may also arise when a response intended to ameliorate vulnerability has the paradoxical effect of exacerbating existing vulnerabilities or generating new ones'. Pathogenic vulnerabilities, then, are those that violate basic human rights, accentuating vulnerability and eroding agency.[4]

Examining these different forms of vulnerability, and the violations as well as the possibilities they give rise to, this book focuses on the meaning, nature and experience of vulnerability as an organizational phenomenon. It explores three sets of distinct but interconnected social relations that help us to reflect on how our desire for recognition as viable subjects, worthy of rights, responsibilities and recognition, comes to be organized in ways that oppress and exploit us, but which potentially also provide scope for rethinking how we might live and work together in ways that are more reflective of a relational ethics: breathing, grieving and staring.

Some important starting premises from recent feminist writing help us to set out what we might broadly understand as a radical vulnerability, providing the basis for a theoretical lens through which to approach these three different sites on which the organization of our desire for recognition is played out. These are, first, that ethics and politics stem from the way in which we are fundamentally interdependent; second, we are driven by the desire for recognition of ourselves as socially viable beings. Finally, this desire for recognition is what drives our need for organization – it renders us mutually, inescapably vulnerable in an existential and embodied sense, a scenario that we do not somehow 'grow out of', meaning that we are interdependent as our lifelong way of being, or as Butler (2009b: 33) has put it, 'vulnerable by definition'. This means that we rely on organizations, and organizing, as a coordination of rights, resources and modes of relating to one another throughout our lives.[5]

Yet as feminist writing has also shown us, our social positioning is such that if we are all mutually vulnerable, and reliant on the infrastructures that organizations can (ideally) provide throughout our lives, we are not equally so – 'exposure', as Butler (2020b: 199, emphasis added) has also emphasized, 'is *a socially organized relation*'. As Alyson Cole (2016: 260) has also said, 'all of us are vulnerable, but some are more vulnerable than others'.[6] Understanding this helps us to fully engage with what vulnerability means as an organized and (potentially) radical phenomenon, a challenge that has been taken up in feminist thinking, and in elements of postcolonial theory that shape the theoretical ideas that this book draws from.

In Butler's earlier writing, vulnerability is understood in the largely Hegelian sense, as relating both to our need for recognition, and to its absence – the 'vulnerable' being those who are denied recognition because of their unintelligibility in relation to (governmental) norms. Butler's more recent work extends this through a preoccupation with how embodied vulnerability comes to be socially situated in ways that result in induced precarity for those whose social positioning makes them vulnerable to privation and injury. For Butler, therefore, as living beings who need recognition in order to survive physically and existentially, we are all vulnerable, but this vulnerability, while socially shared, is by no means universally so. This is a valuable line of argument for understanding the role that organizations, and organizing as a social process, play in instantiating and perpetuating vulnerability as both an existential and social condition.

Understanding vulnerability *as* organization in this way highlights the centrality of our obligations towards one another in comprehending and responding to humanitarian crises. As Marianna Fotaki has put it, referring to the 'migration crisis' in contemporary Europe:

> The future of our societies may be decided by the meaning we give to solidarity now, based on either narrow definitions that divide us into categories of deserving subjects, or on a notion of interdependency without which no form of life is possible. *We must protect the dispossessed who arrive on our shores, because their fate concerns us all. In offering protection, we value their lives as equal and accept the vulnerability of the dispossessed as our own.* (Fotaki, 2022: 318, emphasis added)

Judith Butler's theory of subject formation on which Fotaki draws, itself based largely on Arendt's writing on what it means to be human, positions vulnerability as a shared but socially situated ontological condition. Understood in this way, especially in Butler's more recent writing, mutual interdependency provides both the relational grounds for ethics, and the recognition that is necessary for political solidarity and action. Foregrounded in this work is the idea that social justice can only emerge from a reimagined interdependency, a line of thinking that has also been developed by other feminist writers, notably Lynne Segal (2023) in her book, *Lean on Me*. Such work emphasizes how the task is not to overcome vulnerability, but to recognize that it is our way of being.[7] Such an approach understands vulnerability beyond an essentialist ontology, or more specifically beyond the idea that some individuals, groups or populations are simply more vulnerable than others because of who, what or even where they are. Rather, the focus is on vulnerability as a situated, relational aspect of the human, social condition, one that is both the basis of our openness to being wounded, and our simultaneous capacity for interconnection with other living beings and the natural world. In other words, recognition of the mutual vulnerability engendered by our lifelong interdependency is understood to be a, perhaps *the*, condition of social justice.

And yet, *contra* this way of thinking about vulnerability as constitutive of the human condition, it seems that we are unable to collectively see and sense our mutual interdependence, even in the wake of a global pandemic, and amid a climate emergency and ongoing humanitarian crises and conflicts across the world. Instead, we doggedly pursue a necropolitics[8] of borderization, reinforcing our differences, as Achille Mbembe (2019) has put it, allowing violence to assault 'the living interdependency that is, or should be, our social world' (Butler, 2020b: 25). Rather than a recognition-based relationality, our lives have come to be organized more and more in ways that demarcate and divide us, including in landscapes that are opposed to, but also within, social movements such as feminism (for example, in relation to current debates over what it means to be a 'woman' as the subject of feminism [see Butler, 2024]). This borderized way of being is what feminist philosopher Adriana Cavarero (2016: 6, 11) describes as one in which the upright man (*l'uomo retto*) shapes our geometrical imaginary, functioning as the principle and norm for a self-assuredly vertical 'ethical posture', idealizing the autonomous, self-reliant and independent subject. Drawing variously on Freud, Levinas and Arendt, Cavarero contrasts this individualistic ethic with a relational ontology in which we are 'inclined' towards one another. Not without its problems, not least its essentialist and homogenizing connotations, this approach nevertheless urges us to rethink subjectivity as formed by 'exposure, vulnerability, and dependence', foregrounding, as Cavarero (2016: 13, emphasis added)[9] puts it, that we are '*consigned to one another*'.

Developing this point in a slightly different way to Cavarero herself, we might argue that this understanding of the human, social condition requires us to reframe ethics not in an ontological sense 'from the perspective of the vulnerable' (Cavarero, 2016: 14), but from the viewpoint of vulnerability as a mode of relationality, that is, from a perspective that foregrounds the ethical significance of mutual, socially situated vulnerability rather than one which understands ethical relations with reference to the fair treatment of those deemed 'vulnerable' as a group or class of people, or as those who are subject to a specific social positioning. This seemingly semantic but potentially important shift encourages us to think about how we might open up inclination to the other as the ethical and political basis of relationality premised upon recognition of our mutual but socially situated vulnerability *and* on the basis of a reflexive understanding of the ethical significance of relationality, and hence of the political power of persistence, of simply appearing to and for one another. Responding to this question requires us to begin from a relational perspective, one that sees our lives as defined by interdependency and the social ties we both bear and depend upon. Such an approach understands the 'I' as defined by the social relations through which we are constituted, and that both articulate and situate our most basic interdependencies, so that 'there is no sustaining a singularity outside the context of constitutive sociality and ecology' (Butler, 2021c: 59, 60). Foregrounding this relational ontology, we might argue, is not only necessary as a philosophical or theoretical move; it provides the starting point for a vital effort to sustain life and to limit the ontological claims and political reach of the hyper-individualism that currently dominates our lives. But as Butler and others have argued, the ties that bind us, our 'bonds of interdependency' are not simply primary, but also ambivalent, so that we are largely 'disinclined' towards the other, to borrow from Adriana Cavarero (2016, 2021a), if not outrightly hostile, as Mbembe describes it. This disinclination and hostility threatens not only social bonds and relations of mutual recognition, but also access to the rights, resources and representation that depend upon them, giving rise to a 'destructive inclination' (Butler, 2021c: 61), a borderization as Mbembe (2019) has framed it, shored up by the widely pervasive apathy or disinclination shaping our contemporary social, political and ethical landscapes.

In this book, I hope to contribute to current interest in how the mutual vulnerability engendered by our desire for recognition comes to be socially situated, and to respond to the question of why we cannot recognize and act on our shared vulnerability but instead reinforce the boundaries between us or are hostile towards or ambivalent about them. I do this by considering the three sets of social relations referred to earlier as sites on which the struggle for recognition, the conditions attached to it, and the vulnerability its organization engenders, are enacted and experienced. Why these particular sites or sets of social relations? I am interested in these because my sense is that they tell us something about how our desire for recognition comes to be organized in ways that both oppress and exploit us and others, but which also (potentially) open up opportunities for a more recognition-based, relational way of living and organizing for and with one another. Each site is explored here as a manifestation of a particular social imperative or lived aspect of our desire for recognition, and therefore as a setting through which this desire comes to be organized in ways that make us more or less vulnerable. These are: respiration as a site on which our need to exist is experienced; grieving as a setting through which our need to endure comes to be organized; and staring as a manifestation of our need to appear to one another in ways that are more or less likely to be accorded recognition.

Existing: the social relations of respiration

Breathing is clearly fundamental to human life. As such, it forces us to focus on how 'liveability' as a condition of social existence, of living a life that is endurable, is socially striated by differential access to perhaps one of our most basic requirements – breathable air.

As human beings we need access to breathable air in order to live, for our cells to reproduce and for our vital organs to function. But as successive waves of viral, ecological, racial and gendered violence have shown us, access to the right to breathe is not evenly spread but is organized along axes of race, gender, age, social class and geography (Butler, 2022). The whiter a person is the less likely they are to be asphyxiated at the hands of a police officer, the more hegemonically male they are, the less likely they are to be choked by a violent predator or partner, the place and circumstances in which a person lives shapes their chances of having access to ventilated oxygen when their breathing is compromised by illness or injury, and we have known for some time that the more privileged we are, the cleaner the air we breathe is likely to be. Respiratory poverty has a long history, starting with at least the early stages of industrialization, and remains a significant cause of preventable death in many parts of the world, accentuated by a climate crisis and intersections of precarity and exposure to pollution that make access to clean air the preserve of the privileged few. In Butler's words, access to breathable air is 'both what we share and what we share differently' (Butler, 2022: 77). But philosophers, notably Merleau-Ponty, have long since told us that when I breathe in, others breathe out, and vice versa – sharing breath is what makes us vulnerable, but is also what connects us, blurring any pretence at 'borderization' as a possibility for human beings and social relations. Chapter 2 explores the relationship between breathing, vulnerability and organization with these issues in mind.

Enduring: the social relations of grievability

When we are dead, we are arguably at our most vulnerable. I say this with some degree of hesitation because of course, in a technical sense, when we are dead, we don't exist anymore, so it is perhaps more the anticipation of this vulnerability rather than any 'experience' of it that I am thinking about. Nevertheless, when we are dead, we are entirely dependent on others to treat what remains of our bodies and our humanity with dignity and respect, to recognize any wishes or requests we may have expressed about what will happen to us at the end of our lives, and to care for us even (perhaps especially) when we are no longer able to extend our credit, because for most of us, whatever resources we might have become fixed and finite when we die. This means that what is available to us in terms of funerary rites and memorials is only what we can cover the cost of ourselves (entrusted to others to honour), or what other people, be they kin or strangers, or the state, are willing or able to provide. Butler and others' writing on the ethics and politics of commemoration shows how the conditions attached to recognition shape our likelihood of 'enduring', governing social perceptions of who and what counts, and on what basis, and shaping the likelihood of our lives being deemed worthy of remembrance.

Understanding grievability as a condition of social persistence through an organizational lens, and approached with reference to feminist writing on ethics and relationality, again provides insight into the conditions of recognition as these are shaped by where and how we live (and when), and indeed, who we love – themes explored in Chapter 3. Here we consider how the question of who gets to 'endure' and on what basis brings to the fore insights into how our desire for recognition comes to be organized in ways that affirm or designate who and what 'counts' as a life, or a community, worthy of endurance. Again, these are highly situated and structured phenomena through which our desire for recognition comes to be organized in ways that oppress, exploit and negate, but which in turn open up possibilities for more relational, recognition-based ways of being to emerge, as we will explore.

Enacting: the social relations of appearing

The third and final theme examined in this book connects labour to liveability, considering this link with reference to 'workability' as a condition of social viability; that is, of living a life that is sustainable, endurable, and which is recognized as having 'capacity' in a social world in which the parameters of who and what counts are shaped by a conception of value that is almost exclusively market-driven. Chapter 4 explores how this evaluation takes place within the context of social relations that mark some lives as affectively recognizable, others as less so, or not at all, a distinction that in turn marks out as perpetually precarious those whose workability can't be 'redeemed' even with the acquisition of the right goods and services (for example, through the ever-growing global cosmetics and aesthetic surgery markets). Chapter 4 considers the social dynamics of three politically and ethically distinct aspects of what we might call the ocular-centric 'conditioning' of what it means to be human (to borrow from Arendt) – staring, looking and appearing. We will explore how the former – staring and looking – are conditions of other- and self-objectification, respectively, while the latter, with reference to Hannah Arendt's (1998 [1958]) writing and the way it is taken up by Judith Butler, can be thought of as a potential space of assembly, of appearing together in order to embody and enact social relations of recognition-based solidarity.

Hannah Arendt reminds us that 'appearing' to one another is part of the human condition, referring to what she describes as 'the naked fact of our physical appearance' (Arendt, 1998 [1958]: 176–177). We make an entrance into the world, in physical form, soliciting recognition of our existence and ensuing needs, and this is how we relate to one another throughout our lives so that as human beings we are constitutively exposed to one another, always 'naked'. In this 'appearance' resides our way of being and, Arendt argues (in a way that Butler has developed in their[10] discussion of assembly), our politics. For Arendt, the space of appearance is 'the space where I appear to others as others appear to me', it is where and how we assert our existence explicitly, so that 'to be deprived of it means to be deprived of reality' (Arendt, 1998 [1958]: 198–199).

And like breathing and grieving, our claim to the right to occupy the space of appearance, to persist in this realm, comes to be organized in ways that might be affirmative, but which might also be denigrating or negating. For instance, one of the ways in which we might be denied access to the space of appearance in the way that Arendt understands it is through the profoundly antisocial act of staring. In the context of an ocular-centric social world, particularly a labour market, staring organizes our desire for recognition in ways that render some people particularly vulnerable, as subject to a process of objectification that reifies difference and disavows agency. Being stared at demands a response, forcing the one stared at into a dynamic struggle (Garland-Thomson, 2009: 3) in which they are 'called to account', so that (their) appearance becomes subject to a demand for accountability. In this sense, staring might be understood as a form of interpersonal, or rather intersubjective, violence, one that arrests scope for mutual recognition and which in doing and being so, negates a person's most basic human dignity ('look at *that*!'). Looking, however, might be thought of as a parallel or corollary form of ocular-centrism, one that compels or commands attention in a way that also arrests opportunities for intersubjectivity ('look at *me*!'). Influencers and the narcissism of selfie culture are perhaps the most obvious contemporary manifestations of this phenomenon, one that *organizes* our desire for recognition in ways that are (self-)affirmative for some, yet profoundly negating for others, and which, in this sense, denigrate the relationality that is, or should be (as Butler and other feminist thinkers would have it), the basis of our human condition.

As an alternative to the negativity of both phenomena, Hannah Arendt's notion of appearing potentially opens up a different set of social relations, one that mobilizes the conditions of possibility – or space – for a recognition of the basic interdependency that underpins sociality. In contrast to staring, as an other-orientated form of objectification and looking, as a self-centred objectification, appearing (to borrow from Arendt) offers scope for a more relational way of occupying the same physical, virtual or imagined space, potentially (therefore) in recognition-based solidarity. The ethical and political scope of this connects to recent feminist writing on embodied ethics, assembly and action, in ways that provide a focal point for more reflexive modes of organization as resistance to emerge that are explored in Chapter 4.

Towards a radical vulnerability: organizing for workable, vulnerable lives

To recap, if we accept that social justice can only emerge from a reimagined interdependency, enacted through modes of assembly organized within and through spaces of appearance that challenge dominant social arrangements and norms, the task is not to 'overcome' vulnerability, but to recognize that it is our way of being, that is, that recognition of the mutual vulnerability engendered by our interdependency is perhaps *the* condition of social justice.[11] A vital question for us to reflect on, then, is why we can't collectively see and sense this.[12]

In the chapters that make up this book, we consider existing, enduring and enacting as three distinct but related phenomena that provide insight into why this is the case, and to how things might be otherwise. The focus is on how the vulnerabilities our socially situated desire for recognition engender also open up important possibilities. To think through how these might connect to feminist action, we need to ask several questions that are the focus of the book's final chapter (Chapter 5): What kinds of organizational infrastructures or relations might enable such possibilities to be enacted, individually and collectively, as transformative ways of being and of relating to one another? We might think here of disability movements and trans rights groups whose persistence as simply a 'presence' within and through organization in its broadest sense is of (re)significance, and also about the claims to recognition and rights made by indigenous or dispossessed, stateless people. Key questions for us to explore then, include: What (organizational) forms might a relational mode of co-existence take? And what possibilities might it open up? In what ways are vulnerability, liveability and grieveability organizational phenomena? How do liveability and grieveability relate to workability? What kinds of agency can be found in vulnerability and what role might organizations play in assembling the communities, networks and infrastructures necessary to the conditions of possibility for that agency to be exercised? How might recognition be understood, and rethought, as a vehicle for social change in the context of a world in which, while the COVID-19 pandemic forced us to acknowledge our embodied interdependence (Butler, 2022), social goods and resources are increasingly 'shored up' through the pursuit of a necropolitics of borderization (Mbembe, 2019)?

Organizations can potentially play a vital role in reimagining and realizing radical vulnerability as the basis of social relations, not least because, as Butler and Athanasiou (2013: 165) have put it, they constitute 'the environments, the machines and the complex systems of social interdependency' upon which we all rely, conditioning our embodied existence and differential exposure to socially situated vulnerability. And as Isabella Scheibmayr (2024: 1386, emphasis added) has put it more recently, 'organizations co-constitute the infrastructures that *organize vulnerability*'.

Scheibmayr (2024) proposes three ways in which vulnerability can be understood through an organizational lens: vulnerability *through* organizations (how organizations produce vulnerability through exclusion and exploitation); vulnerability *in* organizations (because most organizations consist of embodied beings, vulnerability exists in organizations rather than simply being produced through them); and the vulnerability *of* organizations. By the latter, Scheibmayr refers to organizational exposure to the wider contexts within which organizational forms exist and operate, including, for instance, via their vulnerability to political or financial support for their activities and goals being withdrawn. Scheibmayr (2024: 1400) goes as far as to say that what work and organization studies is, in this sense, is the study of 'infrastructures of vulnerability'. Understanding vulnerability and its relationship to organization in this way opens up scope, she argues, to understand, first, how organizations respond to the vulnerabilities constituted through, in and of organizations; second, to consider how organizations are constituted in the building and maintaining of the social infrastructures that make life possible; and, third, to better grasp the issue of for whom organizations are currently producing new vulnerabilities and failing to provide the social infrastructure necessary for living.

Such an approach emphasizes how our shared but socially situated interdependence underpins our need for organizations, at the same time as foregrounding our vulnerability through, within and upon them. It reflects Butler's view that vulnerability is a 'feature of the relation that binds us to one another and to the larger structures and institutions upon which we depend for the continuation of life' (Butler, 2021a: 46), including beyond death, as we will explore in Chapter 3, and as Butler has in their own writing.

We begin our consideration of the relationship between vulnerability and organization, then, from the premise that, as Butler has also put it, 'we are, from the start, given over to the other', noting how this renders us perpetually vulnerable to a range of responses to our desire for recognition of ourselves as viable social beings, from 'the eradication of our being at the one end' to 'the physical support for our lives at the other' (Butler, 2004a: 31). Organizations play a vital role at both extremes, and in shaping the circumstances in which our existential, ontological, bodily vulnerability – what Butler calls 'the condition of primary vulnerability' (Butler, 2004a: 31) – is lived and experienced. The terms shaping recognizability mean that as our primordial vulnerability is socially structured, situated and contoured in ways that mean 'lives are supported and maintained differently' in, by and through organizations, so that there are radically different ways that existential and social vulnerability is distributed across social groups, and globally: certain lives will be highly protected, others less so, or on terms that are not of their own making.

Crucial to Butler's writing on vulnerability is the ubiquity of our interdependency as constitutive of the human, social condition. For Butler, this is of course not a scenario that we can 'organize' our way out of: 'There are others out there on whom my life depends, people I do not know and may never know. This fundamental dependency on anonymous others is not a condition that I can will away' (Butler, 2004a: xii). Understood in this way, our mutual, but socially situated, vulnerability is not a political or even ethical position, but an ontological premise underpinning the human condition, one that provides scope for reimagining what organizing, and organization, might mean in and through vulnerability, where the latter refers both to our ek-static existence (to our need to 'lose ourselves' in order to enter into the struggle for recognition), and to our exposure to the Other (to the potential threat to our existence that this exposure engenders, and that this struggle brings about). As Butler puts it, this situation makes 'a tenuous "we" of us all' (Butler, 2004a: 20).[13]

Vulnerability, in this sense, might be understood as our embodied way of being together in a scenario shaped by shared, but differently positioned and experienced, exposure to one another and the world around us:

> Each of us is constituted politically in part by virtue of the social vulnerability of our bodies – as a site of desire and physical vulnerability, *as a site of a publicity at once assertive and exposed*. Loss and vulnerability seem to follow from our being socially constituted bodies, attached to others, at risk of losing those attachments, exposed to others, at risk of violence by virtue of that exposure (Butler, 2004a: 20, emphasis added).

And for Butler this has not only important existential (intersubjective) qualities; we are vulnerable in our very materiality, our 'flesh', for of course, 'the body implies mortality, vulnerability, agency: the skin and the flesh expose us', including to the gaze of others (Butler, 2004a: 26), as we will discuss in later chapters. Our vulnerability therefore means that we are always 'at a loss', living outside of ourselves in a perpetually exposed ek-stasis.[14] In the following chapters, we consider how this is lived, experienced and played out in three different settings, or sets of social relations – breathing, grieving and staring.

First, though, Chapter 1 examines the relationship between interdependency, vulnerability, recognition and organization. It explores the idea that vulnerability is the outcome of a process of organization, namely of the way in which our desire for recognition of ourselves and others as viable living beings comes to be organized. Its starting point is the idea that vulnerability exists in a complex relationship with organization, taking the latter to refer to both a process through which rights and resources come to be allocated, and as the infrastructural settings or site of this process. It considers how, on the one hand, organizations, or rather 'better' (for example, more effective, more just, more inclusive, more accessible, more sustainable) organizing, might provide the means through which to tackle the worst extremes, and exploitations, of vulnerability. Yet it also examines how, on the other hand, socially structured and situated vulnerability is itself the outcome of organizational processes and imperatives, including those that respond differently to appeals to recognition. In this latter sense, vulnerability can be understood *as* an organizational phenomenon – as a positioning that responds to the desire for recognition in ways that designate living beings as more or less 'vulnerable'.

Chapters 2–4 examine three themes that bring together an understanding of vulnerability in/as resistance with a relational ethics and a politics of interdependency. Chapter 2 focuses on liveability as a condition of social existence, of living a life that is endurable within the context of global pandemics, respiratory poverty and a climate crisis in which access to the most basic requirement – breathable air – is socially contoured and, for many, restricted or entirely foreclosed. Chapter 3 explores grievability as a condition of social persistence, of living a life that is (re)markable, including with reference to norms shaping the conditions of recognition based on where and how we live, and who we love. It considers how commemoration, grieveability and mourning play out in social relations that organize who and what 'counts' as a life, or a community, or entire population, worthy of memorialization, imbued with the capacity to endure. Chapter 4 examines workability as a condition of social viability, of living a life that is sustainable, and which is recognized as having capacity in a social world in which the parameters of who and what counts as 'doable' are shaped by a conception of value that is almost exclusively market driven, including according to an affective idealism that marks some lives as aesthetically recognizable, others not, including those whose workability cannot be redeemed even with the acquisition of the right goods and services. The dynamics of staring, looking and appearing are considered, exploring the former as a condition of other- or self-objectification, and examining the latter, with reference to Hannah Arendt's work (1998 [1958]), as a potential space of assembly. The discussion in Chapter 4 draws insight from feminist thinking and activism, and from Judith Butler's reminder to us that 'we are never quite "done" with being undone' (Butler, 2015b: 16). Again, drawing on Arendt, as well as other feminist writers such as Adriana Cavarero and Lynne Segal, the final chapter, Chapter 5, explores how organizing and organizations might be reimagined through the lens of vulnerability, in ways that might make as many lives as possible more 'workable'.

In combination, existence, endurance and appearance provide a recognition-based counter to discourses on resourcefulness and resilience that dominate managerial perspectives, including on equality and difference, in contemporary organizational life. They are considered here as examples or instances of vulnerability and/as forms of resistance that constitute both political and ethical phenomena. The former are understood to relate to modes of acting together in solidarity via a recognition-based sense of vulnerability in/as resistance, while ethical imperatives are taken to refer to modes of relating to one another, underpinned by an ethic of relationality. The latter we can understand as a reflexive awareness of both the mutual vulnerability engendered by our interdependency and, at the same time, an understanding that while we are all therefore vulnerable, we are by no means equally so.

Taken together, these chapters aim to show how feminist perspectives on vulnerability and a recognition-based ethics of interdependency offer new pathways through which to approach how we might tackle urgent social issues, such as borderization, nationalism, struggles over individual and collective identities and territories, the growing care deficit, and the need to intertwine our sense of compassion and shared responsibility for each other's lives with the resources we have available to us. By accounting for interdependency through a relational ontology, the approaches that each chapter draws on potentially provide ethical and political insights into these issues and offer alternatives to dominant paradigms of invulnerability that frame current understandings and experiences of subjectivity as the desire for autonomy, resilience and self-mastery. In sum, the book aims to show how *recognizing vulnerability* and organizing our lives in order to protect and preserve rather than overcome mutual interdependency might open up possibilities for living and working together in ways that connect our need for (shared) agency, care and community with social justice and responsiveness, via sustainable access to the rights, resources and representation that safeguard liveable and workable lives for all.

1

Vulnerability and/as Organization

> We don't live alone. We are members of one body.
> J.B. Priestley, *An Inspector Calls*, 2000 [1947]: 207

Introduction

Mohammed Bhar was a Palestinian man with Down syndrome and autism who was 24 years old at the time of his death in July 2024, having been mauled by an Israeli military dog following a raid on his home in the Shujaiya district of eastern Gaza City. According to BBC news coverage at the time, Mr Bahr and his family had been displaced around 15 times since Israel's war on Gaza began in October 2023. The Bahr family reported that Israeli forces raided their house with a combat dog that attacked Mr Bahr across his arms and chest. His family were forced to leave their home, having been told (at gunpoint) that Mohammed, who needed 24-hour care, would remain behind for medical treatment. When the Bahr family returned to their house a week later, they found Mohammed's decaying body covered in blood on the floor, a tourniquet on his arm. Israeli authorities later confirmed that the soldiers left Mr Bahr in the apartment, saying that they had to leave to help other injured soldiers.

To accept that as human beings we are all inherently vulnerable does not necessarily imply a belief that we are all uniformly so; to say that we are all 'one' body, somebody, as J.P. Priestley's inspector does, does not equate to claiming that we are the same body, or that we are embodied in the same way.[1] Vulnerability does not exist, and is not experienced, in a social, political, economic or ethical vacuum. People living (and dying) in circumstances like Mohammed Bahr's are vulnerable in ways that are different to those of us who are, relatively speaking, less reliant on the care of others and are, therefore, less at risk of suffering because of others' neglect or violence. This complexity raises the question of how we can develop a theoretical understanding of vulnerability and its relationship to the human condition that grasps both vulnerability's ubiquity *and* its social contours. In other words, we need to be able to account for how, as living beings who are dependent upon each other, we are all vulnerable, yet our lives are not all shaped by that vulnerability in the same way.

The Bahr family's hope is to seek social and legal justice for Mohammed, in part by raising awareness of what happened to him, and by securing a full inquiry into the cause and circumstances of his death. How can we theorize this relationship – between vulnerability and agency, between devastation and action – in ways that understand both the inhumanity of what happened to Mohammed, as well as the ability of the Bahr family to seek redress, and to grasp the contexts that place limits on the nature and scope of any agency that can be exercised in these kinds of circumstances?[2] As feminists, we need to interrogate how we understand vulnerability theoretically and as the basis for political action, and we need to do so reflexively, appreciating how our own positionality shapes the ways in which we relate to one another, including through perceptions of how our vulnerability is shared yet also socially situated. In part, this requires an understanding of how vulnerability comes to be organized; that is, of vulnerability as an organizational, and organizing, phenomenon. It needs us to appreciate vulnerability as an aspect of social existence that shapes, and is shaped by, our desire for recognition of ourselves as worthy of the protections necessary to our survival.

Bereft of the rights and resources that ideally follow from an affirmative response to an appeal for recognition, those who are most vulnerable are generally thought of as living beings who are without access to the kinds of infrastructural support that organizations can provide, and which those of us who live in highly organized societies and circumstances often take for granted. For some, organizations as infrastructural entities, and organizing as an agentic social process, can proffer the means to mitigate against some of the worst extremes of vulnerability, although of course, this is by no means the case for everyone, or in all circumstances, as the Bahr family's experience illustrates. For many, if not all of us (in different ways), organizations cause, exacerbate and perpetuate vulnerability.[3] This means that the relationship between vulnerability and organization is complex as organizing, including of resources, rights, people and so on, is both the cause of vulnerability, or at least of its exacerbation, *and* the potential way in which its worst extremees might be mitigated. The relationship between vulnerability and organization is also inherently precarious: if we are dependent upon the organizational processes and resources, and social structures that make our lives possible, then it is also the case that 'when they falter, so do we' (Butler, 2020b: 46).

In this sense, vulnerability itself might be understood as the outcome of a process of organization, perhaps even to the point that it becomes a form of organization in itself, one through which our desire for recognition of ourselves as beings who are worthy of leading 'liveable' lives, to borrow from Judith Butler, comes to be organized, often in categorical and hierarchical ways that serve to negate, oppress and exploit this desire.[4] But organization, and organizing, also has the capacity to resist and redress the effects of negating, oppressive or exploitative responses to our desire for recognition, providing a focal point and mechanism through which it becomes possible to assemble in opposition, and in solidarity, and through which to persist.[5]

Exploring these kinds of issues, this chapter examines how vulnerability and organization are interconnected, considering how what we think of and experience as vulnerability might be understood as an organization of our desire for recognition of ourselves as viable subjects who have the right to exist, endure and appear. It examines vulnerability as the outcome of how this desire comes to be organized in ways that negate, oppress and exploit us, but which also potentially open up scope for rethinking how we might live, work and organize our lives in ways that are more relational and recognition-based, and orientated towards care and solidarity, now and in the future. Drawing together insights from current debates within critical social theory and contemporary feminist thinking, including on the complex, evolving and ambivalent nature of recognition and its relationship to vulnerability, we will consider questions about the nature of the 'more than human' world, and about how social relations are characterized by differently contoured and situated, that is, organized, vulnerabilities.

The chapter begins by considering the relationship between vulnerability and inclination in recent feminist writing on politics and ethics which sets out what we might broadly think of as a social ontology of vulnerability, before considering the significance of care within current feminist thought. It then moves on to discuss the ambivalent relationship between recognition and vulnerability, before developing a deeper consideration of the question of what makes some lives more unliveable, by virtue of their untenable vulnerability, than others. The chapter concludes by examining vulnerability and its organization with reference to recent feminist writing on an ethics of relationality.

Vulnerability and inclination

In her critique of rectitude, through which she elaborates on her understanding of the relationship between an ethics of nonviolence, relationality and care, Italian feminist philosopher Adriana Cavarero (2016) proceeds from the observation that human beings have been figured or depicted as upright throughout human history, the effect of which is to obscure our 'natural' inclination towards one another.[6] Cavarero sees *'l'uomo retto'* as embodying 'upright manhood' (the self-proclaimed subject of simultaneously physical and moral superiority) which is, for her, both an ontological predicament and an ethical proposition embodied as a geometric structure.[7] For Cavarero, idealized principles of autonomy and independence in western cultural history, philosophy and ethics, stoke *Homo erectus*'s fear of a return to perceived childlike states of dependency and submission. Acknowledging any perceived need for others, Cavarero argues, undermines the 'egocentric verticality' shaping hegemonic subjectivity. What is required, she argues, is 'a different, more disruptive, and revolutionary geometry' (Cavarero, 2016: 131) to counter this dominant mindset.

Reminding us that the etymological root of inclination is to bend, to lean down or to lower – from the Greek *klinè* (bed, or bed in), Cavarero sets out two opposing postural paradigms correlating to two distinct modes of ethical subjectivity that provide frameworks for questioning the way in which the human condition comes to be organized hierarchically, as she sees it: the first relates to an individualistic ontology (rectitude), the second to a relational ontology (inclination).[8] Her critique of the former draws directly from Hannah Arendt's (1998 [1958]) account of the human condition that, in Cavarero's reading, 'frames inclination in postural terms and relates it to the geometry of the subject' (Cavarero, 2016: 11). For Cavarero, Arendt's writing evokes a politics of inclining the subject towards the Other in a relational ontology that requires a rethinking of subjectivity as shaped by 'exposure, vulnerability, and dependence' (Cavarero, 2016: 11). Inclination is thus an ethical and ontological, as well as a political issue, as the verticality signified by the line of the 'I' stakes a claim to recognition of an autonomous, self-referencing and self-supporting subject,[9] a scenario that Cavarero (2021a: 44) describes as a 'pathetic blunder' in western philosophy and politics. In contrast, and drawing on Arendt, inclination is posited as 'a powerful force that pushes the self outside of itself', an *ek-statis* (Cavarero, 2016: 7).

Despite its essentialist undertones, Cavarero's engagement with Arendt is important to us here, highlighting how Arendt's notion of what she calls the 'naked fact' of our original physical appearance (our natality) helps us to think about vulnerability as a vital part of the inauguration of subjectivity, a line of argument that is also reflected in Butler's Arendtian claim that we are, from the start, 'given over' to the other.

As well as Arendt (and also like Butler), Cavarero turns to Levinas's (1969) rejection of the autonomous and 'discrete' subject in order to counter what she sees as the intersubjective violence brought about by an egocentric ontology. Drawing on Levinas, Cavarero argues that inclination requires a radical ontological shift in how subjectivity is understood. As she puts it, '*[e]mphasizing vulnerability is* not a matter of correcting individualistic ontology by inserting the category of relation into it. It is rather *to rethink relation itself as originary and constitutive*, as an essential dimension of the human' (Cavarero, 2016: 13, emphasis added). Here Cavarero's notion of the 'consigned self' resonates with Butler's understanding of the precarious subject, when she argues that what makes us human is 'our being creatures who are materially vulnerable and, often in greatly unbalanced circumstances, *consigned to one another*' (Cavarero, 2016: 13, emphasis added). In its radical version, what animates this relational model, premised on an understanding of subjectivity as a state of being given over to the other, is that it opens up possibilities for understanding mutual interdependence not simply as the basis of ethics, but also of politics, providing the starting point for a radical vulnerability, one in which we reflexively recognize, and act upon, our shared but socially situated interdependency. This radical understanding emphasizes that the constitutive interdependency of our lives is one that positions vulnerability as the basis of solidarity and transformation, rather than as precluding it. In this sense, Arendt's model opens up scope, Cavarero (2016: 14) argues, to reframe ethics as inclination and, we might surmise, politics as our shared capacity to act not in spite of, but precisely because of, our mutual reliance upon one another.

In this respect, Cavarero's (2016: 24) critique has an important grammar to it – a geometry based on a rejection, as she puts it, of the 'autonomous "I", self-sufficient and exemplarily vertical'. To develop this point, Cavarero turns to Virginia Woolf's observations on the impact of the vertical 'I' on the page, considering its affective power to overshadow words and letters around it. As she notes, through her reading of Woolf, the English 'I' stands alone – always capitalized, self-sufficient and solitary, rigid and solipsistic; as Woolf reflects, its typographic form is able to synthesize in just one letter 'the quintessence of *homo erectus*' (Cavarero, 2016: 38); its verticality assertively rigid.

In opposition to rectitude, and drawing directly on Arendt (1998 [1958]), Cavarero (2016: 105) argues that inclination is a more ethically relational, postural response to the human condition, one in which we find ourselves compelled to respond to the naked appearance of one another, and in which 'the vulnerable creature carries the *vulnus*, the wound, in its very name'. In this sense, following Arendt, Cavarero (2016: 109) argues that the political designates 'a relational space of reciprocal appearance', one that rests on an 'initiative' from which 'no human being can refrain and still be human'. The space of appearance in this sense is a 'theater of action' (Cavarero, 2016: 115), in which (borrowing further from Arendt) everyone appears 'in their incarnated uniqueness, actor and spectator together on a shared, hence public, space' – a crucial point to which we return in later chapters. As Cavarero observes, reciprocity and interdependence are the essential elements of the interactive context that Arendt calls politics, and this is the basis of her understanding of how an ethics of inclination might underpin action.

Most notably in her essay, 'Schemata for a postural ethics', Cavarero (2016: 122) develops this latter point, noting how Arendt's imaginary of natality is a critical resource for ontology, as well as ethics and politics, shifting attention from a subject modelled on the idea of autonomy to a subjectivity 'structurally characterized by dependence and exposure', moving from the assertion 'of a self-consistent and partitioned subjectivity' to a subjectivity 'that is open and relational'. For her, erect topologies are characterized by an absolute orientation of corporeal verticality, so that the urgent task is to ask 'what consequences this geometry produces for our discourses on subjects, human relations and community' (Cavarero, 2016: 128).

Crucially for Cavarero, inclination offers a radical point of departure for rethinking the ontology of the vulnerable, together with its constitutive rationality; contrary to an 'axis of uprightness', inclination offers the possibility of arranging social relations 'along multiple coexisting lines'. In this sense, for Cavarero, inclination may then become 'a new fundamental schematism' – the 'gestural mark of a new postural geometry, a new mode for evaluating the terrain of the encounter' between Self and Other. Through Arendt, Cavarero comes to the view that understood through a relational ontology, all schemata (ethical and/or political) based on verticality are 'in essence, an anomaly'. To theorize a subject that 'shores itself up ... at the price of denying its own vulnerability, its dependency, its exposure' is, in her view, a catastrophic, if not comical, error. Arendt, she argues, offers a warning against such mistakes, alerting us to the extent to which, as a model for subjectivity, verticality is a pretence that has no correspondence in lived experience, for the vertically imagined subject 'is a fictitious entity, a mirage' (Cavarero, 2016: 130). Problematically, however, Cavarero postulates how a specifically 'maternal inclination could work as a module [*sic*] for a different, more disruptive, and revolutionary geometry whose aim is to rethink the very core of community' (Cavarero, 2016: 131), and her specific reference to 'maternal inclination' here is a point to which we return.

In her final essay in *Inclinations*, 'Coda', Cavarero (2016) engages with Levinas's notion that ethics, at its most basic, is a lack of indifference to the Other's death. Here Cavarero reminds us that the Latin *vulnus* has two meanings, the first referring to a wound (a break in the skin, resulting from the skin's outward-facing nature, and hence exposure); the second to the skin as smooth, hairless and naked. Cavarero makes this (characteristic) etymological distinction in order to explain how the two meanings open up two imaginaries that, while distinguishable, are not entirely distinct: both relate to the skin as a boundary or border between Self and Other, inside and outside, and as 'a radical and immediate exposure' (Cavarero, 2016: 159) – the vulnerable here being the human (in Arendtian terms), in its absolute nakedness, giving rise to an understanding of vulnerability 'as the human's essential condition'.

The nakedness of the skin – exposed and natal – inspires the caress that is so central to Levinas's (1969) thinking in *Totality and Infinity* in which he understands the caress as a response to the Other's vulnerability, emphasizing the ethical responsibility that ensues from this in a way that postulates, for Cavarero, 'a radical relational ontology'. Ultimately, her reading of Levinas through Arendt leads Cavarero to prioritize an etymology of *vulnus* as nudity over an etymology of *vulnus* as laceration, reiterating this meaning of vulnerability as 'exposure of the one to the other' (Cavarero, 2016: 161), her response to which is to emphasize inclination as the ontological, relational basis of ethics and of caring social relations.

Vulnerability and/as care

Caverero's study of vulnerability's etymology asks us to reflect on the ontological basis of the myth of 'invulnerability' and, in doing so, to consider how social relations, historically and in contemporary societies, seem to be shaped by an enduring, reactionary fear of vulnerability (a 'vulneraphobia', so to speak). In this sense, her account asks us to consider how this fear shapes and perpetuates the stigmatization, alienation and abjection of those situated (reified) as vulnerable, and of their living (and working) conditions. Indeed, a vulnerable positionality, Cavarero emphasizes, enforces power relations in part through an ideological construction that promotes mastery and selfishness while denigrating dependency and care. This is a scenario that reflects itself in what Achille Mbembe (2019) calls 'borderization' – what we might think of as the spatial-political organization of vulnerability, amounting to a materialization of an illusory (and elusive) form of self-mastery and impermeability.[10] The result, as Joan Tronto (2015) has emphasized, is nothing short of disastrous for the possibility of a caring democracy ever being widely valued, let alone realized.

Relationality not only rejects borderization as a way of living, working and organizing together on ethical grounds; it refuses what it implies as an ontologically feasible way of being, emphasizing instead that what it means to be a subject is to be constitutively interdependent with others and, hence, to be ethically responsible for one another. Further, rather than politics seeking to 'liberate' us from our mutual reliance, relationality emphasizes the radical, transformative potential of this openness, implying that emancipatory practices can only proceed from mutual recognition of our shared yet situated vulnerability and a conscious rejection of the illusions under which a vulneraphobic society labours. Understood in this way, vulnerability is not a problematic state to be 'overcome' (as is proffered in neoliberal discourse premised upon the misconceived existence of an autonomous, self-sufficiency),[11] or addressed (as in reformist policies), but our way of being, to be cherished, nurtured and cultivated as the basis of an ethical life, so that care becomes 'the outcome of a recognized condition of vulnerability', as Valentina Moro (2022: 46) has put it. The way that Joan Tronto frames this in her writing on care is particularly helpful to us here as the basis for understanding how a relational ontology of vulnerability relates to care, and to a disavowal of the social relations underpinning, in her analysis, caring *about*, caring *for* and caring *with*, one another. Care, Tronto argues, makes us attentive and responsible, competent and responsive in the ways in which we relate to one another. For her, care

> [i]n the most general sense ... is a species activity that includes everything we do to maintain, continue, and repair our world so that we may live in it as well as possible. That world includes our bodies, our selves and our environment, all of which we seek to interweave in a complex, life-sustaining web. (Fisher and Tronto, 1990: 40, cited in Tronto, 2015: 3)

This is the kind of approach to vulnerability as vital to the human condition and as the basic premise of care that is developed by Lynne Segal (2023) in her book, *Lean on Me*, in which she engages with both Cavarero and Butler to map out a politics and ethics of radical care, and in her work with the Care Collective (2020). Segal both reflects on how vulnerability comes to be organized and articulates possibilities for a radical politics of care in place of Cavarero's *homo erectus*,[12] reminding us of how, at every stage of our lives, '*we lean upon others for recognition and sustenance*', simply because this is our way of being; we are mutually vulnerable because 'we have no other choice' (Segal, 2023: 2, emphasis added).

As well as Butler and Cavarero, Segal brings several other thinkers into dialogue in framing her critique of how our conceitful sense of independence relies upon a constant disavowal of the respect, recognition and care we need from others throughout our lives; in other words, of our relational ontology. From Erich Fromm (1977: 87) she takes the idea that what is surprising about this and the way in which it shapes social relations is that our need for reciprocal care 'could be so repressed as to make acts of selfishness the rule in industrial (and many other) societies and acts of solidarity the exception'. The result, she concurs with Cavarero, is the 'veneration of the "self-made man"' (Segal, 2023: 3).

Segal, not surprisingly, also references Butler's (2004a: xiv) book, *Precarious Life* in which they argue that, in the face of persistent global violence, we must proceed, politically and ethically, on the basis of mutual recognition of our 'inevitable interdependency'. This also (again not surprisingly) leads Segal to Levinas (1969: 51), for whom we are 'born into relationality' so that we must always take ethical responsibility for others. And she turns to Freud (2001 [1917]: 142), who (as Segal notes) memorably argued that 'the ego is not the master of its own house' because of the significant role played by the unconscious in shaping our thoughts, feelings and actions, ensuring that our earliest formative experiences and relationships characterized by our need for care, and our reliance upon others, are never fully 'overcome' and can never be so, as Freud famously argued, of course.

For Segal, these different but overlapping ways of foregrounding our lifelong dependency and shared vulnerability help us to destabilize 'presumptions of the rational, autonomous subject'. Yet *Lean on Me* also emphasizes how we can grasp this, perhaps best of all, through simple introspection, and via knowing through experiencing and observing those around us that 'we depend upon one another' (Segal, 2023: 6).

In this sense, Segal's analytical interest, both in her own work and in that co-produced with the Care Collective (2020), is in the question of why the notion of vulnerability, by which she means 'our reliance upon others and on our basic infrastructures of care', continues to be 'perceived as a weakness, facilitating the disparagement if not pathologization of those who are labelled "dependent"' (Segal, 2023: 7). Segal frames this, in part, as an organizational question when she says: 'We all need both to give and to receive care, but we also need time, support, and resources, for this to be done well. Care can turn into forms of control, abuse, even cruelty, from care giver or receiver, if there is no mutual recognition' (Segal, 2023: 8).

In her essay, 'Admitting vulnerability', Segal notes that 'throughout our lives we need each other':

> We all rely upon the shared structures and evolving social relations that protect, feed, educate, and sustain us wherever we reside. This is why *vulnerability is not simply an individual or even a collective attribute, but as aspect of our shared life*. … Our goal should not be to surmount dependency to achieve self-sufficiency, but rather to *recognize our interdependence*. (Segal, 2023: 122–123, emphasis added)

Segal foregrounds how the work of disability activists especially has been vital in unfolding the complexities bound up in the language of vulnerability, revealing dependence as a pretext for exclusion – a synonym for misrecognition and/or negation. On this point she cites Margrit Shildrick (2009) who raises concerns that activism as 'overcoming' or defying disability resonates too closely with neoliberal rhetoric on self-reliance and resilience, fostering a 'dangerous denunciation of dependency in social welfare policies and practices' (Segal, 2023: 127). Segal also turns to Tim Dartington (2010), who notes how this equation between activist discourses associated with overcoming dependence and neoliberal extolments of self-reliance risks a distressing denigration of dependency that perpetuates a formulaic approach to social relations which, at the risk of crude oversimplification, might be construed as follows: disabled people = dependent, dependency = less than human, therefore disabled people = disposable, framing the latter as a 'moral act' that equates to alleviating suffering from a life not worth living, or a difficult 'resource-driven' decision based on cost–benefit.

To illustrate this point, Segal reminds us of the UK government's own statistics showing that 60 per cent of deaths attributed to COVID-19 in 2020 were people with disabilities. Similarly, she cites Margaret M. Gullette's (2024) book *American Eldercide* that reports that, at the height of the pandemic, the elderly were simply declared expendable, especially those residing in care homes. In *Natural Causes*, Barbara Ehrenreich ridicules the idea that, with enough self-care, we can remain fully in control of our minds and bodies, arguing that what is needed is better mutual care, but as Segal reflects, in a time-poor social world, there is limited space 'for care or solidarity, let alone friendship, across the generations' (Segal, 2023: 150). Understood in this context, she argues, ageism 'is actually a prejudice against our dreaded future selves', the second of the two life course markers (the first being childhood) that stoke society's vulneraphobia[13].

In this context, finding ways to collectively reimagine social justice and to reconsider how it is organized on the basis that 'we are all in need of support and care: *all of us some of the time, and some of us all of the time*' (Segal, 2023: 135, emphasis added), can be understood as an urgent – perhaps *the most urgent* – social issue we face, particularly in the context of climate destruction and ongoing global conflict, and the humanitarian crises that both are causing. Regarding the former, as Anne Karpf (2021) notes, those suffering most are arguably those who are least culpable; the world's richest nations are estimated to be responsible for 86 per cent of global CO_2 emissions, caused primarily by burning fossil fuels. For Segal (2023: 156, emphasis added), 'when it comes to understanding the climate crisis, *we are all connected*. But many still refuse to recognize those ties, whether historically or in the present'. She cites Kim TallBear (2019), who notes that the physical elimination of indigenous people in the United States resulted in a settler dispossession that 'objectifies the land and water and other-than-human beings as potentially owned resources' (cited in Segal, 2023: 171).[14]

Segal argues that only sustained efforts at climate justice can take us to the heart of the problem: 'Thinking globally means richer nations assisting public ownership of clean energy projects in poorer ones, along with resources for the expansion of quality public transport, water and housing infrastructures, accompanying universal public healthcare provision' (Segal, 2023: 181). Her essay, 'Caring futures', is perhaps the clearest articulation of a radical vulnerability in *Lean on Me*. Here, Segal notes that in the aftermath of COVID-19, essential workers in health, transport and education took to the streets to demand better wages and contractual terms, showing how far their wages and working conditions had deteriorated because of decades of underfunding.

> It seems clear that more people than ever are coming to see that we can only ensure human survival once we start to place care and concern

for each other at the heart of our politics, and the centre of our lives. *If we are to avoid a calamitous future, we have to move away from a world based on private accumulation and replace it with a politics of care, solidarity, and equality*, cultivating a caring consciousness in all our social interactions. (Segal, 2023: 186, emphasis added)

Cultivating a 'caring consciousness' must involve starting from the premise of an understanding of care as encompassing 'all activities that enable human life to flourish, alongside the nurturing of non-human and planetary well-being', requiring an agentic approach – a radical vulnerability, we might say – focusing on recognition-based solidarity that is 'quite distinct from benevolence or pity' (Segal, 2023: 189). One of the theoretical challenges associated with identifying the basis for such an approach is that of conceptualizing vulnerability as both universally shared *and* as socially contoured.

Responding to this challenge, and reflecting insights from Cavarero and Butler, Valentina Moro (2022: 62, original emphasis) distinguishes between a universalistic understanding of vulnerability (as a shared human condition), and a more particularistic, or we might say 'situated', political and legal identification of specific groups of people or individuals as being 'vulnerable subjects'. The problem with a universalistic account, she argues, is that it fails to witness the unequal distribution of precarity in the lives of those who, consequently, risk ending up not being represented in the democratic and/or juridical realm, while the particularistic account 'reproduces and even fosters the isolation and marginality of groups and individuals identified as needing *protection*'.[15] For Butler (2015), the latter negates the agency of those designated as vulnerable, or more specifically the agency of vulnerability itself, as a potentially politically mobilizing force, and as the basis of ethical critique and action. Following this line of argument, what Moro (2022: 63) calls 'performances of vulnerability' are '[a]ssemblies and public interactions in which bodies gather with a political goal, while adopting a specific narration and interpretation of vulnerability as being a shared condition that all individuals embody, although each one does so in different ways using different resources and opportunities'.

Framing vulnerability as performative in this way – crucially through an understanding that does not neglect its materiality or status as a site of embodied struggle, foregrounds how recognition of our mutual, but socially situated, vulnerability is vital for social justice, and for reimagining a future in which our lives might be organized according to principles of care (Segal, 2019) and interconnectedness rather than borderization (Mbembe, 2019) or verticality (Cavarero, 2016). Yet recognition, as Butler and other commentators have argued, is a complex and ambivalent concept, itself vulnerable to co-optation in and through exploitative and oppressive organizational imperatives and contexts.

Vulnerability and recognition

Judith Butler's (2004a, 2004b, 2009a, 2009b, 2015) writing on vulnerability emphasizes how the latter emerges from mutual recognition of the shared predicament that is the human condition as a precarious one, while at the same time recognizing how that precarity is unequally distributed between groups of people within and across different societies and circumstances. At the heart of Butler's theory of how vulnerability relates to precarity is the question of recognition, or more specifically, a concern to understand how the desire for recognition comes to be organized in ways that render all of us vulnerable, but by no means universally or homogeneously so. Understanding how and why this is the case, and with what consequences for how we live and relate to one another, has arguably been Butler's most enduring philosophical and political preoccupation.

Returning to Cavarero for a moment before exploring this in more depth, it is useful to remind ourselves that Cavarero's writing discussed earlier has been subject to critique for its postulation that inclination is ideally embodied by the maternal caregiver. Although this is an approach that Cavarero (2021a: 42–44) says she sets out to interrogate in her critique of the dominant model of the self-sufficient individual, stating, for instance, that maternal inclination offers an analytical model 'to be strategically exploited in order to make inclination a … point of departure … from which to rethink the ontology of the vulnerable and its constitutive relationality' in effect, her writing arguably ends up reinforcing this association in ways that essentialize the maternal feminine as the ideal, ethical basis of social relations. In doing so, she ends up in a position from which she argues that women especially are inclined towards those in need of care and have a greater capacity to provide it. Commentators have noted that this is, effectively, to the exclusion of other possibilities (Bernini, 2021), including within the mother–child relationship (Devenney, 2021) and broader kinship and non-kinship relations (Woodford, 2021). Indeed, in phrasing that appears to contradict that cited earlier, Cavarero (2021a: 44) goes on to argue that maternal inclination can become 'the founding gesture of a new postural geometry', appearing to invert rather than critique the hierarchy of subjectivity she traces historically and philosophically in her account of inclination. In other words, here Cavarero arguably simply replaces verticality with inclination as the ideal ethical posture, rather than subjecting the assumption of self-reliance as the optimal way of being to critique, her precise use of the term 'founding' constituting another problematic reference to maternal essentialism.

Butler responds to this tension in Cavarero's writing in several ways that are important to our discussion of here, developing a more radical, non- (or more precisely, anti-) essentialist critique of verticality.[16] They do so, first, by emphasizing the importance of ambivalence in our affective ties and ethical relations and, second, by reminding us that ostensibly 'upright' bodies pre-suppose support that comes from an originary, primary inclination. As they put it, the upright self 'was not born into the world a standing person, which means that the upright body is *formed in dependency*' (Butler, 2021c: 46, emphasis added). Referring indirectly to Arendt's notion of nascent vulnerability, Butler's point here is that 'in the beginning, no one stands'. Further, Butler draws attention to the material, technical and infrastructural support that exceeds interpersonal caring relations, such as the maternal and familial, which Cavarero foregrounds, but also the sororal and platonic, as Bonnie Honig (2021)[17] has also emphasized in her critique of Cavarero.[18] In this sense, Butler highlights the significance of both how recognition comes to be organized *and* how it becomes an organizing principle through which, for instance, access to healthcare, education, legal recourse, and so on is filtered. As Butler puts it, 'all bodies from the start require support to stand on their own, if they are able to stand atall, and they never outgrow that requirement' (Butler, 2021c: 46). For Butler, then, everyone requires, from the very beginning, and throughout our lives, support to stand, figuratively speaking and often literally as well. This largely nascent rather than maternal framing of subjectivity as a postural geometry sees verticality as both the outcome of an organizational process, and as a disavowal of that process, or perhaps more specifically, as the (fictional) corollary of the vulnerability that our original 'nakedness', to borrow from Arendt, engenders. So, for Butler (2021c: 47, emphasis added), 'uprightness ... *is the result of* an established domain of infrastructural support ... eliding the infrastructural conditions of its very possibility'.

Further reflecting Arendt and diverging even more from Cavarero in doing so, Butler (2021c: 47) goes on to elaborate: 'this means as well that the sort of standings that humans do is conditioned and formed by objects and material conditions that are constituent moments'. Being upright is therefore an inherently precarious endeavour, as well as a pretence – a postulation, so to speak. While this critique is not a complete rejection of Cavarero as such, it is certainly a development of her account of the ethical posture of the subject in a different direction, namely by offering a recognition-based critique of verticality as a reification of relationality, rather than an advocacy of a maternal feminine postural alternative (Cavarero, 2016), and in this sense, Butler's critique is one which lays the basis for a quite different theory of vulnerability and its relationship to recognition and organization. As Butler (2021c: 50–51) puts it, 'when uprightness serves as the geometrical imaginary for masculinist individualism, it does so precisely by forgetting or projecting that history of dependency, exposure, inclination, and falling'. The task Butler sets us, in this respect, is that of tracing the *mechanism* of that externalization and disavowal. For Cavarero, this is to be found in the history of western philosophy and art, and its insistence of conflating the maternal feminine with inclination, a trap she herself arguably falls into, as noted above and as others have commented on.[19] *Contra* Cavarero, for Butler and Segal alike, this mechanism takes the form of institutional support which itself is too precarious, is the cause of the harm underpinning the need for support (the 'wound' as it were), *or* is organized according to principles that hierarchically structure access to the recognition, resources, rights and representation necessary for meaningful support.

But Butler does not stop there. They further complicate Cavarero's analysis of verticality as the antithesis of vulnerability through a dialectical reading of her critique of this juxtaposition, one that emphasizes the extent to which erect and inclined figures are never fully separate; for Butler (2021c: 49, original emphasis), 'the two are *not* radically distinct and never fully oppositional'. Rather, the upright figure can falter and fall, and both figures require infrastructural support, with the pretence of verticality as a disavowal of precarity being revealed *especially* when the provision of support 'turns out to do the very damage from which one needs protection and repair' (Butler, 2021c: 50). Instead of the inclined and erect figures being two opposed geometries of subjectivity, therefore, the one vulnerable, the other labouring under the myth of invulnerability, Butler emphasizes how we move between forms and extremes of inclination and rectitude throughout our lives, often depending upon the degree to which we are accorded or denied recognition, and on what or whose terms.

It is perhaps not too much of an overstatement to say, then, as Heikki Ikäheimo et al (2021: 1) have, that 'few concepts in contemporary social and political thought have attracted as widespread an interest as the concept of recognition'. Philosophical treatment of recognition within the Hegelian tradition, understood here as 'the social ascription of a desirable status' (Stahl, 2021: 170), frames recognition largely as a source of social affirmation based on the premise that 'if others are involved in shaping our lives through the way they see and treat us, recognition designates those forms of this process that are successful' (Ikäheimo et al, 2021: 2). Yet recognition is also 'a deeply ambivalent phenomenon' (Ikäheimo et al, 2021: 3), not least in terms of its relationship to vulnerability, and especially so within feminist thinking.

Recognition has been a central concern of Butler's writing on vulnerability since their earlier work. Drawing largely on Hegel, Butler has explored how recognition relates to vulnerability in at least three ways that are important to our discussion here. First, Butler shows how our desire for recognition renders us vulnerable in an ontological sense,[20] and in ways that are socially situated and structured, so that recognition is not equally available to, or possible for, all, operating as a conditional phenomenon, dependent upon an individual, group or entire population's capacity to meet its normative terms, or what Butler (2021a, 2021b) calls recognizability. Second, our desire for recognition also results in political vulnerability: those who are denied recognition lack access to the rights, resources, recourse, representation and so on that makes lives more or less liveable, and workable, and those who challenge the normative terms shaping recognition risk 'excessive' vulnerability, including being denied access to the resources necessary to support life (for example, to dignified, fairly paid work), but also to extreme violence or death.[21] Yet, third, Butler also foregrounds how recognition is also necessary if these various forms of vulnerability – ontological, social, political – are to be mitigated, implying not simply a cognitive process of 'knowing again', or re-cognizing our mutual interdependence, but also the ethical and political relationship that ensues from that process.[22]

Butler (2021a, 2021b) emphasizes how it is the 'framing' of recognizability that both affirms the exclusion of some and shores up the inclusion of others, disavowing mutual interdependence as the basis of social relations. Butler reminds us that for Hegel, recognition 'establishes the social relation between the I and the other' (Butler, 2021a: 35), and Butler takes seriously the *ek-static* character of the subject constituted within and through this relation, noting how we continualy find ourselves 'outside of ourselves', and that '"outside" proves to be a necessary feature of our self-understanding' (Butler, 2021a: 35). This mutual recognition of the difference between us is 'one of the most important roles of *determinate negation* in social relations' (Butler, 2021a: 35, emphasis added), constituting a primary dislocation as the basis for whatever social relation emerges between us.[23] Crucially, for Butler, this is one that renders us vulnerable in *both* an ontological and a socially situated, relational sense. To clarify, for Butler our mutually shared desire for recognition makes us all vulnerable in a constitutive sense, while our socially contoured experiences of recognizability add a 'double', socially situated – relational – layer to that existential, pre-social vulnerability.

To illustrate this point, in *Who's Afraid of Gender?* Butler (2024) reminds us that performativity, as a process of gender subjectivation, is an ontology that enables us to grasp, critically and reflexively, how the attribution of subjectivity (gender recognition) takes place within a matrix, or scene of constraint that consists of an 'entry point' to personhood, to which we are all differentially subject. Making precisely this point in earlier work, Butler argues that:

> Human beings come into the world through a gender matrix, such that being called a girl or boy is a mandatory gateway for becoming human. In this way, gender is there as a matrix of subject formation ... not merely a set of characteristics attributed to an already existing subject. (Butler, 2021a: 41)

Their performative theory of gender, and of recognition, insists, however, that 'freedom can be found within the scene of social constraint' (Butler, 2021a: 38) precisely because it is possible to oppose subjection to power regimes while being subject to those very regimes. For Butler (2021a: 39), this is 'the central paradoxical structure of subjugation and agency'. In other words, we are able to reflexively occupy the categories by which we are constrained 'and to give them new meaning' (Butler, 2021a: 39). But doing so, as Butler is also at pains to acknowledge, risks becoming subject to the vulnerability that ensues from opposing, standing up to or speaking out against regimes or scenes of constraint that render some people extremely vulnerable in a relational, recognitive sense.

Responding to this and drawing on Levinas (1969) in a way that is similar to Cavarero (2016) and Segal (2023), Butler argues that while our desire for recognition renders us vulnerable, often excessively so, it also opens up scope for how we relate to one another ethically and politically.[24] From the passage in Hegel's (1977 [1807]) *Phenomenology of Spirit* in which he tells us that we are each outside of ourselves, lost to or rather 'in' the other, Butler derives a rejection of the pretence of individual autonomy as the basis of social justice, arguing that: 'When we find a way to live among one another with a full understanding of our interdependency, and with a commitment to refrain from acts of destruction, we then are able to formulate and affirm a version of equality that acknowledges that profound and precarious form of interdependency' (Butler, 2021a: 51–52).

Understood from this perspective, recognition can lead to vulnerability in several important ways that connect its ontological and ethical dimensions to political solidarity via recognition: first, our only choice is to be recognized in ways and according to terms that are 'beyond us' and which can, therefore, lead to our subordination or negation. Second, even when we achieve recognition that might be acceptable ('recognizable') to us, the meaning of the terms we are subject to is never fixed or stable, and we are perpetually vulnerable, or rather we are vulnerable 'in perpetuity' – a premise that is key to understanding Butler's theory of vulnerability as a vital aspect of the human condition. Finally, our subjection is conditional (dependent) upon acceding to norms beyond our control, and further vulnerability is risked by those who challenge a position of conditional recognition and the norms on which it depends. How this position of vulnerability 'translates' into political capacity as the basis of struggle, as its 'vital' force, needs to be accounted for in recognition theory; in other words, we need to ask, how might a situation of precarity become one of possibility in ways that transform unlivably vulnerable lives into ways of existing – together – that have the capacity to endure, appear and 'work'?

Vulnerability as/at the extremes of liveability

In *The Force of Nonviolence*, Butler (2020b) explains how the unliveable life is one that persists unfeasibly. As discussed earlier, Butler understands vulnerability's ontology as follows: if exposure is co-existent with life, so that to live is to risk violence and death, and our existence means that we are all interdependent upon one another, our mode of living means that we are mutually vulnerable in our embodied intertwining.[25] But, as we also discussed earlier, Butler and others emphasize how this vulnerability is socially situated in ways that mean life is more exposed, and unliveable, for some individuals, groups and populations than others.

In Butler's discussion on the relationship between vulnerability and liveable lives with Frédéric Worms (Butler and Worms, 2023), both emphasize that in the concept of an 'unliveable life', seemingly not just a semantic contradiction, but an ontological (and by implication, ethical) one, resides the possibility of political and social critique of how our inherent, primordial vulnerability comes to be organized in ways that make life unliveable for many, and untenably so for some. Their discussion foregrounds the problem of how we can understand, and therefore respond to, the 'problem' of what it means to say that some lives are unliveable. Both agree that if this claim means to assert that some people's lives ought not, for ethical reasons, to be lived as they are, then it also (always) implies a critique of the conditions to which those lives are subject, and to express the urgent need for circumstances to be otherwise. The concept of the 'unliveable' life is therefore at once (1) an empirical descriptor – referring to lives that cannot be lived as they are, that are unfeasible or unsustainable, (2) a normative critique – a claim that lives such as these should not be lived as they are, that they are unendurable, and (3) a political imperative – asserting that society must find ways for lives that ought not to be lived as they are, to be lived differently.

In dialogue, Butler and Worms (2023) examine the unliveable as the most extreme point of human suffering and injustice, considering what can be done to prevent and repair lives that are unliveable. Butler criticizes the norms that make life precarious *in extremis*, while Worms appeals to what he calls a 'critical vitalism' as a way of allowing the hardship of the unliveable to reveal what is essential to us for physical and social survival.[26]

Worms gives three meanings to critical vitalism: a refusal to not exist (for example, to die), a discernment (for example, between different kinds of life) and a mode of reflexivity. By the latter, he refers to an ethical and political criterion for understanding what is 'vitally' necessary to life. For Worms, this refers largely to a necessary minimum, that is, a socio-political guarantee of the *vita minima* that makes lives liveable, and he lays out three polarities that structure the act of discerning between lives that are viable from those that are not: between life and death, between attachment and violation, and between care and power. With echoes of Honneth (1995), Worms argues that all living beings are mortal, and no attachment relationships are immune from the risk of violence and violation, so that all care is permeated by power dynamics. Critical thinking, he reminds us, while committed to values of life, attachment and care, understands these tensions as an essential ambivalence in social and interpersonal relations. For Worms, such tensions are intrinsic to all vital phenomena, and to which care responds. When life is deprived of care in all its forms it is made unliveable. The possibility of care is therefore the first criterion of life's liveability (see also Segal, 2023); for Worms, a life without care is simply a 'damaged' life.

Drawing on and responding to these lines of argument, for Butler it is impossible to disentangle precariousness as a shared existential condition from precarity – the social and political processes that position some individuals, groups and populations as more at risk than others, for example, in ways that endanger life.[27] In *Notes Toward a Performance Theory of Assembly*, Butler (2015: 17) places the question of what a liveable life means, and what the conditions of liveability are, at the forefront of politics, for example, referring to mobilizations that formulate their demands 'in the name of the living body, one entitled to life and persistence, even flourishing'. This develops ideas introduced in Butler's (2009a: 33) earlier work, *Frames of War*, focusing on the social ontology of the body to foreground the relational conditions of our embodied way of being.[28] Such an approach establishes unliveability as a social ontology that provides a way for Butler to 'situate the living body in relation to material, infrastructural, intersubjective, and, more generally, social and environmental conditions, *without which this body can hope neither to survive nor to flourish*' (Charpentier and Barillas, 2023: 7, emphasis added). Butler's philosophical reflections on this underpin their socio-political critique and the ethical-political obligations that stem from them. Ultimately, this is the critical requirement that Butler believes must serve as the norm for political action: 'to secure the conditions for liveable lives, and to do so on egalitarian grounds' (Butler, 2015: 21). For Butler, it is only by securing these conditions that the possibility of becoming, of living and of futurity can be secured. Without this possibility '*a life is merely existing; but it is not living*' (Butler, 2020b: 100–101, emphasis added).

For Worms (in Butler and Worms, 2023: 14, original emphasis), liveability is 'a notion that cannot be reduced to a strictly biological level, although it points toward what is *vital* for us'. Worms recognizes intersubjectivity as key to liveability, which he defines as 'one person's recognition of another as the subject of "their" own life' (Worms, in Butler and Worms, 2023: 16). For him, the unliveable is a scenario brought about by a negation of subjectivity, 'a situation in which "life" continues without "someone" to live it'. Worms notes the significance of recognition to liveability when he says, 'just as we can die, in the classical sense of the word, from hunger and cold, so our life can be made unliveable (and therefore mortal) by a lack of recognition' (Worms, in Butler and Worms, 2023: 20). In response to a life that becomes unliveable due to a lack of recognition, Worms posits critical vitalism as a life preoccupied with 'taking care', by which he means '*arranging for the conditions of a liveable life* in all senses, in all the vital dimensions of living humans' (Worms, in Butler and Worms, 2023: 20, emphasis added). To live a liveable life, in this respect, means 'to be the creative and social subject of one's life' (Worms, in Butler and Worms, 2023: 22).

This phenomenological approach to liveability, one that is developed in both Butler's and Worms's writing, and in dialogue with one another, is concerned with integrating the vital and the critical, enabling us to connect vulnerability to ethics and politics, and to understand those who are 'vulnerable' as those who are denied recognition and all that it implies. It also posits 'taking care' as a process of organizing – 'arranging', as in making provision for, and structuring, the conditions that make a liveable life possible. And in this sense, it strikes me as significant that in English the phrase 'taking' care is largely used to refer to minding ourselves, and to providing care to and for others. The origins of the verb 'to take' in English are interesting to note here, referring to the Old Norse word '*taka*', meaning 'to grasp' or 'get hold of', which has connotations of both a physical activity and a process of understanding, perhaps even of recognition. I note this because it suggests that when we 'take care' and encourage others to do so in everyday conversation and social relations, we are arguably inviting a recognition of our shared, situated need for care as the basis of how we relate to one another.

Thinking relationally: vulnerability *contra* resilience and paternalism

Not surprisingly, in thinking through what liveability means in the current socio-political context, Butler is highly critical of the discourse of resilience that has been widely mobilized in contemporary neoliberal invocations to 'overcome' vulnerability. For Butler, what makes otherwise vulnerable lives more liveable is if they are organized according to norms that seek to safeguard and further the conditions necessary for liveability. This further develops Butler's reading of Hegel's (1977 [1807]) philosophical concern with intersubjectivity, situating the struggle for recognition, understood not as a resilient desire to 'overcome' vulnerability but rather as a reiteration of its relational ontology, as more than phenomenological. The political imperative that Butler adds here is that of the need to recognize that the desire for recognition is not simply of one's self, but of the shared but social situated nature of one's vulnerability, in a way that requires an understanding that the self does not emerge or persist without a supportive infrastructure for mutual interdependency. And for Butler, it is not simply recognition of one's vulnerability that is crucial to ethical social relations, but recognition that mutual vulnerability is our shared (albeit socially contoured), relational way of being. In Butler's words:

The reason the subject has to be referred to intersubjectively is that *my life is not liveable without your life being liveable, without a number of lives being liveable, because we are commonly dependent on each other and social structures for common life.* The subject that I am is dependent on care not only in infancy but throughout life, and 'care' is meant here less as a maternal disposition than a social and institutional provision for a liveable life. (Butler, in Butler and Worms, 2023: 30–31, emphasis added)

Butler's use of the term 'care' here is particularly important (in the commonsensical use of that term, and in the way in which Worms mobilizes it), decoupled from its essentialist connotations and situated in organizational life as crucial to liveability, based on an understanding that care is 'relational, *and* also institutional' (Butler, in Butler and Worms, 2023: 36, original emphasis). Here Butler concurs with Worms (and Segal, 2023 – see earlier discussion) that a liveable life is a cared for life, a cared about life and a 'cared with' life, but this care requires 'infrastructures that nourish the living'. In their discussion, this link between liveability and care is further elaborated on by Butler and Worms with reference to equality, which Butler defines as 'the mutually dependent relations of people in social and economic life … a feature and result of interdependency'. Underpinning Butler's understanding of how a liveable life connects to care and equality is their view that the intersubjective conditions of liveable life imply a fundamental obligation towards the life of the other; for Butler, this is how liveability links to ethics and politics. In this sense, as well as the political imperative of liveability, Butler emphasizes that the recognition of intersubjectivity described earlier provides the basis for the ethical obligations that we have towards one another. The latter involve a commitment 'not just to protect the life of the other, but to affirm … the institutional conditions that support interdependent lives as part of a community without borders' (Butler, in Butler and Worms, 2023: 32), emphasizing the relationship between intersubjectivity and infrastructure as crucial to sustaining the conditions that might enable interdependency to flourish.

In reflecting on the terms of liveability in dialogue with Butler, Worms also thinks about the unliveable as 'the unnarratable' (Worms, in Butler and Worms, 2023: 33). Butler responds to this by noting that unliveability can mean living life 'in a contradictory way without solving the conceptual contradiction that structures that life', living in tension, ambivalence 'or perhaps through a certain kind of splitting' (Butler, in Butler and Worms, 2023: 34). Speaking in dialogue with Worms in 2022, Butler refers to refugee situations as illustrative of life as physically, psychically and politically unliveable, as 'unnarratable'. Butler also links unliveability to a recognition-based understanding of abjection as intersubjective, noting that 'something about the unliveable makes us turn away because we don't want to imagine that we could be in that situation.

And yet we know we could. And that denial intensifies the suffering' (Butler, in Butler and Worms, 2023: 48). And it is this 'turning away', a 'disinclination' in Cavarero's terms, that reproduces unliveability, rendering unliveable lives abject or mis-recognized. Referring to abjection in this sense, Butler (Butler, in Butler and Worms, 2023: 49) notes that 'ambivalence is also part of its reproduction', and this ambivalence – which we may think of as a disavowal of our mutual vulnerability and interdependency – has both a temporal and situated dimension. For Butler, a necropolitical logic that 'allows toxification and destruction to go on elsewhere as long as it does not happen here' stabilizes 'there and here' and 'them and us' (and 'then and now') 'in the service of denial and abandonment' (Butler, in Butler and Worms, 2023: 55) – a crucial, perceptual organizing device perpetuating the disavowal of recognition that is necessary to liveability.

For Butler and Worms then, much like Moro (2022), Tronto (2015), Segal (2023), the Care Collective (2020) and others who have advocated networks of solidarity based on care, what are required are new modes of action underpinned by a collective commitment precisely to 'not looking away'. Framing liveability as a political concern, Butler poses the question of what form these might take as an organizational one, asking:

> If we agreed that there is a minimal set of conditions for liveability, then the question of how that set of conditions gets implemented and organized is a political question ... that brings us back to basic questions ... of global governance ... Through what established units does it work, and *what kinds of new organizational structures does it require?* (Butler, in Butler and Worms, 2023: 65, emphasis added)[29]

Butler goes on to ask Worms if it is possible to make a distinction between critical and uncritical vitalism, with the latter referring to what does 'damage in the name of life' (Butler, in Butler and Worms, 2023: 71) by understanding vitality in terms of personal liberty that comes at the expense of others, while linking the former – critical vitalism – to recognition-based interdependency. This is potentially an important concern to connect to Butler's (open) question, *'what kinds of new organizational structures does [liveability] require?'* (Butler, in Butler and Worms, 2023: 65, emphasis added). As a starting point for responding to this question, Butler and others have considered what scope there might be for an ethics and politics based on principles of nonviolence.

Vulnerability and the ethics/politics of nonviolence

To recap, we have considered so far how those who are positioned, or who experience life, as vulnerable are also those who are at most risk of being subject to the other's violence or neglect, and our desire for recognition clearly comes to be organized in ways that perpetuate, accentuate and realize this. Our bodies materialize this: they are not simply the threshold of personhood; they are also 'the site of passage and porosity ... evidence of an openness to alterity that is definitional of the body itself' (Butler, 2020b: 16). In *The Force of Nonviolence* (Butler, 2020b), Butler considers the philosophical and political nature of responses to the other's vulnerability ('porosity'), examining how oppressive regimes such as racism are mobilized to inform justifications for governmental and bio-political violence, and noting how violence is often attributed to those most vulnerable to its destructive effects. Their ontological starting point in developing a critique of this is a sense that 'violence done to another is at once a violence done to the self' (Butler, 2020b: 9). While somewhat idealistic, as an organizing premise, a principle of nonviolence might be a way, Butler argues, of acknowledging that each self is implicated in the other, *and* 'of affirming the normative aspirations that follow from that prior social relatedness' (Butler, 2020b: 9).

Crucially, this relationality extends beyond intersubjective human relations, 'the dyadic human encounter', which is why 'nonviolence pertains not only to human relations, but to all living and inter-constitutive relations' (Butler, 2020b: 9), the basis of which is the crucial point that the self is made up only through relations with others, including the beyond human, or 'more than' human, sphere of existence. Recognizing this requires a critique of ego-logical ethics as well as of the political persistence of individualism so as to open up an ontology and ethics of intersubjectivity 'as a fraught field of social relationality' (Butler, 2020b: 10).[30]

In their essay, 'Nonviolence, grievability and the critique of individualism', Butler (2020b) revisits their earlier work on grievability in developing a relational theory of vulnerability, emphasizing the importance of social bonds for a nonviolent politics and ethics of relationality. The Hobbesian view (that assumes that one individual wants what another has) is a 'powerful fiction', Butler (2020b: 30) argues, providing a point of view from which to comprehend how the organization of passions and interests (and resources) props up the verticality and borderization about which Cavarero (2016) and Mbembe (2019) are so concerned. In developing their Hegelian critique of Hobbes, what troubles Butler most is the subject at the heart of this 'powerful fiction', one that (seemingly), Butler wryly observes, 'was never provided for, never depended upon parents or kinship relations, or upon social institutions, in order to survive and grow and (presumably) learn' (Butler, 2020b: 37); rather, 'he' stands in independent verticality from the start, as Cavarero (2016) has described it.

And like Cavarero, Segal and others, Butler emphasizes that if we wish to develop a critique of this fantasy in order to think and act beyond it, we have to be able to imagine ways of being and of relating to one another that do not neglect or negate dependency but rather foreground and resource it. Resonating with Cavarero's account of verticality and its relationship to self-sufficiency and moral rectitude, the scene of subjective inauguration is read by Butler with characteristic humour, as follows: 'He sprang, lucky guy, from the imaginations of liberal theorists as a full adult, without relations, but equipped with anger and desire' (Butler, 2020b: 38). In Butler's view (and in accordance with Cavarero), we must concede, therefore, that an annihilation has taken place prior to this narrated scene, or rather 'that an annihilation inaugurates the scene: everyone else is excluded, negated, … from the start' (Butler, 2020b: 38). This annihilation of alterity, and by implication of mutual vulnerability, constitutes what for Butler is an inaugural violence, giving a history to the fantasy of the 'lucky man' on the basis of 'a murder that leaves no trace' (Butler, 2020b: 38). Many feminists have of course argued that the social contract is always already a sexual contract (see Pateman, 1988); but Butler argues further that somewhere in this inaugural scene 'an expulsion of some sort has taken place, and within that vacated place is erected the adult man' (Butler, 2020b: 38).

Further, and developing Cavarero's (2016) critique, Butler argues that this adult man is understood to encounter others only in a conflict-ridden way, his goal being annihilation of the Other and total self-sufficiency. Butler's Hegelian perspective does not, it is important to stress, lead them to argue against the primary character of conflict; Butler insists that every social bond is in part a conflict. Rather, their concern is with what keeps this potential for conflict, for annihilation, 'in check' – it being the case that if nonviolence is to make sense as an ethical and political position, it cannot simply repress aggression; rather, 'it emerges as a meaningful concept precisely when destruction is most likely or seems most certain' (Butler, 2020b: 39). What accounts for that 'check'? While some might argue that it is the superego, others that it is the law or coercive state power, and others that it comes from a calm region of the soul that we ought to cultivate through spiritual practices, Butler argues that this destruction is and can only be checked by recognition of the obligations that stem from our mutual interdependency, because 'we were all … born into a condition of radical dependency' (Butler, 2020b: 41). Again, and developing points noted earlier, this takes Butler in a different direction to Cavarero (2016), for whom feminine maternalism provides the vital antidote to *homo erectus*' (conceited) self-determination, and in this sense (as in other respects), Butler arguably builds upon Cavarero's work, while also reading Cavarero against herself.

And to reiterate, for Butler, this is not a scenario that we somehow 'grow' out of or overcome; our ontology means that no one ever actually 'stands' on their own. In Butler's words:

> Our enduring dependency on social and economic forms of life itself is not something we grow out of – it is not a dependency that converts

to independence in time. When there is nothing to depend upon, when social structures fail or are withdrawn, then life itself falters or fails: life becomes precarious. That enduring condition may become more poignant in care for children and the elderly, or for those who are physically challenged, but *all of us are subject to this condition.* (Butler, 2020b: 50, emphasis added)

In this sense, Butler's critique is in part one of the conflation of vulnerability with chrononormativity, here framed as an ontological or more specifically relational assertion rather than a sociological one. That assumptions are made about certain achievements or life course markers is premised, Butler suggests, on the idea that we are from the start self-sufficient.[31] As disability scholarship and activism has long since shown us (see Boys, 2017), however, it is not only those who are disabled who require support to live: 'all … basic human capacities are supported in one way or another' (Butler, 2020b: 41). Dependency can be defined, at least in part, 'as a reliance on social and material structures and on the environment' (Butler, 2020b: 41) right from the start, and throughout our lives.

In this sense, the task is not to 'overcome' dependency in order to fulfil the fantasy of self-sufficiency (in the way that resilience discourses urge us to)[32] but rather to 'accept interdependency as a condition of equality' (Butler, 2020b: 47), *at the same time* as reflexively understanding how that interdependency is socially situated and differently structured. In *The Force of Nonviolence*, Butler illustrates this point with reference to the chronologic of colonial power (in a discussion that has important parallels with disability politics, critiques of normative ageing, and so on). As Butler reminds us, colonial power seeks to establish the pathological dependency of the colonized through a scene in which the colonizer imagines himself (*sic*) as the 'adult' responsible for the childlike colonized population. Of course, the colonizer depends on the compliable willingness of the colonized, 'for when the colonized refuse to remain subordinate, then the colonizer is threatened with the loss of colonial power' (Butler, 2020b: 48). Butler's critique of this scenario lays the groundwork for a practice of nonviolence as 'a new egalitarian imaginary' (Butler, 2020b: 49), premised on the view that nobody can sustain life independently – to believe otherwise is to perpetuate a harmful fantasy that is detrimental to our most basic relationality and its articulation within social relations.

As Butler puts it, the embodied paradox of 'the social organization of life' (Butler, 2020b: 49) is that we all start by being given over, 'a situation both passive and animating' (Butler, 2020b: 49). Recognition of this is crucial to Butler's understanding of vulnerability, and its relationship to ethics and politics, not as simply ontological ('universalistic', in Moro's terms – see earlier discussion), or solely as socially situated ('particularistic', as Moro puts it), but more precisely, as *relational* – as the outcome of how our desire for recognition comes to be organized according to norms that condition the outcome of the inaugural scenario in which we are each given over to the other, but as Butler emphasizes (especially through their concept of 'recognizability'), never according to the same terms or circumstances.

The radical equality that this way of understanding vulnerability might make possible, as a precondition for a nonviolent ethics of relationality, is not an absolute principle but (in Hegelian terms) 'an open-ended struggle' (Butler, 2020b: 56), and this struggle is shaped, ultimately, by a preoccupation not with annihilation but with preserving the life of the Other. Exploring this further requires Butler to consider how 'the "I" and the "you", the "they" and the "we" are implicated in one another', and how that implication is 'lived out as *an ambivalent social bond*, one that constantly poses the ethical demand to negotiate aggression' (Butler, 2020b: 69, emphasis added). This is the basic premise of a nonviolent, relational ethic as Butler sees it, but it is one that is problematized by notions of vulnerability that presume a certain paternalistic divide (see Butler, 2016) between those situated as 'vulnerable' and those who are not.

As Butler sees it, a designation as vulnerable enables certain individuals and groups (and other animate and inanimate beings) to claim protection, as discussed briefly earlier. Yet the question then becomes: 'To whom is that claim addressed, and which group emerges as charged with the protection of the vulnerable?' if not society as a whole (Butler, 2020b: 71). There is also the related risk that those responsible for protecting particular individuals, groups or populations of vulnerable beings become divested of responsibility for causing or perpetuating others' (situated, structured) vulnerability. Thinking through these issues, Butler (2016, 2020b) argues that paternalistic perceptions of vulnerability are based on two problematic assumptions. First, they reify vulnerability, treating vulnerable beings as if they were somehow already 'inherently' constituted as more vulnerable than others. Second, and most pertinent to our immediate discussion, such perspectives fortify established power relations 'at the very moment in which reciprocal social obligations are most urgently required' (Butler, 2020b: 71; see also Pianezzi, 2025). These two concerns are related of course, as the process of designation 'fixes' those deemed vulnerable as distinct from those who are, by implication, framed as inviolable. Further, this paternalism unreflexively reiterates ('recites', to use Butler's earlier terminology [see Butler, 1988, 1990]) precisely the hierarchical social relations it ought – as its ethical and political preoccupation – to dismantle.

Grappling with these issues in their essay, 'The ethics and politics of nonviolence', Butler reminds us that 'a life can register as a life only within a schema that presents it as such', so that the annihilation or foreclosure of whole groups or populations amounts to a 'genocidal epistemology' (Butler,

2020b: 112). Here Butler draws on Fanon's (1967) notion (reflected in earlier writing on the heterosexual matrix [see Butler, 1990, 1993]) of a historical-racial schema that functions as a perception and projection of what is viable, '*an interpretive casing* that enfolds the black body and orchestrates its social negation' (Butler, 2020b: 113, emphasis added). This, Butler notes, bears a direct relation to Merleau-Ponty's (2002 [1946]) 'bodily schema' – '*the organization of tacit and structuring bodily relations* within the world' as well as the act of 'constituting oneself within the terms made available by that world' (Butler, 2020b: 113, emphasis added). Butler poses a series of questions about how this works to establish relative values for different lives that serve to socially situate, or striate, lived experiences and perceptions of vulnerability, asking: 'How do we account for the differential ways in which lives and deaths matter or fail to matter? ... How do such differentiated modes of perception ... operate, as a set of uncritically accepted presuppositions' (Butler, 2020b: 114–115)?

To address these questions, Butler turns to Foucault's (2004) discussion at the close of *Society Must Be Defended* where he opens up the proposition that populations who are precarious or abandoned are 'not yet' constituted as subjects of rights and, by implication, are denied access to representation and resources. Foucault abandoned this project, but it is one that Butler feels can and perhaps should be revived, their concern being to supplement Foucault by bringing Fanon to bear on questions of how and why regulatory schemas become subjective configurations that inform perceptions of liveability, or what Butler (1993) calls intelligibility, or recognizability in later work (see Butler, 2021a, 2021b). Such questions, Butler reminds us, are always 'bound up with ... recognition' (Butler, 2020b: 116) so that, for instance, racism works as a 'thought sequence' that serves to negate 'the life claim of the person whose life is at stake' (Butler, 2020b: 116), themes that Butler explores more fully with reference to trans people's rights in *Who's Afraid of Gender* (Butler, 2024).

For Butler, lives rendered unintelligible or unrecognizable are lives 'not deemed worthy of safeguarding' (Butler, 2020b: 120). Understood in this way, asylum seekers, as but one possible example, become people 'we' would rather let die than let in, 'they are treated as beyond losing ... never having been entitled to life' (Butler, 2020b: 121). Drawing from Merleau-Ponty, Butler argues that negation of their 'unintelligible' lives occludes the social bond within a schema in which aggression becomes justified through a perceptual field that endorses destructive violence 'because from the start, such a life ... did not register as a life' (Butler, 2020b: 121).

In response to this scenario, the task, Butler (2016, 2020b) argues, is not to reify a class of persons designated as vulnerable in order to 'protect' or exploit them. Rather, it is to raise awareness of those who lack basic human requirements, or whose freedom and rights are routinely denied, or violated. As they put it, '"subordinate or die" may seem like a hyperbolic imperative, but it is the message that many ... know is addressed to them' (Butler, 2020b: 189). But, as Butler also emphasizes, violence 'constitutes a dense site for *complex histories of oppression as well as of resistance struggles*' (Butler, 2020b: 190, emphasis added). The dual meaning of struggle as both unable to cope/do otherwise and of resisting is important to understanding its relationship to vulnerability in this respect, in Butler's writing and in contemporary feminist work on ethics and politics more widely.

Towards an ethics and politics of vulnerability

Returning to an ongoing dialogue with Adorno, Butler argues that a life will only ever be a good life if and when it is lived with others, as the 'I' always requires a 'you' 'in order to survive and flourish' (Butler, 2020b: 200). Yet beyond this, the 'I' and the 'you' require a sustaining world – an organizational infrastructure for social relations that can fully protect and support the obligations we bear towards one another, and which in doing so, provide the conditions within which those obligations can be honoured. This is what we might mean by a caring society premised upon mutual recognition of our shared, but socially situated, interdependency – one in which recognition brings with it rights, resources and representation for all who need them.

Feminist writing on ethics often emphasizes how beginning with the concept of bodily vulnerability can help us to understand how conditions can emerge that enable or deny a more or less liveable life to exist, including in and through organizational life (Kenny and Fotaki, 2023). At the same time, feminist writing also challenges a view of vulnerability as 'injurability', reinstating its dialectical meanings in the way that Butler does by emphasizing the potential for solidarity attached to vulnerability's relationality, including, for instance, with reference to feminist activism and knowledge production, recognizing that vulnerability carries 'salient, ethical meaning, and significance' (Kaasila-Pakanen et al, 2024: 268).[33] Such an approach foregrounds vulnerability as 'unavoidable receptivity and openness to the ability to affect and be affected by other' (Gilson, 2014: 37), and as crucial to a just and sustainable social world, one premised upon an ethics of openness to one another (Hancock, 2008).

Feminist writing on relationality frames vulnerability as premised upon our socially situated mutual interdependency. As such, it provides the basis for an ethics and politics that understands the moral premise of the connection between vulnerability, recognition, ethics and agency to be relational. Such an approach challenges a normative equation of dependency with a lack of agency, understanding it instead as the foundation for solidarity. It also challenges the bifurcation of vulnerability, discussed earlier and returned to here, as universalistic or particularist (Moro, 2022), a critique that has important origins in and parallels with critical disability studies, with struggles for trans recognition and rights, and with critical race studies, indigeneous people's struggles for recognition and rights, and migrant community activism.

To recap, the etymology of vulnerability has led to the term being used largely to refer to a state of being more likely than is usual in any given social context to experience harm. This, combined with the socially situated nature of vulnerability, has led to ongoing debate over whether vulnerability is best understood as a universal feature of all human lives or alternatively as a circumstance that is experienced more in some lives and less so in others. This distinction would not be so problematic if vulnerability were not also associated with an implied lack of autonomy and agency, which, in most contemporary societies, is generally perceived – and experienced – negatively.

A universalist, or ontological, perspective understands vulnerability as meaning 'to be potentially subject to harms' of various kinds, especially those that are commonly regarded as natural or inherent to what it means to be a living being such as illness, injury or death. Seen through this lens, all human beings are vulnerable, because constant exposure is constitutive of the fabric of human life in both a physical and existential sense; this is what Cavarero (2021a: 42) calls 'congenital vulnerability' – the vulnerability that we are born with and into, as Hannah Arendt's (1998 [1958]) understanding of the human condition emphasizes. Understanding vulnerability as a constitutive feature of human relationality means that, in practice, none of us can ever hope to escape the fear, threat or actual experience of harm entirely. For Arendt, this is the case precisely because we begin in the intensely vulnerable state of infancy, and most if not all of us will die much the same. With exposure to risk being a constant presence throughout our lives, vulnerability is simply our way of being, definitive of the human condition in all its plenitude and generosity, as well as its selfishness and stupidity.

A widely cited reference point for thinking about vulnerability in more socially and/or politically particular terms than Arendt's constitutive ontology and its influence in feminist thinking is that of Giorgio Agamben's (1998) notion of the 'bare life', a term developed largely to refer to a form of living death or abjection through which some people, groups or populations come to be understood and treated as dispensable. Consumed solely with their own physical or psychic survival, those living a bare life are deemed to lack the agency to challenge or change their situation. Bare life, in other words, is life divested of any political agency, or capacity to signify anything other than a subsistence level of existence.[34] Philanthropic, paternalistic responses to this positioning often presume a duty of care, to step in to provide those who are destitute with the shelter, care, support and protections that they cannot provide for themselves. Urgent though this can be, especially in the context of ongoing climate destruction and catastrophic, humanitarian crises, through this positioning, a reification of vulnerability is implied, one that, on the one hand, tends not to differentiate adequately between the diverse ways in which some people may become more vulnerable than others, and on the other, because paternalistic approaches are based largely on a model that ascribes agentic capacity on one side and dependency on the other. This raises several related problems already discussed: it negates mutual interdependency – vulnerability as a shared human condition in Arendtian terms; it shores up the ascribed 'power' of those deemed invulnerable; and it ignores the ways in which vulnerable individuals, groups and populations actively oppose, challenge and resist the conditions that render them disproportionately vulnerable. Finally, and perhaps of most significance to our discussion here, paternalistic responses to vulnerability as a social positioning organize the distinction between the 'vulnerable' and the 'invulnerable' hierarchically, the latter being idealized within neoliberal discourses of independence, resilience and self-reliance that negate the intersubjective relationality that *is* the human social condition from the more constitutive perspective adopted by Arendt and others.

Disability rights activists and theorists especially have challenged precisely this kind of paternalistic, binary distinction between vulnerability and invulnerability on both ontological and ethical grounds, problematizing not only this bifurcation but also its hierarchical organization. A notable critic of the assumption that disabled people have 'special' vulnerabilities distinct from the ontological exposure that is constitutive of all living beings is bioethicist, Jackie Leach Scully, who has argued that vulnerabilities are socially ubiquitous rather than limited to disabled people as an 'especially' vulnerable category. For Scully (2013: 204), '[t]he line between "normal" and "special" vulnerability is not natural but established through social and political decisions that determine when a dependency will be taken for granted and when it is marked as exceptional'. In this sense, Scully helps us to understand how disabled people might be vulnerable in an organization sense (for example, through patterns and experiences of exclusion, and inaccessibility), and how they might be vulnerable through organizations (for example, as political support and often, concomitantly, financial resources are withdrawn from advocacy organizations, and other infrastructures that make life liveable and workable). But most important for our discussion here, Scully helps us to make sense of how a paternalistic approach that positions disabled people as 'especially' vulnerable in a reificatory sense means that (their) vulnerability is also *the outcome of a process of organization* – of a framing of the desire for recognition, and the rights, resources and so on that (ideally) go with it in ways that 'organize' disabled people, and disability, as vulnerable.

Scully's (2013) socio-relational understanding of disability illustrates this, working through the apparent dichotomy between autonomy and dependence by arguing that the latter is a necessary condition of human existence. She illustrates this point with reference to a discussion of how a person with disabilities who requires adaptations to the built environment is often perceived as socially vulnerable, while a person who does not have disabilities, yet who needs similar infrastructural support to exist and act, for example, roads, pavements, staircases and so on, tends not to be perceived as vulnerable, but (paradoxically) as independent and self-reliant, even as they make use of these essential and enabling forms of material and organizational support. Scully argues that by bringing this anomaly in the relationship between social perceptions of vulnerability and lived, embodied experiences of mutual interdependency to the fore, we can begin to move beyond a reifying conception ('organization') of some individuals and groups of people as being 'more' or somehow 'especially' vulnerable than others in ways that, by implication, often negate their capacity to exercise agency. Her key point is that such an approach, a relational one, provides a more nuanced understanding of ontological vulnerability that takes account of differently situated vulnerabilities as constitutive of what it means to be human, as a socially situated being, in the sense in which Arendt and others understand it.

Using conceptual reference points similar to those we have engaged with so far in her examination of the range of vulnerabilities that disabled and non-disabled people experience, Scully (2013) makes a distinction between different types of vulnerabilities that are helpful to our discussion here: those that are 'inherent' (for example, those which are the direct result of an impairment), those which are 'contingent' (that is, are caused or accentuated by social and/or environmental responses to impairment) and those that are what she calls 'ascribed global vulnerabilities'. The latter refer to the tendency to generalize from a particular vulnerability in one aspect of a person's life to a globally increased dependency stretching across the entirety of that person's existence, with often negative consequences for that person's social positioning and life chances.[35] To appreciate the full effects of this, the (organizing) process of ascribing what she calls global vulnerabilities has to be placed, Scully argues, within historical and cultural contexts in which disabled people's lives have been deemed not to be liveable, and in which objectification is a persistent feature of their ontological, social and political landscape, themes returned to in Chapters 2–4.

Borrowing from Scully, we might argue that the reificatory effects of globally ascribed vulnerabilities are, on the one hand, a negation of the right to ethical treatment, or even to exist, and on the other, a denigration of people's capacity for agency and solidarity. Yet the normative logic of a paternalistic perspective not only conflates dependency and vulnerability, rather than understanding how the latter can (for example, through lack of adequate social resources, recognition and organizational infrastructures) lead to the former. Perhaps more problematically, dependency is often negatively equated with vulnerability within discourses premised upon perpetuating an idealization of individual autonomy, one that frames agency and vulnerability as antithetical, resulting in a logic that to be dependent is to be, by default, vulnerable in some excessive or 'special' sense. Reflecting feminist writing on relationality, such inherent, contingent and globally ascribed vulnerabilities are distinct from those which are 'generated intersubjectively', Scully (2013: 216) argues, and which are intrinsic to the human social condition.

Against this backdrop, Scully (2013: 217) asks, why is it the case that some forms of dependency become so reified that they 'globally' ascribe vulnerability to someone's entire personhood, while 'permitted dependencies are naturalised and normalised'? In response, Scully situates this question in a critique of liberal or Kantian accounts of personhood in which autonomy is an attribute possessed by an individual and exercised to a greater or lesser degree both in making and in effecting self-determined choices, and in doing so, exercising moral agency.[36] A growing body of work in feminist philosophy attempts to replace such liberal models of autonomy and moral agency with more relational views of the human condition that foreground the various ways in which it is interconnections rather than borders and hierarchies that enable people to exercise agentic capacity. Drawing from this work, Scully (2013: 212, emphasis added) notes how, while traditional models see autonomy as exercised more or less against the rival claims of others, 'relational accounts see the networks of social and institutional interdependencies within which people are embedded not as compromising self-determined choice and action but rather as *providing the … conditions of possibility for them*'. Relational perspectives, understood in this way, provide one reason that being more than usually dependent on others because of disability can't simply be equated with an overall decrease in the capacity for agency. From this perspective, dependency becomes a condition of autonomy rather than a threat to, or negation of, it.

Building on relational approaches to the question of vulnerability's ontology and its implications for ethics and politics, organization theorist Marianna Fotaki (2022) offers a feminist conception of solidarity that rejects the ideal of homogeneity and the notion of common interests as its foundation, proposing instead a non-exclusionary obligation to care for the irreducible other. As she explains it, 'this theoretical proposal of a holistic, relationally reconfigured notion of solidarity that is situated and embodied, allows us to formulate a political strategy to counteract the neoliberal predicament that threatens all forms of life with extinction' (Fotaki, 2022: 297). Drawing on both Butler and Levinas, Fotaki explicitly connects existential and socially structured vulnerability with the notion that interdependency obliges us to protect human life and the dignity of irreducible others. For her, mutual recognition of our shared but situated vulnerability as the basis of an ethic of relationality is 'a first crucial step in creating solidarity' (Fotaki, 2022: 316), a theme we return to in later chapters. In this sense, Fotaki responds to an important issue raised by Scully's discussion of different forms and lived experiences of vulnerability, one that has arguably plagued feminist approaches to social justice for many centuries; namely the question of how to act in solidarity as a plurality without risking misrecognizing or negating others' needs and desires at one extreme, or appropriating or reifying the other's otherness, or mobilizing it politically in a tactical sense, at the other, *at the same time* as reflexively recognizing that vulnerability, while existentially shared, is also socially situated and contoured.

Engaging with these concerns, Scully (2013: 206) notes how the two extremes created by a bifurcated understanding of vulnerability, as either universal or particular, present a series of related problems. As she outlines it, concentrating on the generality of vulnerability may detract from attesting with empirical rigour to the particular conditions that do, of course, make some people more exposed to harm than others, and this in turn makes it harder to take action to secure rights and resources to change those particular conditions for the better, including via securing necessary and sustainable infrastructures that are meaningful and recognition based. On the other hand, focusing only on the 'special' vulnerabilities of defined individuals, groups or populations risks reinforcing rather than problematizing the notion that although some people need specific or additional protections, the 'norm' of human life is to be, or aspire to be, invulnerable.

At best, this perpetuates paternalistic and/or philanthropic responses to the need for vulnerability (Pianezzi, 2025), including in a restorative sense (that is, according to a normative perception that the ideal is to 'restore' vulnerable people to normality). At worst, it might be exploitative, objectifying and/or abusive, negating subjectivity and the capacity for agency, and opportunities for recognition-based solidarity. As discussed throughout this chapter, in a way that will frame our focus in subsequent, more thematic ones, feminist perspectives on vulnerability have developed an alternative view to this bifurcation, noting not only the artificial separation of the 'vulnerable' from the 'invulnerable', but also developing both a critique of the hierarchical organization of this dichotomy, as well as a commitment to recognizing and organizing on the basis of relationality, care and solidarity. This is what we might think of as a radical vulnerability, providing the basis for an ethics of relationality premised upon the reflexive recognition of our shared, but always socially situated, vulnerability and a politics of solidarity underpinned by a concern to secure the rights, recognition and resources necessary for vulnerability to be understood and experienced as a vital aspect of the human, social condition rather than a limitation to be overcome.

Concluding thoughts

This opening chapter has examined some of the questions and challenges that a feminist approach to vulnerability needs to engage with, considering how these relate to the ways in which our desire for recognition comes to be organized. It has emphasized, with reference to feminist insights from philosophy, sociology and ethics, that to insist on the universality of vulnerability is not the same as to assert its uniformity (Moro, 2022), and in this respect, vulnerability can be understood to describe both the relational and embodied nature of living beings (ontological vulnerability) *and* our necessarily situated and unpredictable, yet also highly organized, existence (situational vulnerabilities). The question of what vulnerability means and of how it shapes social relations raises complex concerns that go to the heart of feminist conceptions of obligation, justice and agency that seek to find ways to reframe vulnerability as solidarity, beginning from the premise that while vulnerability is an ontological human condition, it is always also socially situated and structured. Understanding vulnerability as the outcome of how our desire for recognition comes to be organized in ways that, normatively speaking, can be affirmative, but also negating, is central to the relational approach considered and advocated here, drawing from work by Arendt, Cavarero, Segal, Butler and Mbembe, and its development in feminist writing on relationality and vulnerability. It is also key to grasping how vulnerability plays out in different social contexts. It is to this latter issue that we turn in the next three chapters.

2

Existing: The Social Relations of Breathing

> Respiration is a way of living in vulnerability.
> Magdalena Górska, *Breathing Matters*, 2016: 283

Introduction

In this chapter, we will explore the question of why we are ambivalent about or hostile towards one another when (especially when) it is so apparent that we breathe the same air, failing to recognize the most basic, mutual vulnerabilities shaping the human condition considered in Chapter 1; a critical question in the wake of a global pandemic and in the midst of a global climate emergency. Drawing together insights from the critical, feminist and postcolonial thinking discussed in the previous chapter, we will explore how examining the social relations of something as fundamental as breathing helps us to understand how our desire for recognition comes to be organized in ways that oppress and exploit us, but which also open up scope for thinking about how we might live and work together more relationally, in (reflexive) recognition of our shared but socially situated vulnerability, now and in the future.

By focusing on the social (organizational) relations of respiration, we will consider the forms of recognition that might be necessary to realizing some of the possibilities attached to more relationally affirmative modes of organizing that are currently in evidence as instances of activism and social movements across the public and social media spheres, including those directly concerned with respiratory poverty and precarity. With this in mind, the chapter sets out to consider how public engagement for hopeful and solidary-orientated futures might be understood and enacted through more radical forms of organizing that are recognition-based in their grounding in relationality and reflexivity, contrasting these with the more reified, rhetoric modes of recognition currently in circulation in social, political and organizational life, focusing on how respiration helps us to make sense of how these different modes of recognition are lived and experienced in relation to vulnerability and its organization.

We will begin with a discussion of respiration as a 'problem' of (and for) organization, considering its relationship to shared yet situated exposure, and the desire for recognition. We will then explore what it might mean to reimagine breathing through the lens of vulnerability, drawing on insights from phenomenological and sociological perspectives on the social relations of respiration, and insights from recognition theory drawn together from Judith Butler's (2016, 2021a, 2021b, 2022) writing on ethics, and Achille Mbembe's (2019) work on necropolitics. These different perspectives are discussed as offering, respectively, insight into the social relations and politics of respiration as bound up with our vulnerability and relationality. The discussion then moves on to focus on how the organization of respiration might be understood with reference to recognition and recognizability, making a distinction between reified forms of recognition based on a 'forgetting' of our mutual vulnerability, and more reflexive forms that connect to current feminist thinking and activism as the potential basis for more relational ways of organizing premised upon mutual recognition of our shared, yet socially contoured, vulnerability. In conclusion, we will reflect on how these theoretical insights can potentially provide the ethical basis for organizing in and through vulnerability, and for organizational modes of recognition that are more relational and solidarity-orientated, now and in the future.

The social organization of respiration

Despite its centrality to bodily existence,[1] social theory has paid only relatively limited attention to breath, and to breathing as an individual and collective endeavour (Allen, 2020). Yet there is growing recognition of the catastrophic problems caused by industrial air pollution, and of its connections to poverty and precarity as one of the world's biggest and most inequitable public health crises. The COVID-19 pandemic highlighted stark inequalities in access to breathable air among the world's population. Both issues – climate destruction caused by the polluting effects of global capitalism and a respiratory pandemic – brought our sense of similarity, even commonality, to the forefront (albeit the latter for a relatively brief period), foregrounding the interdependence brought about by our shared need for unrestricted access to safe, breathable air (Butler, 2022). And yet at the same time, and in ways that reflect respiration as an intertwined process of inhalation and exhalation, one existing as part of the other, these same circumstances shone a spotlight on the differences, not least the social inequalities that place limits around access to breathable air, between people living in different regions and situations across the world. To put it simply, our recent and ongoing circumstances illustrate to us, in no uncertain terms, the myriad ways in which the social relations of breathing are very much an 'organizational' problem in the broadest sense.

Yet the apparent lack of interest in breathing in social theory and in the social sciences more widely is largely replicated in the field of organization studies, within which respiration as an organized (or disorganized, or unjustly organized), social phenomenon has received only relatively limited interest to date – although for a recent exception, see Pérezts et al (2024). To rethink this, this chapter sets out to examine respiration as an organizational phenomenon, hoping to encourage a more critical, reflexive discussion of why we can't collectively see and sense our interdependency, but instead doggedly pursue what Achille Mbembe (2019) calls a necropolitics of borderization – an approach to organizing our lives that involves a shoring up of our differences and resources, including something as fundamental as air, negating our shared vulnerability and accentuating socially striated lived experiences of it.

Before we begin, it is perhaps helpful to remind ourselves at this point of the basic ethical premises discussed in Chapter 1 that enable us to set out what we might broadly call a phenomenology of respiration as a lens through which to understand how breathing connects to vulnerability. These are, first, that ethics and politics stem from the ways in which we are fundamentally mutually interdependent – to put it very simply, we breathe the same air (as Merleau-Ponty emphasized, when I breathe out, others breathe in and vice versa).[2] Second, we are driven by the desire for recognition of ourselves as socially viable beings worthy of rights, responsibilities and resources – we depend upon access to breathable air, and on other people and organizational infrastructures to provide this when needed. Finally, and in this respect, this desire for recognition is what drives our need for organization – it renders us mutually, inescapably vulnerable in an existential and embodied sense, a scenario that we do not somehow 'grow out of' – sometimes we simply cannot breathe unaided. Our life course 'bookends' this but it can happen to any of us, at any time. And in organizational terms, this desire for recognition constitutes an inherently exploitable form of human capital rendering us vulnerable in a political and economic sense as well as an existential one.

Thinking about breathing in this way, and in this context, reminds us of just how mutually interdependent we are, highlighting (to borrow from Butler and other feminist writers on ethics) that social relations and solidarity can *only* emerge from a mutual recognition of our embodied, relational multiplicity and shared intercorporeal vulnerability, and breathing is a poignant illustration – an embodied locus – of this. Taking this as a starting point enables us to explore how a more relational approach to organizing premised upon recognition of our embodied, mutual vulnerability might open up new possibilities for care and solidarity, and for more ethical and sustainable modes of organizing in the future that reflecting on the social relations of breathing enables us to grasp.

And yet, of course, such an endeavour also needs to proceed from the reflexive recognition that our social positioning is such that if we are all mutually vulnerable, we are by no means equally so, as discussed in Chapter 1. To go back to Merleau-Ponty's point, as successive waves of viral, racial and gendered violence have shown us, access to the right to breathe is not evenly spread but is organized along axes of race, gender, age, social class and geography.[3] If COVID-19, MeToo, Black Lives Matter and the climate emergency have taught us anything, it is that 'exposure is … a socially organized relation' (Butler, 2020b: 199). We have known for some time that the more privileged we are, the cleaner and safer the air we breathe, and the more liveable and workable the environment we inhabit, is likely to be. The use of gas in wartime is perhaps one of the more extreme examples of the axes and circumstances according to which these latter points come to be experienced and organized (Sloterdijk, 2009).

Respiratory poverty has a long history, starting with at least the early stages of industrialization, and remains a significant cause of preventable death in many parts of the world, accentuated by a globally contoured climate crisis and intersections of precarity and exposure to pollution that make access to clean air the preserve of the privileged few, as studies highlighting the 'embodied, entangled and emotional' experiences of people living in regions with high levels of industrial air pollution have shown (Jokela-Pansini and Militz, 2022: 742). According to the United Nations' Breathe Life campaign, which seeks to ensure that more people have access to a breathable environment by 2030, only one in ten people across the world currently breathe safe air.[4] And even for those fortunate enough to have unrestricted access to breathable air, the latter has rapidly become the subject of strategic interventions into the management of our everyday lives and ways of being. 'How to' manuals on effective breathing methods designed to enhance productive output abound, although we should note, of course, that midwives and doulas, and professional performers, have long since known about and practised careful breathing technniques, recognizing the importance of understanding how air moves in and out of us.

The dialogical nature of the boundaries between the social and material, and between bodies, that is epitomized by breath and breathing, and by the socio-material relations of respiration, is explored by feminist researcher Magdalena Górska (2016) in her project, *Breathing Matters*, in which she offers a post-humanist analysis that attends to the relationalities enacted through breathing. Górska's work emphasizes the transformative nature of breath, which she describes as a continuous metabolism extending the human beyond conventional boundaries of embodiment. For her, 'fighting for breath and for breathable lives is, therefore, *a matter of not only acts of and aspirations for change but also recognition*' (Górska, 2016: 264, emphasis added). Framing breathing as 'a vulnerable process of recognition and openness', Górska's is an approach that echoes Sloterdijk's (2009: 31, emphasis added) contention that air is 'the element, not of our exposure or containment, but of our *immixture with, our inextricability from* the outside world'. Górska and others' phenemonological way of understanding breathing frames respiration as a socio-material process, foregrounding the ways in which it problematizes enduring notions of our bodies and selves as discrete entities, understanding instead how we are not simply situated within, but are intertwined with, the environments we inhabit.

The social relations of respiration have also been considered within sociological thinking, highlighting that clearly not everyone has equal access to breathable air or experiences the same vulnerability to polluted/ contaminated environments. Brown et al (2020), for instance, show how for people with cystic fibrosis, achieving safe breathing spaces relies on a multitude of socio-technical elements, highlighting the need to 'think laterally' about the political and ethical contours of environmental conditions that lead to struggles to breathe, particularly in relation to race, class and caste, and in settings in which access to breathable air can be severely compromised. Such approaches foreground the need to be attuned to the social, political and spatial configurations that mediate and produce situations of exposure as starting points for reimagining how access to breathable air might be shared more equitably, based on recognition of our mutual, but contextually specific, vulnerability. They also highlight how taking deep breaths, finding the 'space' to breathe, might bring joy and an empowering and liberating sense of freedom, individually and/or collectively for some; yet at the same time, racial, class-based and other social injustices create very visceral, existentially threatening experiences of having no air to breathe for many others. Through a sociological lens, therefore, we can begin to understand how just as capacities to breathe are not equally shared, the quality of breathable air is not the same everywhere, as Jokela-Pansini and Militz's (2022) study of living and working in a highly industrially polluted community shows. As they note, the question of who breathes what kinds of air and where is one that is shaped by environmental inequalities, as well as racial, class-based and regional injustices.

In combination, phenomenological and sociological approaches to respiration emphasize how breathing, as a seemingly self-evident process of taking air into, and expelling it from, the lungs, can be considered as a mode of relating to the world – of engaging with others, objects, environments and technologies in ways that both provide the potential for connection and community, yet which can also act as the site for a perpetuation and exploitation of precarity and vulnerability. Understanding respiration in this way highlights its relationship to mutual interdependency, framing breathable air as a material, affective and aesthetic phenomenon, one that we should relate to not simply more gratefully and vigilantly (Pérezts et al, 2024), but also more reflexively and relationally. Scholars arguing for such an approach have studied the ways in which bodies enact politics through breathing, showing how breathing extends what it means to be a living being beyond conventional boundaries of embodiment (Górska, 2016), highlighting how breathing is a relational phenomenon, a process through which we are all 'deeply entwined' (Allen, 2020: 95).

Robin Wall Kimmerer (2013) makes this very point in her book, *Braiding Sweetgrass*, which draws from her indigenous and scientific knowledge of plant life to understand respiration in post- or non-dualist terms, emphasizing instead that all social and beyond human life is composed of movements of the inhalation and exhalation of shared breath. As Wall Kimmerer (2013: 165 and 179) reminds us, in this sense, all respiration is reciprocity – 'self-perpetuating cycles of giving and receiving'. And as she also encourages us to reflect on, 'cautionary tales of the consequences of taking too much are ubiquitous in [indigenous] cultures'.[5] Speaking of the urgent need for us to develop a regenerative, restorative relationship with the natural world, in which human beings exercise our caregiving responsibility for the ecosystems that sustain us via a relationship of mutual recognition and respect, Wall Kimmerer (2013: 144, emphasis added) explains what this might mean for how we understand and enact co-respiration. As she puts it, 'my breath is your breath, your breath is mine. *It's the great poem of give and take*, or reciprocity that animates the world'. Understood in this way, responsible respiration as a restorative act (taking only what is needed, and seeking to allow others and the rest of the world to 'breathe') becomes what she describes as a moral covenant, one that calls us to honour what we have been given, and acknowledge and atone for what we have taken, recognizing 'the privilege of breath' (Wall Kimmerer, 2013: 184).

What all of these insights point to, especially Robin Wall Kimmerer's understanding of breathing as reciprocity, is the need to think about breathing as much more than a physical act, but as a mode of relating to the world, and of engaging with others, through what Oxley and Russell (2020: 4) call 'the nebulous essence of being-in-the-world'. This is not least because, as they emphasize, breathing bodies complicate dualistic notions of inside/inside, self/other, presence/absence, opening up the necessity for more dialectical, dialogical ways of understanding, embodying and enacting social relations that acknowledge mutually shared, but situated, vulnerability. As they go on to note, while much of the research on breath focuses on its correlation to life, death, healing and illness, we need to find ways to explore how 'socio-economic contexts are embodied in the act of breathing' (Oxley and Russell, 2020: 17).[6]

Some of this work is beginning to emerge in research foregrounding the impact of industrial pollution on the social relations and organization of breathing. Anna Lora-Wainwright's (2021) study of how residents in China's so-called 'cancer villages' have to 'fight for breath', in a way that shows how interconnected the physical, emotional and economic hardships that result from living and working in an industrially polluted region are, is a notable example.[7] In these kinds of areas, toxins in the air, soil and water lead to a higher risk of early mortality, reproductive problems and respiratory diseases (Leogrande et al, 2019). Similar points of concern are raised by Pérezts et al (2024) in their recent work on breathing as a political mode of organizing, in which they reflect on the question of whose breathing 'counts' (that is, is valued, protected, resourced and so on), noting how the air that we breathe is too quickly becoming a commodity instead of a common resource. Breathing, as they put it, 'is as much about being able to breathe, as about letting others – including the more-than-human others – breathe' (Pérezts et al, 2024: 2). Echoing Franco Berardi's (2018: 11) point that breathlessness – what he calls 'the suffocation of abstraction' – is the leitmotif of our time, their starting point is the observation that the world we are currently living in is one characterized by both breathlessness and carelessness, and by purely instrumental and extractive relationships between ourselves, others and the world we inhabit. The intersubjective, intercorporeal and social significance of 'inhabiting' rather than 'having' our bodies and social world highlighted in phenomenological traditions invites us to claim back and restore a more liveable, breathable rhythm for our social existence, they suggest.[8] Reflecting phenomenological thinking, their account frames breathing as both a material exchange and as a metaphor for our times, stressing the importance of sharing spaces and resources for making our lives more liveable (Butler, 2004a). Holding our breath, they contend, can open up space for critical reflection, signifying hope and resistance by speaking out instead of simply struggling for survival in an era of breathlessness.

Accounts such as these, that approach breathing as an embodied, simultaneously material and metaphorical phenomenon, provide important starting points for thinking about how the organization of recognition shapes both our mutual vulnerability and the differential distribution of that vulnerability in ways that social movements and activism seek to address, as these are materialized in the social relations of respiration. Such an approach is an important part of any critical reflection on the socio-material relations of respiration and recognition, if 'breathable lives' are understood to be those which are both more sustainable and just, and it is to the question of recognition, and its relationship to breathability, that we now turn.

Reimagining breathing through recognition

So far, in Chapter 1 and here, we have reiterated how our embodied interdependence and relationality is a way of being that we cannot 'choose' or will away *contra* dominant political discourses and imperatives, and in this chapter, we have considered phenomenological, sociological and indigenous ways of thinking about respiration that highlight how breathing seems to illustrate this in a very fundamental way. Acknowledging this points to the idea that social (respiratory) equality can only emerge from a reimagined interdependency that foregrounds mutual but also socially situated vulnerability as the starting point for ethics and politics. As Judith Butler has argued (2016, 2022), and as we discussed in Chapter 1, the task is not to 'overcome' vulnerability, but to recognize that it is our way of being, that is, that recognition of the mutual vulnerability engendered by our interdependence is perhaps *the* condition of social justice. Vital for us to reflect on then (as noted at the start of this chapter), is the question of why we can't collectively recognize this, even in the wake of a respiratory pandemic, and in the context of an ongoing climate emergency.

Achille Mbembe (2019) responds to this question with reference to what he sees as a self-righteous necropolitics, one that reinscribes a spurious distinction between what Butler (2022: 28) frames as grievable and ungrievable lives, that is, between those who feel and assert their sense of having a right to be protected at all costs, at the expense of those whose lives are considered not worth recognizing or safeguarding, or as not mattering at all (see also Butler, 2009a). For Mbembe (2019: 1), the contemporary world is one that embraces the destructive desires that drove global histories of colonialism, with 'the force of separation' being its organizing principle. In his book, *Necropolitics*, Mbembe describes a scenario in which the Other's burden has become not only overwhelming but intolerable, with the desire to separate oneself from their presence being 'our' overriding imperative. In these circumstances, our most urgent problem is that of how to find 'a relation with others based on reciprocal recognition of our common vulnerability and finitude', as Mbembe (2019: 3) puts it. We return to Mbembe's work in more depth in the next two chapters, but for now, it is important to note his view that the key question of our age is that of how we reconcile what we come to perceive as 'our' right to live safely and freely, alongside the urgent need to recognize that such rights can only be meaningful if they are shared equally with those we perceive as different from ourselves in a social world in which 'it has become impossible to breathe' (Mbembe, 2019: 3). For him, this is because of our incapacity to share a respiratory rhythm between ourselves, others and the world in which we live, so that our orientation towards organizing our world via a shoring up of rights, resources and representation only for ourselves and those we understand to be 'like us' is literally choking everyone, including the natural environment on which we all depend.

Echoing Freud, in *The Force of Nonviolence* Judith Butler (2020b) recognizes that hostility is part of our psychic constitution so that the field of social relationality, rather than being unproblematically harmonious, is inevitably a fraught one. Characterized by negativity, our relationality is not simply 'a good thing', a sign of love, care or interconnectedness, but is rather 'a vexed and ambivalent field in which the question of ethical obligation *has to be worked out*' (Butler, 2020b: 10, emphasis added). Much the same can of course be said and thought about respiration, which, understood as a dialectical phenomenon, helps us to grasp how social relationality comes to be organized and experienced not as unproblematically harmonious, but as the outcome of ongoing struggle.

As Mbembe and Butler both emphasize, recognition is easier to comprehend with reference to those we identify with, see as like us, wish to protect and so on, but is more complex when applied to those we are hostile towards, including those whose beliefs, ways of life, and so on we might find abhorrent, or who we are simply ambivalent about. The dialectical and socially situated nature of relationality means that this 'working out', as Butler puts it, is a process of struggle, one played out through the body, as the social relations of respiration illustrate. Further, while our way of being is one that is situated in interconnection, dominant political discourses and modes of organization frame idealized subjectivity largely in terms of autonomy, so that we come to relate to one another primarily, or even only, through a frame of reference that posits dependency as negativity (see Segal, 2023) and which, in doing so, erases our basic and ongoing mutual vulnerability and the potential it holds for a more relational way of living, working and organizing together. An example of the result of this is the perception that a dependent life is not a 'real' life, or a life lived fully, and many people experienced this during the COVID-19 pandemic when told that elderly and/or disabled loved ones in hospital or care homes were being labelled 'do not resuscitate' so that oxygen and breathing equipment could be reserved for those deemed more 'deserving'.

If we wish to call this fantasy (of discrete autonomy) to account so that we might open up scope to think, organize and act beyond it, we have to be able to imagine ways of being and of relating to one another that do not effectively write dependency out of the picture, *and* which keep our hostility in check. Hegel (1977 [1807]) narrates the scene of (inter)subjective inauguration as one of struggle between master and slave through which each comes to recognize the other. In phrasing that resonates with Adriana Cavarero's (2016) critique of rectitude, Butler's reading of Hegel leads them to argue that an annihilation has already occurred prior to this narrated scenario, one that shapes its scenography: 'an expulsion of some sort has taken place, and within that vacated place is erected the adult man' (Butler, 2020b: 38) – unencumbered and self-reliant.⁹ Further, this adult man is understood to encounter others only in a conflict-ridden way, his goal being total self-sufficiency, as noted in Chapter 1. Butler's Hegelian perspective does not, of course, lead them to argue against the primary character of conflict, or to imply (as Cavarero does [see Chapter 1]) that the male conflict-ridden subject ought to be replaced by a more 'caring' maternal feminine in order for ethics to flourish. On the contrary, Butler insists (like many other critical thinkers) that every social bond is in part one of conflict. Rather, their concern is with what prevents this conflict from becoming destructive, in circumstances in which social relations are already premised upon a primordial annihilation. Their thesis is that, if nonviolence (a politics based on keeping destruction of the Other, and hence self-destruction, contained) is to make sense as an ethical and political position, it cannot simply repress aggression; rather, nonviolence emerges as a meaningful concept 'precisely when destruction is most likely or seems most certain' (Butler, 2020b: 39). A question Butler poses for us is that of what accounts for that 'check'? As discussed in the previous chapter, for recognition theorists such as Butler this destruction is and can only be 'checked' by mutual affirmation (re-cognition of what we have ostensibly 'forgotten' or written out of sociality), that is, of the obligations that stem from our mutual interdependency, illustrated by the social relations of respiration and the shared but socially contoured vulnerability they embody.¹⁰

However, Butler's own articulation of what an alternative to this might entail is somewhat vague – they simply say that 'critical patience is required' (Butler, 2020b: 145). A key challenge, therefore, is to consider how vulnerability might be rethought through recognition and relationality (in other words, beyond reification) within the context of how we live and work together, and to reflect on what light respiration can shed on how we might apprehend and approach this. The task in this sense is not to designate a class of people as 'vulnerable' and to offer them paternalistic protection as a result, as reificatory organizational policies and practices tend to, but rather to take seriously Butler (2016) and other feminists' view (see Segal, 2023) that vulnerability and resistance are not opposing forces or ways of being but are dialectically interconnected, so that presence, persistence, simply existing becomes a political act – a theme we return to in later chapters.

Writing in early 2020 in the midst of the first COVID-19 outbreak in the United Kingdom, when the pandemic felt like a 'critical moment' that might hold some promise for more radical ways of organizing to emerge (Parker, 2020), and echoing Butler's (2016) perspective on vulnerability in/as resistance, Neil Howard (2020: 22) argued that in order to organize our lives more relationally we ought to proceed by acting as if 'each individual life is all our lives'. As he put it, the pandemic brought home the extent to which 'we are all made of the same stuff, we are all human, vulnerable, and thus in need of care'; for him, 'this embodied experience of our shared vulnerability is extremely connecting' (Howard, 2020: 22). But as Lynne Segal (2023) has written more recently, the sense of connection and commitment to activism and commonality that was in evidence at some points and in some places during the pandemic dissipated very quickly once lockdowns and other COVID-related restrictions were lifted,[11] arguably resulting in social worlds that in the years since have felt increasingly borderized (Mbembe, 2019), especially given the scale and brutality of humanitarian crises in Gaza, Ukraine and across many other parts of the world.

Howard (2020: 24–25) described four overlapping scenarios that, he argued, might help us to realize some of the radical potential attached to the (albeit relatively fleeting) 'moments' of recognition that many experienced during the pandemic into something more meaningful and sustainable. In his account, Moment One occurs when we begin to recognize that the system that we live within leaves too many people uncared for or unsafe, or vulnerable to being so. Moment Two is when we sense that other ways of doing things are possible. Moment Three is marked by the 'irruption of long-suppressed needs into the mainstream of public and political life', with care returning as a central principle of our collective being, and Moment Four is characterized by the critical hope that 'it might be possible for us to live in a world set up to care for and attend to our needs rather than one focused on accumulation'. Our human nature, Howard optimistically suggested, is primed for these successive moments of connection 'because we are born into and sustained by webs of care'. Our individual and collective, shared needs (for example, for access to breathable air, food, shelter, connection and meaning) are threads of vulnerability that bind us and also (in being so) are 'threads of possibility' (Howard, 2020: 26). Evoking Ernst Bloch, Howard concluded that in the re-emergence of care as 'the always-ever-there foundation of our lives' there exists a profoundly critical, reflexive hope; our challenge 'is *to organize that hope* towards the caring alternative reality' that he feels began to make itself visible during the pandemic (Howard, 2020: 30, emphasis added). Yet the process he maps out seemed to stall somewhere between Moments One and Two, with hopes for more affirmative, affective bonds of recognition-based organizing being thwarted, if not actively reversed in what Lynne Segal (2023) describes as a 'care stripping' process.

A very different perspective to Howard's is offered by Achille Mbembe (2019) in his discussion of necropolitics. As discussed earlier, for Mbembe (2019: 1), necropolitics constitutes 'a force of separation rather than one that is bond-intensifying', a scenario in which the Other's burden is intolerably overwhelming and we become indifferent to the Other's suffering, in part because we become fixated on the Other's difference. Mbembe (2019: 59, 3) illustrates this with reference to the way in which nano-racism infiltrates into 'the pores and veins of society ... into the air one breathes', and asks, in these circumstances, how can we find 'a relation with others based on the reciprocal recognition of our common vulnerability' when confronted with the challenges of exercising life and freedom among those we can only regard as different from ourselves. Nano-racism, he argues, captures the spirit of our times, taking pleasure in ignorance and claiming a right to stupidity and immunity from responsibility for the violence it engenders. In Mbembe's account, this has resulted in an ongoing struggle over difference with no possibility of mutual recognition and instating instead, a way of living in which 'the experience of being unrecognized, humiliated, alienated, and mistreated' (Mbembe, 2019: 65) has become hidden in plain sight, with individuals, groups and populations subject to what Butler calls de-realization, embodying a human condition of mis/non-recognition. The latter is defined (in reificatory terms) solely by difference from an idealized, illusory position of invulnerability. The challenge then becomes how to respond to this scenario when recognition is de-coupled from desire, that is, through encounters with those whose mere existence or proximity is deemed to represent a physical or existential threat to 'our' own lives and whose recognition we neither seek nor proffer, coming to regard Others' bodies as polluting by their very presence. It is a scenario that, Mbembe (2019: 100–101, 159) argues, is 'on the verge of defining the times in which we live', in an era rapidly emerging as 'an age terrified of itself and of its own excess', shaped by forces of separation and 'fixity' in which (for some, quite literally) 'it becomes impossible to breathe'.

Radical vulnerability as a response to the impossibility of breathing

So, what can we do? It seems that the concerted actions of our bodies, assembled physically and virtually in whatever way we can to resist and protest against precarity, as the destruction of the conditions of liveability, must be combined with an assemblage of resources, rights and forms of representation so that a liveable life becomes more possible for more living beings, an issue we return to in Chapter 5. For now, an important question for us to ask, in considering the relationship between vulnerability and organization, is that of what role organizations could or should play in responding to the disavowal of our mutual but socially situated interdependency, and the apathy that this disavowal gives rise to. Does it become a question, to revisit some of the emancipatory potential in say, Honneth's (1995, 2008, 2021a, 2021b) writing on recognition, to struggle for a shift from a (reificatory, recitational) organization *of* our lives (for example, through matrices of cultural intelligibility) to a more relational and reflexive recognition-based organization *for* our lives? What (organizational) form might this latter mode of co-existence take? And what possibilities might it open up for our critique of more reificatory modes of organizing our desire for recognition, and the vulnerabilities that ensue from these?

Clearly, when understood as an organizational 'problem', recognition becomes more complex than hopeful perspectives such as Howard's suggest, and it is not necessarily so easily thought of, or experienced, as the social 'good' that recognition theorists such as Honneth might have us believe. But considering different ways of understanding recognition, and of reading Hegel's (1977 [1807]) writing on the desire for recognition on which Butler, Fanon and in turn Mbembe draw, opens up possibilities for thinking critically and reflexively about recognition as the potential basis for more relational ways of organizing that affirm rather than disavow our shared, situated vulnerability.

Recent debates on recognition in social theory, engaging with different ways of reading Hegel's work, and its uptake in Althusser, Butler and Honneth, think about recognition as an ambivalent phenomenon and hence provide an interesting starting point for considering some of the issues discussed so far in this chapter and in the previous one – namely that we are all interconnected, but the mutual vulnerability that this engenders all too easily becomes the basis for exploitation and appropriation *and* our social positioning means that while we are all vulnerable in an existential/philosophical sense, we are not equally so. In other words, while we all breathe the same air, some have a perceived right or access to more breathable air than others (and we can think both literally and metaphorically here). As Peter Sloterdijk has observed, as simultaneously biological entities and social beings, we breathe and are breathed upon; we are 'bonded by an intimate complicity', existing as what he calls 'ontological twins' in our shared reliance on the air that we breathe (Sloterdijk, 2011: 44). Arguably, in this sense, 'in the sharing of breath lies the very essence of human conviviality' (Ingold, 2020: 162), or, of course, otherwise. And it is this 'otherwise' that draws together a philosophical and more sociological approach to respiration, highlighting that the social relations of respiration are always shaped by the political contours of inequality and injustice. And this relationship between respiration and social exclusion reminds us of the extent to which the dialectical nature of the obligations we bear towards one another mean that 'our persistence is relational, fragile, sometimes conflictual and unbearable', yet also 'sometimes ecstatic and joyous' (Butler, 2020b: 64).

The complexity Butler alludes to here can be found in, for instance, those experiences when someone we love 'takes our breath away', or when we find ourselves unable to breathe because of physical or emotional pain. Our basic need for respiration, combined with our relationality, renders us doubly, mutually vulnerable – in a physical and existential sense, but not equally so, and to understand how and why this is the case it is important to think dialectically, about the relationship between our need for recognition and our differential experiences of the conditions attached to it. Understanding how these phenomena are conceptually distinct but empirically and theoretically related helps us to grasp, as we examine in what follows, how the reproduction of social inequality depends upon a reification of the attribution of different values to different lives in ways that shift individuals, groups or whole populations from shared (existential) precariousness, to socially induced (situated) precarity, accentuating, denigrating or exploiting their relative vulnerability.

Building on earlier writing on intelligibility, Butler's (1993, 2021a, 2021b) more recent account of how the desire for recognition might turn out to be a vehicle of, and for, domination makes a critical distinction between recognition and *recognizability*.[12] At the risk of oversimplification, it seems that in making this distinction, Butler does two important things with their reading of Hegel that, in combination, open up critical scope for thinking about the crucial question of why we seem to have become stuck between the two 'moments' of recognition that Howard (2020) outlines, and to grasping how and why our (apparent, and albeit fleeting) commitment to a more caring way of living together has faltered so badly (Segal, 2023), giving rise to increasing borderization (Mbembe, 2019) and violence. Returning to a question we posed earlier in this chapter, Butler's concept of recognizability helps us to make sense of why we cannot 'see' our mutual interdependency (by recognizing that we breathe the same air), even in the aftermath of a global pandemic and amid an ongoing climate emergency. First, Butler takes Hegel back a step, foregrounding the importance of understanding how our desire for recognition comes to be organized according to normative (not simply cognitive or classificatory – Honneth, 2021a, 2021b) terms of *recognizability* that, in the context of contemporary organizational life, require us to 'forget' or reify our primary interdependency and mutual vulnerability. So, when we ask who emerges as an intelligible life, as a recognizable subject (for example, as a person, group or population worthy of protection from a deadly virus, or being granted access to oxygen treatment when ill or injured, or being able to live somewhere where clean, safe, breathable air is available), '[w]e are asking about the matrices of subject formation, the fields of intelligibility and recognizability into which and by which any of us emerge. They make some of us very recognizable and cast some of us as nearly unrecognizable, *depending on the terms of recognition* themselves' (Butler, 2021a: 46, emphasis added).

Second, Butler takes Hegel on a stage,[13] highlighting how the differential terms of recognition mean that while we are all vulnerable (precarious) in a philosophical, existential sense, we are not equally so, emphasizing how the exploitation of the former – the vulnerability engendered by our mutual interdependence – can provide the social, political and/or economic basis of the latter, an *organization* of vulnerability that affirms its unequal distribution, and differential experiences of it. Taken together, these lines of argument present recognition in a much more complex and ambivalent light than Hegel's original narrative, or Honneth's (2021a, 2021b) sophisticated, but largely affirmative, teleological development of it.

Showing how recognizability and recognition are related (we might even say, dialectically 'organized') enables us to understand the epistemological conditions governing what it means to be accorded recognition, and its normative consequences. Butler's non-teleological reading of Hegel has important implications, or possibilities for responding to the kinds of questions we are considering here, in so far as it highlights that our desire for recognition renders us socially (organizationally) vulnerable in at least two important ways. First, often, our only choice is to be recognized in ways and according to terms that are 'beyond us' and which therefore can lead to our subordination, or at least our constraint, or of not being recognized at all (this may happen to us unreflexively, or sometimes more 'tactically'). Second, even when we achieve recognition that might be liveable or 'workable' for us, the meaning of the terms we are subject to is never fixed or stable, *and* 'there is … no recognition of all that a person is *or may be*' (Butler, 2021a: 34, emphasis added) hence we are perpetually vulnerable, or to put it more specifically (as noted in Chapter 1), we are vulnerable 'in perpetuity' and organizations are important social contexts in which these dynamics are played out. We can perhaps identify an example of this in relation to the subjection of health and social care workers to the rhetorical, largely self-interested and reificatory forms of recognition that were in widespread circulation during the pandemic, and which were articulated through a discourse of heroism in many parts of the world, including but not limited to the United Kingdom, Europe and the United States, at the same time as denying health and social care workers a fair wage, humane working environments, and access to adequate protective equipment to keep them safe while providing vital care work.[14]

But this vulnerable positioning also opens up important possibilities that might be transformative, and which raise critical questions for thinking about the kinds of work, and organizational forms and relations involved. If, for example, 'norms are "resignified" by bodies that are not supposed to embody them, and that can change the way we think about embodiment, norms and social transformation' (Butler, 2021a: 40–41), what kind of *work* do such bodies do? How might we understand the nature of this resignificatory labour, and (to stretch the metaphor a little), what kinds of 'breathing spaces' do they open up? What kind of organizational infrastructures or relations might enable such bodies to enact, individually and collectively, transformative ways of being and of relating to one another? We might think here of disability and trans rights groups whose persistence as simply a 'presence' within and for organizations is of political significance, and about the claims to recognition and rights made by indigenous and/or stateless people, and the kinds of ethical possibilities that radical vulnerability opens up – a theme we return to in Chapters 4 and 5.

For now, it is useful to remind ourselves that Judith Butler's view has long been that recitation constitutes a possible resource for emancipatory change, especially when emanating from the domain of non-intelligibility. At stake here is the question of a radical, agentic vulnerability, a 'refusal' to be recognized according to terms that perpetuate one's negation and that of others and instead recognizing that, as Robin Wall Kimmerer (2024: epitaph, 33, 72) has put it, 'all flourishing is mutual'. For some (for example, Stahl, 2021), the possibility of emancipation lies in standing in solidarity with those threatened by exclusion/expulsion from the sphere of recognition and those rendered non-intelligible by its terms of recognizability, but arguably this carries with it a heavy risk – at least in organizational contexts – of shoring up paternalism in the name of recognition, and of reaffirming established norms in the process (see Bernini, 2021).

Perhaps a more critical way in which the Hegelian narrative might be extended to our current sphere of interest is by combining political and philosophical lines of argument that connect post-recognition solidarity and pre-recognition vulnerability in order to develop a more reflexive, relational understanding of recognition and (its) ambivalence, one that has the potential to form the basis of a more reflexive, ethically and politically orientated theory of our encounters with one another. Such an approach might enable us to develop a response to the question of why we don't see/sense our mutual vulnerability, even – especially – when we know that we breathe the same air, which is our key concern in this chapter. Drawing on Butler's work that takes Hegel both back and forwards a step in the ways discussed earlier, we might start to tease out distinct forms of recognition as organizational phenomena that, through the lens of respiration, help us to understand more about how vulnerability comes to be organized in ways that negate subjective viability, at the same time as opening up possibilities for ways of being that reflexively recognize mutual but situated vulnerability, not only as our way of being, but as the basis of a more relational politics and ethics.

First, we might think of a rhetorical, largely (negative) ideological form that is not simply cognitive or classificatory in Honneth's (2021a, 2021b) terms but which establishes the very terms of intelligibility or recognizability in Butler's (2021a, 2021b). An example of this form or mode of recognition might be employee recognition or accreditation schemes. Philip Hancock (2024: 381) has recently argued that such programmes, replete as they are with pathological tendencies towards compelled identification, effectively undermine 'the ontological conditions necessary for recognition to flourish'.

Restricting expressions of value attribution solely, or even primarily, to the level of the symbolic means that so-called employee recognition schemes provide, in his account, little beyond a 'cheap and instrumentally effective ... *normative grounding* for organizational life' constituting a form of recognition that is 'all too easily appropriated' (Hancock, 2024: 388, emphasis added).

As noted earlier, this way of thinking about recognition as reification is illustrated in the discourses and practices that hailed health and social care workers as heroes during the pandemic, at the same time as denying them the rights and resources to lead workable lives. Such practices 'constitute recognition less as a process of mutual attentiveness – as an associative, intersubjective outcome – and more *as an object or property*' (Hancock, 2024: 392, emphasis added), reifying the subjectivities, labour and social relations of mutual interdependency involved. Taken together, this results in a false or alienating form of recognition that undermines the conditions necessary for its own realization, reducing recognition to a reified, 'thing-like status' (Hancock, 2024: 395). For Hancock (2024: 392–393), recognition is both a process of mutual attentiveness and an associative, intersubjective outcome, while organizational forms of recognition such as those encountered in accreditation or award schemes and other managerial discourses operate from a premise of recognition as an object 'to be individually coveted and possessed', especially as they are often characterized by what Hancock terms 'compelled over-identification' involving a colonization of recognition's ethical and political capacity.

Second, we might think of what for Honneth (1995, 2008, 2021a) is 'full' (affirmative/normative) recognition that reinstates our social bond and is hence, to a degree, more transformative. Yet when read through the lens of the questions considered here, and a combined phenomenological and sociological understanding of the relationality and mutual interdependency embodied in and through respiration, we can begin to see how this more affirmative recognition carries with it two significant risks as the potential basis for a more relational mode of organizing. This 'fuller' mode of recognition, as espoused by Honneth (2021a, 2021b) and other recognition theorists, risks, first, a paternalistic shoring up of subjective hierarchies, marked by a lack of reflexivity in framing and imposing particular terms of recognizability (Butler, 2021a, 2021b). Second, such a mode of recognition risks, in doing so, failing to fully grasp the ambivalence engendered by these terms (that is, of the normative effects of what Butler calls 'recognizability'), such that 'we' may be accorded recognition, but the basis of that recognition is beyond our sphere of agency, if (as is the case) we are entirely, if differentially, dependent upon being recognized in order to sustain liveable, workable (for example, breathable) existences.

Third, focusing on the social relations of respiration in the way that this chapter has, enables us to start to think about a more reflexive version of recognition, infused by feminist writing on ethics and relationality, as the basis for social and organizational life, one premised upon a mutual appreciation of the degree to which, to put it at its simplest, we breathe the same air. This form or mode of recognition involves a more critically reflexive, solidarity-orientated 'problematization' of the relations and terms of recognition as they are currently in social circulation, and of our differential investments in them, including of the norms that govern recognizability (Butler, 2021a, 2021b). Examples might include, for instance, the kinds of actions and activism orientated towards not simply extending pre-existing, heteronormative models of matrimony to LGBTQIA+ couples, and instead critically rethinking established ideas shaping what it means to marry, and be married, and to constitute a family, opening up – reflexively – alternative ways of recognizing one another and the bonds we form, and that sustain us, when we build lives that intertwine with those we love and care for, with and about. Another example we might think of relates to the activist work undertaken within critical disability studies and movements, that sets out to rethink the meaning, perception and lived experience of disability as a social norm. Understanding recognition more relationally in this way arguably enables us to foreground – critically and reflexively – how claims to recognition are always already normatively embedded in socially situated relations of mutual vulnerability and are grounded in a 'forgotten', reified relation of mutual interdependence. This latter approach is a way of thinking about what recognition might mean that links to feminist work on ethics and solidarity that envisages recognition as being orientated towards collective agency, bringing theoretical understanding into conversation with practice and embodied solidarity (Vachhani and Pullen, 2019; Pullen and Vachhani, 2020; Smolović Jones et al, 2021; Smolović Jones, 2023). In recent feminist writing, the latter is understood theoretically as 'a participative and inclusive endeavour driven by conflictual encounters, constituted through the bodies, language and visual imagery of assembling and articulating subjects' (Smolović Jones et al, 2021: 917–918), enabling alliances to grow and persist, a theme we return to in later chapters. Bringing theory, embodied experience and solidarity into dialogue in this way foregrounds solidarity as a contested practice, 'where difference is experienced and negotiated through corporeal–discursive enactment … involving both positive expressions of empathy, vulnerability and care, but also contest, pain and discomfort', an approach to understanding and organizing social relations, including those embodied in/by respiration, that is more dialogical than either the reificatory or reformist modes of recognition noted earlier allow for.

    Drawing on Frantz Fanon (2007 [1967]), Mbembe (2019: 141, emphasis added) argues that this third form of recognition, one that is more reflexive, is the kind that aims to bring about a more solidarity-orientated set of relations between people, things and planetary resources: 'it engages everything: muscles, bare fists, intelligence, the suffering from which one is not spared, blood. A new gesture, *it creates new respiratory rhythms*'. It is premised on a relational understanding of recognition as a constant, and socially situated, struggle that involves 'organized, collective work and the recognition-based reinstatement of a relation of care premised not on paternalism but *recognition of our primal, and ongoing, mutual vulnerability*'.

Helping us to find new ways to 'breathe' together, such an approach would need to be critically, reflexively aware of how the context in which we are situated results in the homogenization and commodification of normative terms shaping an individual, group or population's capacity to be recognized (their 'recognizability' [see Butler, 2021a, 2021b]) as these are played out within current social arrangements governing organizational/organized life. This kind of communal self-awareness would require a reflexive understanding of how the self and others are positioned prior to, during and subsequent to, struggles for and over recognition, while also acknowledging the often-paradoxical nature of efforts to bestow recognition, or to change the terms of recognition, returning us to the question of according to what form of recognition, and on whose terms, we might be recognized. A reflexive mode of recognition must acknowledge that any such project to alter the terms and field of recognition might simply create a different configuration of established power/knowledge relations. This in itself requires a reflexive, mutual understanding of the ways in which, while seeking to affirm the rights, resources and representation of some, there is always the inherent danger of unintentionally exploiting, marginalizing and silencing others and, further, that this complexity is invested with differential terms and circumstances of recognizability (Butler, 2021a, 2021b).

Reflexive recognition as it is understood here and within contemporary feminist writing on vulnerability, and within theoretical (notably indigenous and postcolonial) work on the social relations of respiration involves, in the most vital Hegelian sense, being moved or changed by encounters with Others. In Sara Ahmed's (2000: 156, emphasis added) words, 'to hear, or to give the other a hearing, *is to be moved by the other*, such that one ceases to inhabit the same place'. When thought about through the lens of mutual vulnerability as it is articulated, or more precisely animated, in social relations of respiration, that is, through a notion of reflexivity as transformative, recognition reflects Hegel's original formulation – central to Butler's reading of his dialectical account – as an encounter through which the One becomes *for* the Other and vice versa. This represents a mode of being that we embody when we recognize that we breathe the same air; as Merleau-Ponty puts it, when I breathe out, others breathe in and vice versa. In other words, reflexive recognition involves each acknowledging the Self in and through the Other in such a way as both are transformed in ways that cannot simply be 'undone', or easily unravelled, each being changed by the other's reciprocity. This contrasts with a scenario that Iris Marion Young describes as that which occurs when 'privileged people put themselves in the position of those who are less privileged', and the assumptions derived from their privilege lead them, often inadvertently or unknowingly, to misrepresent the other's situation (Young, 1997: 48).

This misrepresentation, understood here as a form of epistemic misrecognition (that is, claiming, unreflexively, the capacity to know and articulate what is 'best' for the Other and how to bring that about) is what the first and second forms of recognition, reified and reformist versions discussed earlier, are arguably premised upon in their largely paternalistic framing of social relations. In the third, more reflexive form, collaborative space is potentially opened up through, for instance, what Butler (2015) calls 'assembly'. In this context, unreflexive, reificatory orientations towards the Self and Other might give way to a more relational reciprocity with each coming to realize that knowledge and understanding can only emerge through relations of mutual recognition that acknowledge one another's different positionalities and predicaments, while at the same time recognizing that our social relations are woven into the very air that we breathe. As Cutcher et al (2020: 15) caution us, resonating with Mbembe's postcolonial critique, 'the more one thinks one "understands" the Other, the less the opportunity for dialogue and the more for misunderstanding'. Moreover, as they also emphasize, this relationship – of mutual recognition – is never fixed or stable, but always in a state of flow, consistent with the notion of an evolving, respectful and mutually constitutive narrative of the encounter between ourselves and others, and, of course, also with the flux and flow that characterizes respiration as our embodied way of being together.

Concluding thoughts

In this chapter, we have considered how a reflexive, relational understanding of recognition might help us to grasp how respiration embodies mutual but differently positioned vulnerability as the basis of the human condition. We have considered how recognizing our shared, situated interdependency potentially opens up ways to explore vulnerability beyond the reificatory and reformist versions of recognition we have examined, and to consider respiration as illustrative of how mutual interdependency is literally the air that we breathe, requiring us to imagine a more reflexive, relational mode of recognizing our mutual interdependence upon one another.

Respiration highlights how, as embodied social beings, we can never be completely open or completely closed; we are rather engaged in 'a perpetual and alternating movement of opening and closing, dilatation and contraction. And *that is what it means to breathe*' (Ingold, 2020: 163, emphasis added). That is also, as Hannah Arendt (1998 [1958]) was at pains to emphasize, what it means to be immersed in the human condition. Merleau-Ponty's understanding of the situated, social relations of breathing, based upon his post-dualist ontology of subjectivity, foregrounds the radical potential of rethinking the social relations of respiration premised upon mutual recognition of our most basic interconnectedness as vital to this condition.[15]

Yet differentiating between the different forms of recognition that organize social relations that we have also considered in this chapter, including those associated with our need for access to safe, clean, breathable air, enables us to make sense of why instead of recognizing our mutual, but socially situated interdependence, we doggedly pursue ways of borderizing access to rights, resources and representation on the basis of reifying terms of recognizability that designate some individuals, groups and populations as mattering, others as not. This means that some of us have the space and resources necessary to breathe, while others are asphyxiated, over-worked or polluted into situations that involve literally fighting for breath.

In this sense, respiration can be understood as a site on which the struggle for existence is played out; in other words, through the social relations of breathing, our desire for recognition is organized according to norms and terms of recognizability (Butler, 2021a, 2021b) in ways that can be negating, exploitative and/or oppressive but which also open up the potential for our mutual vulnerability to be lived and embodied more relationally. Recognizing that socially shared but situated vulnerability is as vital to us as the air that we breathe is essential if we are to find more hopeful and sustainable ways in which to respond to the urgent need to reimagine how we relate to one another and the world in which we live than those that have led to the global care deficit, worldwide conflict and worsening state of climate emergency that we currently find ourselves in. Doing so requires a reflexive understanding of mutual vulnerability not as a weakness to be 'overcome', but as the outcome of how our desire for recognition of ourselves, and of the social relations of our existence, come to be organized, and as the basis of our capacity to act collectively and to live and work relationally. In the next chapter, we turn to another site of lived, embodied experience through which our desire to endure – to persist as viable beings worthy of recognition – is organized, one that Judith Butler and others have written about extensively, namely grieving and commemoration.

3

Enduring: The Social Relations of Grieving

> Let's face it. We're undone by each other. And if we're not, we're missing something. This seems so clearly the case with grief, but it can be so only because it was already the case with desire.
> Judith Butler, *Undoing Gender*, 2004: 23

Introduction

This phrase of Judith Butler's has always struck me as being particularly poignant, evoking the 'heart' of recognition and the mutual exposure it engenders in a way that is able to convey both the joy and sheer terror of surrendering oneself to another, knowing the devastating risk of loss that this carries with it, as well as the scope for experiencing mutual interdependency as an ecstatic, joyous form of entwinement that it opens up. For Butler, of course, desire is erotic in its very ontology – as a losing oneself in another. 'Better to have loved and lost', as Tennyson put it,[1] because without having done so, we have never really lived at all. But with all living, as Butler reminds us, comes vulnerability, a vulnerability that shapes us.

In her book *Relating Narratives* and elsewhere throughout her writing, Adriana Cavarero (2000) draws on Hannah Arendt's work (1998 [1958]) to argue that from our inaugural moment ('the naked fact of our original physical appearance', as Arendt puts it), and for as long as we exist, we are constantly – constitutively – exposed to others. The nature and meaning of the life-long vulnerability that this brings about can be understood as an organizational phenomenon, that is, as the outcome of a process through which our desire for recognition comes to be organized. It is also a scenario that is grounded in organizational infrastructures, bringing the potential for the resources, rights and forms of representation necessary to our survival to be provided, but with that, potentially limitless scope for exclusion, oppression and exploitation of the existential and social vulnerability that our need for recognition engenders.

For both Arendt and Cavarero, as feminist philosophers concerned with the 'vitally' constitutive nature of vulnerability, our exposure to others is definitive of the (more than) human condition throughout our lifetime – it forms who and what we are, from the inaugural to the final moments of our existence.

And yet, it is when we are dead that we are arguably at our most vulnerable. We are entirely dependent on others to treat what remains of our bodies and our humanity with dignity and respect, to recognize any wishes or requests we may have expressed about what will happen to us at the end of our lives, and to care for us. In this chapter, we consider the vulnerabilities and forms of agency embedded, and embodied, in the social relations of grieving and commemorating, and in the dynamics of social perceptions of who and what counts as worthy of remembrance, and on what basis. Butler's (2021c: 55) question, posed as part of their critique of Cavarero's (2016, 2021a) writing on the postural geometry of subjectivity, 'what happens when inclination takes narrative form?', is particularly pertinent to our discussion here, especially so in relation to our consideration of the ways in which the politics and ethics of commemoration relate to vulnerability, organization and the desire for recognition.

Butler's writing has emphasized how grieving is a highly organized process, one situated in social relations of vulnerability and our desire for recognition; for Butler, grievability 'governs the way in which living creatures are managed' (Butler, 2020b: 56).[2] And just as vulnerability is both an ontological relationality and a socially situated precarity, if mourning is a shared recognition of loss then, as Butler has also emphasized, it requires a context (for example, infrastructural support and mechanisms) through which to register and enact that loss. Anyone who has had responsibility for organizing the burial of a stateless or trans person will know only too well the extent to which death is very much an organizational problem of and for recognition. This way of thinking about grieving and how the end of a person's life comes to be organized in ways that either affirm or deny recognition, or something in between (for example, proffer recognition only on impossible, unviable terms) is one that reiterates our enduring interdependence. It places questions of relationality and care at the heart of social relations, setting out basic premises for progressive thinking on how we might respond to increasingly urgent global problems such as how to grieve ethically and sustainability in a world marked by borderization (Mbembe, 2019), extreme inequality and climate emergency. For Butler and others, borderization and its manifestation in global conflict seeks to deny the ongoing and irrefutable ways in which we are all subject to one another, vulnerable to destruction by the other, and in need of protection through multilateral and global agreements based on recognition of our shared but always socially contoured precarity, not only throughout but beyond our lifetimes.

Exploring the relationship between vulnerability and organization through grieving, this chapter begins with a discussion of Butler's writing on loss, drawing from insights in their work that help us to frame grieving as a site on which vulnerability as a simultaneously ontological and sociological phenomenon is played out. It then moves on to discuss recent feminist writing on ethics, considering the relationship between narrative, vulnerability and the social relations of endurance.[3] A discussion of registering loss then considers how grievability comes to be organized, framing mourning as a form of organization that perpetuates vulnerability, but which also reinstates its potential for solidarity, community and connection, not least through grieving as a simultaneously ethical and political, agentic act.

Registering loss: vulnerability, dispossession and precarity

At the heart of Judith Butler's writing on loss and its relationship to vulnerability is their view that 'the ek-static character of our existence is *essential to the possibility of persisting* as human' (Butler, 2004a: 33, emphasis added), one that brings an Arendtian lens to Butler's reading of Hegel (1977). For Butler, it is through the ontological vulnerability engendered by our primary relationality, experienced as an 'ek-static movement' (Butler, 2005: 115), or struggle for recognition in the Hegelian sense, that the self emerges. In other words, it is only by being drawn into a sphere of simultaneous dispossession and constitution that we come to 'be'.[4] This understanding of the human predicament opens up important possibilities for thinking about how recognition comes to be organized in their writing on grieving and grievability, not least because there is arguably nothing quite as dispossessing, for the reasons outlined above, as death.

Echoing earlier preoccupations explored in *Subjects of Desire* (Butler, 1987), it is in their book *Psychic Life* that Butler (1997b) emphasizes most clearly that all subjects emerge because of mutual interdependency, but this relationality is then repressed ('forgotten'), or it is exploited and appropriated. This results in a politically induced condition of dispossession, a privative form of precarity, in which certain populations 'become differentially exposed', or come to live their lives in ways that are more vulnerable than others 'to injury, violence and death' (Butler, 2009a: xx). The context and consequences of this for social relations, and the capacity to secure and sustain a liveable life, are what concern Butler most in *Precarious Life* (Butler, 2004a), a text that raises important questions for our understanding of the role that organizations play in responding to our primary (existential) vulnerability, and to inaugurating and perpetuating induced forms of precarity that capitalize on this vulnerability, including through the ways in which our constitutive vulnerability to loss is 'managed'.

Precarious Life strives to reimagine how the inherent vulnerability of human (and beyond human) existence might become the basis for a shared radical, ethical project premised upon 'interdependency ... as the basis for [a] global political community' (Butler, 2004a: xii–xiii). As feminist political theorist Moya Lloyd (2007: 141) has framed it, this raises the important question of how the experience of loss and vulnerability might 'lend itself to a recognition of interdependence'. Butler's own response to this question is to emphasize that grief and mourning expose precarity and mutual vulnerability as signs of the intercorporeal nature of existence, or natality of the human condition in Arendt's (1998 [1958]) terms. Through grief 'something about who we are is revealed, something that delineates the ties we have to others, that shows that these ties constitute who we are' (Butler, 2004a: 22).

Drawing from Freud's writing on mourning and melancholia, Butler argues that the loss of another also becomes self-loss as it reveals the Self and Other's mutual interdependence. Grief and mourning are thus forms of dispossession that serve to 'remind' us of the extent to which our lives are intertwined with others in relations of mutual interdependency; they are 'occasions when one body can be "undone" by another body, and *it is the moment of undoing that reveals that our existence is always a being-with the other*' as Lloyd (2007: 142, emphasis added) has summed it up. Your loss is always also my loss, and so on. For Butler, it is in this 'moment' of mutual (Self and Other) loss that we are reminded of the primacy of our ethical relationality, of 'the condition of primary vulnerability' (Butler, 2004a: 31). Hence (paradoxically) loss can be a transformative, affirmative experience (telling us that we have lived, and loved, to borrow from Tennyson). To reiterate, it is at this moment that we recognize 'we're undone by each other. And if we're not, we're missing something' (Butler, 2004a: 23).

Butler's contention that grief highlights how all fleshy, embodied existence is precarious means that we all can, do and will suffer; this is both the risk and the potential 'reward' attached to self-loss, to being 'given over' to others. But crucial to Butler's thesis is that the way in which this primary vulnerability comes to be organized means that only some lives are deemed to be a 'loss'. Hence, certain deaths count as 'mournable', worthy of grief and commemoration, while others do not. In this sense, as well as our mutual vulnerability, grief and mourning remind us that while, precisely because of our primary relationality, we are all precarious, some lives are more precarious – grievable, liveable, workable, than others. On this point, Butler's reading of Hegel (1977) is important, suggesting that the terms that define what it means to be human for some are precisely those that deprive others of the possibility of 'mattering'. This means that some individuals, groups and populations come to be recognized as subjects and hence are endowed with the resources, rights and forms of representation that are necessary for liveable lives whose potential loss would be registered as a loss, while that possibility is denied to others.[5]

This has, as Moya Lloyd goes on to note, profound implications for ethics and politics, as cultural normativity not only conditions who or what 'I' can be, but the terms on which 'I' might be recognized, raising the important question: 'What happens if a life that is not recognized normatively *as a life* is violated in some way?' (Lloyd, 2007: 144, emphasis added). What, for Butler, is effectively a 'double negation' means that if harm is done to those who are 'unrecognized' then it fails to injure, since those effected are already negated (Butler, 2004a: 33) – this is what Butler describes as de-realization, and it has profound implications for the social relations, politics and ethics of grieving as a site on which the desire for recognition comes to be organized in ways that shape lived experiences of vulnerability.[6] As Lloyd notes, this 'double negation' presents the problem of how to identify with the suffering of those positioned as Other, including within and through organizational mechanisms. If, as Butler maintains, abject deaths constitute 'the melancholic background' (Butler, 2004a: 46) of our shared social – and organizational – lifeworlds, this relationship further negates the humanity of those deemed 'unrecognizable' and whose deaths, by the same token, are ungrievable, or who are grieved only in a reified way that reaffirms their dispossession.[7] Consequently, *'the matter that must be addressed constantly and forcefully is the differential allocation of humanness'* (Butler and Athanasiou, 2013: 31, emphasis added).

In this sense (and echoing Butler, 1993), the political emphasis of Butler's critique of dispossession lies in its capacity to open up radical re-articulations of what it means to matter,[8] the aim being to move 'toward a relational view' of human subjectivity and social relations (Butler and Athanasiou, 2013: 35), by finding ways to reinstate, or re-cognize our primary relationality. Expanding on this in dialogue with Butler, Athena Athanasiou distinguishes between 'that which gets abjected or foreclosed from the human' and 'forms of life that are conferred recognition as human according to the established norms of recognizability, on the condition of and at the cost of conforming to these norms' (Butler and Athanasiou, 2013: 36), producing an 'exclusionary inclusion' (Butler and Athanasiou, 2013: 36). The latter involves being 'conditionally interpellated in the all-too-intelligible categories of the normative human' (Butler and Athanasiou, 2013: 36). Athanasiou maps this out in order to ask: Is it possible to 'trouble' this from the outside; that is, to establish a sustained challenge to the limits of the tolerable, and therefore, grievable?[9]

To set the groundwork for this, Butler recaps on some basic premises, particularly their ongoing concern with questioning 'the power relations that condition in advance who will count or matter as a recognizable, viable human subject and who will not' (Butler and Athanasiou, 2013: 78). Reminding us of their Foucauldian-infused Hegelian understanding of recognition as the normative, disciplinary regime through which human beings become social subjects, Butler's concern is with the regimes of power that regulate intersubjectivity, 'defining what renders a subject legible, recognizable, desirable' (Butler and Athanasiou, 2013: 94).

Being at a loss: grieving and/as organization

Butler's (2004a, 2009a, 2020b) writing on grievability discussed earlier reminds us of how the violation of humanitarian principles that persists across our contemporary social world is predicated on a conscious or ambivalent disregard for the inequality that distinguishes lives that are deemed to be worth living and protecting from those that are unseen and unmarked by their actual or prospective loss (see also Fotaki, 2022). This is a point that Erin Baines (2004) discussed some two decades ago with reference to the 'vulnerable bodies' of those who get displaced as refugees and as a result of humanitarian crises. Baines notes the paradox that, on the one hand, displaced people's bodies are disregarded, rendered disposable, and on the other, refugees especially are often confined to their bodies, rendered speechless and without agency in their 'fixity', becoming positioned as purely physical entities, often *en masse*, so that their uniqueness is subsumed, as they are restricted to the capacity to signify only incapacity. One of the central effects of this process is a dispossessing negation of displaced people's agency, further entrapping them in their bodily circumstances as (paradoxically) simply 'matter'.

Concerned with this very process, and referring to their Althusserian influences, Butler reiterates how grievability relates to precarity, arguing that to be 'grievable' '[i]s to be interpellated in such a way that you know your life matters ... that your body is treated as one that should be able to live and thrive, whose precarity should be minimized, for which provisions for flourishing should be available' (Butler, 2020b: 59). Butler distinguishes between lives that are 'absolutely and clearly grievable' (Butler, 2020b: 73) and others that 'barely make a mark', with the latter signifying 'a loss that is no loss', a fate that the many thousands of European migrants and displaced people believed to have drowned in the Mediterranean Sea embody. Butler tentatively frames these extremes as a continuum but only in order to show that to do so does not allow scope through which to understand the degree to which a life that is actively mourned in one community or context might be fully unmarked or unmarkable in another.[10] While vulnerable to co-optation, mourning, Butler argues, can also be an embodied form of protest, demanding accountability and recognition and requiring a political imaginary orientated towards realizing 'the radical equality of grievability' (Butler, 2020b: 74). The latter, for Butler, means making the claim that a life lost ought not to have been lost, that it is grievable and therefore, retrospectively, was/should have been liveable and workable.

To develop this argument, Butler makes an important grammatical shift, one that parallels their wider thesis about the relationship between recognition and recognizability discussed in Chapter 2 (Butler, 2021a, 2021b), noting: 'There is a difference between someone's being grieved and that same person's bearing, in their living being, a characteristic of grievability. The second involves the conditional tense: those who are grievable *would be* mourned if their lives *were* lost; the ungrievable are those whose loss would leave no trace' (Butler, 2020b: 74–75, original emphasis). This means that precautions are taken to safeguard from harm or destruction, lives that would register as a loss, even (perhaps especially, or even deliberately) if doing so incurs the loss of 'unregistered' lives that are framed, by implication, as disposable. Events during the COVID-19 pandemic illustrated what Butler means when they argue that grievability is a socially situated form of vulnerability. As an example, Jagannathan and Rai's (2022: 426) account of the state's response to the pandemic in India attests to the precarity, violence and inequality shaping 'overlapping planes of marginality', amounting to what they describe as 'an erosion of dignity in both life and death' for India's most marginalized people. They explain how COVID-19 'rendered workers jobless, hungry, exhausted, and on the borders of death', showing how the state's response to the pandemic as a public health crisis was embedded in a necropolitical protection of middle class and elite lives while directing structural violence towards the working-class and Muslim people, 'making their lives disposable'. Their chilling narrative shows how the dead bodies of marginalized people came to be regarded simply as biological hazards ('matter', as noted earlier) 'that needed to be disposed of', rather than as fellow human beings 'worthy of dignity and mourning' (Jagannathan and Rai, 2022: 435).

Another poignant illustration of grievability as a site on which the vulnerability engendered by the desire for recognition is played out is the case of Hart Island, New York. Situated just off the eastern coast of Manhattan in the Bronx Sound, Hart Island is reportedly the largest public cemetery in the world (Raudon, 2022), yet it is practically invisible; hidden in plain sight, it is almost inaccessible to all but those who work there. Described as the City's 'dark shadow', Hart Island is the final resting place of approximately one million of New York's 'unwanted ... lonely, ... forgotten and ... marginalised' people (Byers, 2022: 1); it is a cemetery 'for the nameless and the homeless' (Bowring, 2011: 251). Until 2020, its massed, anonymous graves[11] were dug and filled by prisoners from nearby Rikers Island, in a workforce scenario that bordered on the Dickensian;[12] 'the disenfranchised burying the forgotten' (Raudon, 2022: 89). As an organized space that epitomizes what Butler and others have called dispossession, or de-realization, Hart Island is a mass burial site that is widely regarded by those who know of it as a poignant, barren 'hellscape' (Byers, 2022: 6), a landscape that materializes what it means to live – and die – in precarity.

Catriona Byers's account of the place explains some of the organizational history of Hart Island, which was first used for burials in the 1860s:

> Formerly used as a civil war training camp, it was purchased by the Department of Charities and Corrections in 1869. ... Along with the grid

cemetery for mass grave trenches, a number of penitentiary institutions were established [t]here, such as a psychiatric hospital and a workhouse for delinquent boys. Institutions within this network were utilised throughout the burial process, with inmates at the workhouses put to work building pine coffins and sewing shrouds, and prisoners from the penitentiary burying the bodies. In a time when poverty was largely seen as a personal failing resulting from immorality and inherent criminality, little sympathy was extended to those who ended their days on Hart Island. Instead, contemporary media reinforced existing social and cultural stereotypes about poor, largely immigrant communities. (Byers, 2022: 5)

Reflecting this history over a century later, Hart Island was widely used for interments during the AIDS epidemic in the 1980s and again, during the COVID-19 crisis in the early 2020s.[13] It was only during the latter that media coverage of Hart Island began to shine a critical spotlight on the island's history rendering, albeit for a relatively temporary period, a place that is usually hidden in plain sight becoming publicly 'legible'. As already noted, records indicate that approximately a million people are buried on Hart Island, predominantly those who, largely because of race, immigration status, poverty, lifestyle and disease, have been buried in obscurity, with many ending up, because of the circumstances of their life and/or death, being condemned 'to oblivion's relegation' (Brouwer and Morris, 2021: 160) in almost entirely 'unmarked and unmemorialized' (Raudon, 2022: 84) massed graves.[14] In the words of a New York City council worker: 'the city has always wanted to forget about Hart Island. The city has wanted to forget about the people who are buried there. It's wanted to forget about the fact that there is a potter's field, that there is a place where difficult stories are hidden' (Brouwer and Morris, 2021: 164).

For author and historian Michael Keene (2019: 65), the common denominator for all those interred on Hart Island and places like it is 'mass anonymity, total detachment, and a dark loneliness'.[15] The stigma that surrounds burial sites like Hart Island reflects more than marginalization, however. As social anthropologist, Sally Raudon, puts it:

> Massed graves ... effectively mute social connections. To be buried promiscuously, in the sense of indiscriminately mixed, is a lonely burial, separated from family, faith, community or other groups. Because Hart Island is difficult to visit, rituals celebrating the continuing bonds between the living and the dead are not easily performed publicly or privately. (Raudon, 2022: 91)

For Butler, it is not only that a 'liveable/unliveable' dyad is ethically and politically indefensible; it is ontologically untenable, as the interdependency that constitutes the human condition means that, albeit in socially contoured ways, we are all bound up in our vulnerability, as discussed in earlier chapters. In their efforts to articulate a more egalitarian imaginary in response to this, Butler returns to Hegel (1977) reminding us that 'this "I" that I am ... is *one for whom differentiation is a perpetual struggle and problem*' (Butler, 2020b: 98, original emphasis). This latter point is important to our discussion here as it reminds us that, as a site on which our desire for recognition is played out, grievability is marked by perpetual, socially structured vulnerability. Reimagining grievability as a form of relationality, one premised upon mutual recognition of our shared but situated interdependency requires grieving not only beyond a liveability dyad, but more so, a mode of social organization that provides the infrastructural context within which all losses can register as a loss. This requires, Adriana Cavarero argues, us to bear witness through the narratives that we tell as a relational, reflexive mode of recognition.

Matters of life and death: narrating our existence

It is something of a cliché to say that history is told and written by its victors; but it is also worth remembering Paul Ricoeur's (1983) point that precisely because historical accounts are largely descriptions of actors who have triumphed, there is an ethical duty to remember 'other' narratives so that their sufferings are not submerged within and by triumphalism. Writing out some versions of history while romanticizing and idealizing others constitutes a form of de-narrativization, a biographical corollary of the de-realization that Butler (2009a, 2009b) and others are concerned with, whereby those rendered Other are marginalized and erased from collective memories, not simply because their stories aren't told; their de-realization makes their stories not worth telling, a process on which 'victorious' narratives and heroic tales of course depend. In the process of such de-narrativization, Other stories come to be forgotten, so that narratives become normalizing ideological frames that prevent some lives from being recognized as mattering, that is, as grievable (Butler, 2009a), while reaffirming the relative value of others. De-narrativization then becomes complicit in the reproduction and naturalization of forms of non- or misrecognition and the harm they perpetuate, as the latter are not considered to be injustices that need to be addressed. And the performative nature of narrating loss through mourning and commemoration means that de-realization takes place in perpetuity, as those who are 'written out' of existence cannot easily be reclaimed, or at least not without great political effort, as Butler and others have emphasized. Further, de-realization also negates the capacity of marginalized individuals, communities or populations to deploy their grief as a form of political intervention, limiting scope for this to happen as a recognition-based, relational act. Understood in this way, struggles for recognition are linked to 'remembering' negated people's contributions and suffering, or simply their very existence, foregrounding how 'de-narrativization is not merely a political-discursive enactment but a process of repressing concrete embodied experiences of injustice' as Mahalingam et al (2019: 236) describe in their work on Dalit people.

Concerned with these very issues in her writing on narratives, Adriana Cavarero (2000, 2016) has argued that the stories told about us bear witness to our lives, narrating our existence to and for others, signifying the subjectivities that are visible and sayable, and creating the conditions of possibility for us and others to exist and endure.[16] Narration, for Cavarero, is a set of possibilities that have the capacity to disclose the absolute uniqueness of each existent being, the tale of *who* someone is rather than simply what they are, for example, in categorical, homogenizing terms.

The origins of Cavarero's lines of argument on narrative can be found in Hannah Arendt's (1998 [1958]) linkage of philosophy's failure to grasp 'who' someone is to politics. For Arendt and Cavarero alike, the latter deals only in universals. Hence, for both, narration offers scope for a rethinking of politics proceeding from a recognition, and narration, of the centrality of understanding human interaction as the co-actions of unique existent beings. On this point, it is crucial to grasp that for Cavarero, following Arendt, the notion of human beings as unique 'existents' is not the same as the idea of the individual as a discrete entity that is championed by liberal politics and Kantian philosophy, and whose story is told largely as a series of 'rights'. Rather, the unique existent is understood to be embedded within a constitutive relationship with and for others, so that the first consideration for politics and ethics should be how human beings might live (better) together, beginning from the premise that what it means to be human is to be constitutively exposed to others, vulnerable 'in perpetuity', as we have noted so far. To this viewpoint, Cavarero adds that each of us is 'narratable' by the other; that is, we are dependent upon others for the narration of our own life stories in order for our existence to be affirmed, and to endure. To put it simply, 'to Arendt's notion of the constitutive exposure of the self, Cavarero ... adds the *narratability* of that self' (Kottman, 2000: ix, original emphasis). Both because of, and through, our constitutive mutual exposure, we desire that our own tale be told from the mouth, pen or keyboard of another. The 'narratability' of every person therefore has a bearing upon what story or history that person lives and leaves behind, hence the condition of narratability is linked both to ethics and to politics. Cavarero illustrates this with reference to the reciprocal storytelling of feminist consciousness-raising groups, as scenes in which selves are constitutively exposed to one another in ways that are relational and which, therefore, make a recognition-based political scene, or set of relations, possible.

For Cavarero (2000), the narratable self is one that struggles to protect and project the uniqueness of their existence, that is, of the 'who' someone is in relation to and for others rather than the simple 'what' of who they are. A self that is narratable is therefore a self whose uniqueness is recognized, and whose existence is affirmed.[17] The uniqueness of each narratable existence is thus both revealed and affirmed through the narration of that person's life story, which in part depends upon the temporal extension of that life story as a sign of the capacity of a person's uniqueness to endure.

For Cavarero and Butler alike, because vulnerability is constitutive of the human condition, there is an ethical valence in narrating the life stories of those who are exposed to extreme violence and/or negation. Narrating life stories, for Cavarero, is a process of rehumanization, of redeeming the meaning and value of a life from the ruins of its negation. The 'See, here!' exclamation that this involves is both an ethical responsibility and a political action, a moment of recognition, that reclaims human subjectivity by revealing the 'scandal' of dehumanization, radically reinstating a person's (or group, community, or population's) humanity in opposition to its unspeakable destruction. In this way, Cavarero insists, '[t]here is an ethical and even ontological urgency in the necessity of ... narration, almost as if every recounted story, snatched from oblivion, saves a possible sense of the human from its absolute negation and destruction' (Cavarero, 2016: 14). Narrating is therefore not simply reconstructing the thread of a life story as a 'coherent' account or process; it is first and foremost an opposition to the work of destruction – a 'creating against demolishing, *a doing against undoing*' (Cavarero, 2016: 14, emphasis added). The aim of narration, in this sense (that is, as the work of recognition), is not simply to provide a descriptively accurate account or testimony, but rather to enact an ethical and political intervention into the negation of existence, and to radically transform the latter into a condition of endurance, understood here (therefore) as the relational capacity to persist in defiance of negation.

Like Arendt, for Cavarero the first task of politics is to find ways for human beings to live together, as we are constitutively exposed to one another through our embodied existence. To this, Cavarero adds that we are mutually dependent upon each other not simply for our bodily endurance, but for the very narration of our existence, the telling of our life stories. To Arendt's notion of the constitutive exposure of the self that is inaugurated from birth (or earlier, of course), Cavarero (2000: 67) adds a concern with the vulnerability that our need to be 'narratable' brings about, for narrative is what gives us 'lives-with-meaning' – the term Cavarero uses to refer to 'the principle of a narrated identity as the tangible expression of existence'. The 'narratable self' – a self whose story is deemed to be capable of being told coherently (that is, in ways that can be accorded recognition), is therefore one that is exposed within the interactive sphere of social relations or what, for

Arendt, is the realm of the political, and which for Cavarero is also the site of ethical relationality. As Cavarero (2000: 36) puts it, 'someone's life story always results from an existence, which, from the beginning, has exposed her to the world – revealing her uniqueness'.[18] To be clear, it is the exposure of the self within social relations, and the need for recognition (in the form of narratability) that renders storytelling a political and ethical endeavour; without it, we risk ending our lives simply as 'remains without narration' (Cavarero, 2000: 57). Narration, for both Arendt and Cavarero, then is a response to the desire for recognition – the desire for one's story to be told, and to be deemed worthy of telling. It is an affirmation of viable existence, and a reply to the question of 'who' (rather than simply 'what') someone is in their unique, but relational existence in the form of a confirmatory account of subjective coherence. Hence, narration, as a mode of recognition, is always a political and ethical act. What Butler adds to this discussion is a concern to understand and emphasize how narrative acts become performative processes of interpellation through which, in the Althusserian sense, subjects are hailed into subject positions according to terms that are not necessarily of their own making, including in ways that are hateful (but also, potentially, generatively so [see Butler, 1997a, 1997b]). For Butler then, narratives, including those associated with grieving and commemoration, are ongoing struggles within and through which perpetually vulnerable subjects both effectively lose and (potentially) find themselves through interpellatory processes that set out the terms of recognition for particular individuals, groups, communities and populations.

It is useful, at this point, to remind ourselves of the extent to which Butler's writing continues to engage itself in an ongoing dialogue with Hegel. While the focus of this is largely on the ambivalent meaning and nature of recognition (as discussed in the previous chapter), Butler concurs with Hegel on the centrality of our desire for recognition to social relations.[19] Crucially, for Butler then, is that because recognition is grounded in a relational ethic that both precedes and exceeds it, 'we belong to each other prior to the act of recognition' (Butler, 2021a: 44), so that recognition is entirely bound up with 'the problem of dependency'. In their discussion of what this means for social relations, Butler hints at an important distinction between the (reificatory, recitational) organization *of* our lives (for example, through matrices of cultural intelligibility) and a more relational and reflexive, re-significatory potential of a recognition-based organization *for* our lives: 'In Hegel, the life and death struggle ends with the recognition that my life is bound up with the life of the other, [so] that *a social organization for our lives must be found that reflects and honours this insuperable interdependency*' (Butler, 2021a: 45, emphasis added). Butler goes on to link this distinction, and the questions it raises, to their ethical concerns with how we might live together more equitably and relationally, based upon a mutual recognition of our co-dependence, noting our need to '[d]erive an ethical position from the interdiction against violence and destruction, or rather, [to] base a politics of nonviolence on the postulate that the social bond is a necessary feature of who the subject is' (Butler, 2021a: 45).[20]

Returning to the example of Hart Island through the lens of what we have considered in relation to loss, grievability and narrative in our discussion so far in this chapter, we can reflect on what this crucial (Hegelian) distinction that Butler makes might mean for reimagining forms of commemoration (as a collaborative remembering) that are more relational, premised upon an understanding of vulnerability not as a weakness to be 'overcome', but as the basis of our ethical relationality and capacity to endure in and through one another, as discussed in Chapters 1 and 2.

Founded in 1994 by activist and artist, Melinda Hunt, the Hart Island Project (HIP) has been working for over three decades to destigmatize the island and to find the names and locate the burial places of those known or believed to be interred there. The HIP's work both highlights the racialized and class-based politics of misrecognition that Hart Island represents and draws critical attention to the 'memory impoverishment' (Brouwer and Morris, 2021: 161) that places like it materialize. The HIP has focused in particular on how, during the AIDS epidemic in the 1980s, 'a collective "recoil" characterized administrative logics and labour practices' (Brouwer and Morris, 2021: 166) governing how the bodies of those who had died from AIDS-related illnesses were treated at the time. As depicted in the award-winning FX series, *Pose*, the burial of bodies and access to commemorative opportunities were governed by a heteronormative schema that was, at best, hostile to queer kinship ties and which conflated homophobic hate with a lack of scientific understanding about viral transmission, and of basic compassion – a care deficit, as Lynne Segal (2023) might put it. Buried in lead coffins in quarantined plots, those known to have died from AIDS-related causes suffered 'a double indignity ... to die from such a stigmatized disease and then be buried in anonymity' as Elsie Soto, one of the featured storytellers in the HIP AIDS Initiative web series describes it. And to this double negation, we might add a third, namely that the enduring public perception that a Hart Island burial 'inevitably means a deeply shameful and degrading end to an unfulfilled, unhappy life' arguably limits the ways in which Hart Island's possible futures might be reimagined (Byers, 2022: 2). For those who are aware of its history, Hart Island will always be a place populated by those who have suffered the multiple indignities of 'disposals of last resort' (Raudon, 2022: 84).

Struggling to tackle these multi-layered stigmas that have endured for many decades, the HIP has attempted to narrate the life stories of those buried there in the ways in which Cavarero (2000) describes. Through legal intervention and public memory work, the HIP has pursued commemorative narration by making public records and institutional history more transparent, and by generating remembrance through its Traveling Cloud Museum (TCM), films and web series. As Brouwer and Morris sum it up:

> A key motive of the Hart Island Project is to destigmatize the site, transforming it into a reachable and respectable public cemetery and national monument, via the breakthroughs of rhetorical claimings and tellings. The vision is liberatory but the labour daunting, owing to the deep discursive sedimentation constituting the ignoble status of Hart Island's dead and the forbidding nature of the destination. (Brouwer and Morris, 2021: 164)

The HIP AIDS Initiative in particular aims to identify people who died of AIDS-related illnesses who are buried on Hart Island and is working to preserve their individual and collective stories. HIP's work to find, name and curate the life stories of people buried there is designed, in part, to provide points of identification and reconnection, to commemorate and to problematize the hegemonic terms of AIDS-related remembering, in order to interrogate who counts as a grievable subject, and to critically question the politics and practices of remembering in and through abject spaces such as Hart Island. As Raudon (2022: 85, emphasis added) puts it, 'in most societies, mass graves indicate a bad death, because individual burial crucially affirms personhood by signalling who is "grievable": some lives are recognised as worth celebrating, while others are deemed less than human and disposed of anonymously ... *These burials materially illustrate a nexus between inequality and symbolic violence*'.[21]

In November 2018, HIP released an activist documentary, *Loneliness in a Beautiful Place*, and uploaded it to the Project's AIDS Initiative website. The film features aerial drone footage that aims to render Hart Island more accessible, telling the story of the place itself as a 'See, here!' critical moment, as Cavarero (2000) leads us to understand it. Recognizing growing critique of the uses of drone technology for state and corporate surveillance and violence, Brouwer and Morris (2021: 167–168) view the film as illustrative of how drone technology's oppositional uses for activists and social movements can help in the assertion of counterhegemonic rhetorical possibilities, highlighting how, under what were (at the time) conditions of restricted access to the island, the film and its aerial imagery performed a kind of 'queer reconnaissance ... a rare way of getting there that facilitated the ability for wider publics to see and experience the [island's] AIDS dead'.

Providing unrestricted aerial 'access' to the island for the first time in its history and illustrating its proximity to mainland Manhattan with a commentary that highlights its history and topography, the film implicitly poses the question of why somewhere so close could be so out of reach, hidden in plains sight, and, in doing so, 'performs a critique of limited access', re-narrating Hart Island and, in doing so, the stories of those buried there. In this sense, as part of the wider activist project, the film shows how 'the variegated "unclaimed" AIDS dead on Hart Island struggle to achieve standing as grievable subjects on a national scale [arguing] ... for a reconsideration of the indigent or "unclaimed," including the abundance of those with Latinx surnames, as grievable national AIDS subjects' (Brouwer and Morris, 2021: 169). In doing so, the film and the wider HIP undertake the work necessary to both highlight the negation of those deemed unworthy of recognition at the time of their burial, and to begin the process of recognizing and remembering them as unique existents, as Arendt (1998 [1958]) might put it.

As another of HIP's activist practices, the 'AIDS Burials on Hart Island' web series features storytelling interviews, ranging between ten and 19 minutes in length, largely with family members and other kin of people buried there. Launched in April 2020, the series introduces us to friends, family and other loved ones of the deceased, interspersing personal encounters with family artefacts, street scenes, HIP video footage and photographs, and new footage at and about the island. Across these interviews, the contributors share different perspectives on what it means to be buried there, and to visit Hart Island as a grieving friend, relative or partner. Referring to Hart Island as 'beautiful', 'calming' and even as 'relaxing', some of the short films support HIP's project to destigmatize the island and to reimagine what it might mean to be associated with it.[22]

A third element of the HIP project's narrative work is that of the 'ticking clock' that features on its TCM webpage. This feature counts the time difference between the date of a person's burial on Hart Island, as recorded in the New York City official record, and the precise time when a person confirms that they are known, recognized and 'claimed'. Most of the clocks are still ticking in real time, attesting to the number of (named) people who no one has 'claimed'. Brouwer and Morris (2021: 172–173) note how, as one element of the TCM, the ticking clocks function as an 'affect generator', heightening a sense of urgency to recognize and connect to the unclaimed. Crucially, encountering not just one but so many ticking clocks on the TCM produces a strong affective response marked by the quiet, haunting persistence of each unclaimed person, highlighting the dynamics of vulnerability and recognition that constitute burial places as sites on which a recognition-based 'ethics of claiming' (Brouwer and Morris, 2021: 174), and the social relations of endurance, are played out.

The HIP aims to bring dignity and accessibility to those interred on Hart Island, to help relatives and kin connected to people known or believed to be buried there to access their records and resting places, and to tell their stories as unique human beings, and as part of a community, as well as to rehabilitate Hart Island itself. At the time of writing, the HIP is also working towards designating the island a National Monument to recognize and reconnect those who are buried there. Through the COVID-19 Initiative, the HIP aims to support people in locating gravesites of people who died during the pandemic and who were given a city burial on Hart Island. This project evolved from the longer-standing AIDS Initiative discussed earlier, and underpins the HIP's aim, through identification, connection and engaged storytelling, to make Hart Island an inclusive rather than abject resting place, and in doing so, 'to enlarge the meaning of this landscape' (hartisland.net). In October 2022, the Hart Island Touchstone Coalition organized the first in a planned series of bereavement walks to honour the memory of those interred on Hart Island because of pandemic illnesses, including AIDS and COVID-19.

What the example of Hart Island, and other similar settings, shows us is that the designation of some individuals, groups or populations as 'worth' remembering and others as not constitutes an organizational, and organizing, process, one that reflects wider social relations of precarity shaping the degree to which some of us – alive or dead – are understood to 'matter' more than others, so that some are commemorated while others are forgotten. What they also materialize is our shared, but socially situated, vulnerability, and how the social relations of endurance are always both political and ethical. In the case of Hart Island its future is, as Byers (2022: 14) highlights, 'laden with practical, spatial and ideological challenges'. Some of the most pressing yet seemingly insurmountable issues include the need for a new infrastructure to make the site safe; workable flood barriers, and mechanisms to deal with the problem of shore erosion (Byers notes the gruesome fact that inadequately interred bodies sometimes wash up on neighbouring shores after floods on Hart Island), and better transport links for public access. Access is an important ethical issue, as without it, not only do the bereaved suffer from being unable to attend burials; they are also prohibited from visiting graves. In order to tackle these issues, Byers argues, it is imperative to navigate the complex balance of, on the one hand, finding ways to move away from enduring perceptions of Hart Island as New York's 'forgotten, unwanted shadow', at the same time as to more openly acknowledge – recognize – the complex constellation of organizational policies, prejudices and practices 'that have allowed us to persist in positioning the island this way for so long'. Necessary to this, Byers emphasizes, is a collaborative, collective community-based re-engagement with the complex, multi-faceted circumstances at stake, at a time when singular, polarized narratives are becoming increasingly dominant.

Memorialization is therefore paramount for those currently interred on Hart Island and in places like it, to reconnect the 'doubly dead' within their kinship relations, and to provide some ongoing recognition both of their lives and of the circumstances that led to them being interred there. In considering memorialization as an ethical imperative for Hart Island, Abby Rees (2020) draws on Lisa Guenther's (2013) idea of social death, a concept that encapsulates the experience of living with no kinship connections and no social recognition. 'Social death' is defined as being the effect of a (social) practice in which a person or group of people is excluded, dominated or humiliated to the point of becoming dead to the rest of society. Although such people are physically alive, their lives no longer bear a social meaning; they no longer count as lives that *matter*'. Rees (2020) notes how Guenther (2013: xxi) states that

> it takes a whole network of interconnected obligations, both in the present and extending into the past and future, to create and sustain social personhood, and it takes a network of exclusions, interruptions and violations, not only against individuals but against the social and temporal horizons of their lives to destroy that personhood.

The network of 'exclusions, interruptions and violations' to which she refers include, in the case of Hart Island, a constellation of organizational imperatives, policies, practices and ethical failings, as Rees's (2020) critique foregrounds. These include decisions and actions that result in a person's violent and permanent dislocation from their kinship networks, those that would otherwise support, protect and give meaning to their lives (and deaths), as well as to individuals' and communities' own wishes and points of identification (for example, LGBTQIA+ communities and histories). As poignant illustrations of Guenther's argument, those interred on Hart Island become precarious in perpetuity, wrenched from their pasts, presents and possible futures. As Rees puts it in this respect:

> Traditional cemeteries have mechanisms to keep the dead attached to their social history and life. Headstones stating that someone is a 'beloved mother' are a demonstration of such a mechanism; the individual buried there is identifiable by their kinship relationships and is connected to their social history of past and future. Hart Island has no such mechanism and thus perpetuates a state of social death for those who are laid to rest there. (Rees, 2020: 7)

Butler's recognition-based theory of grievability, vulnerability and precarity, combined with insights from Cavarero (2000) on the political and ethical importance of thinking about grieving as a re-humanizing narrativization, and of challenging what Mbembe (2019) calls borderization as a premise upon which grieving is currently organized, provides a critical lens through which to reflect both on the predicament of those interred on Hart Island, as well as the work of the HIP. If, as Butler (2009a: 38) puts it, 'an ungrievable life is one that cannot be mourned because it has never lived, that is, it has never counted as a life at all', Hart Island shows how this is also the case vice versa, that is, that those who cannot be mourned are reframed as having never existed. Precariousness is a state of being (or rather not being) that is of concern to Guenther as well, and her critique is also grounded (like Butler's) in the view that because humans (and non-/more than-human beings) are interdependent upon one another, we are therefore all vulnerable to loss and thus exist in a state of perpetual, but socially variable, precarity. For both Butler and Guenther, the human capacity for connection to others is what renders us vulnerable, but it is also what makes living in such a vulnerable state bearable; our vulnerability to and with others is what makes life both precarious and liveable, and which imbues us with the capacity to endure in and through others.

For Rees (2020: 9), memorialization is crucial to combating the 'double death' of those interred on Hart Island and in places like it, or who are missing and unaccounted for entirely, as is the case for so many of those who have lost their lives seeking safety and security as refugees across the globe. In this sense, a similar story to that of Hart Island must be told about the unmarked or anonymous graves and unclaimed bodies along migrant routes, including in the waters of the marine cemetery that the Mediterranean Sea has become (Cavarero, 2021c; Fotaki, 2022).

The European Parliament passed a resolution in 2021 that called for people who die along such routes to be identified, and for a coordinated database to be established to collect details of unclaimed bodies that could be shared. But a recognition void persists, with no sustained or consistent collation or sharing of data, and no agreed way of organizing a cross-national response to the scale of the problem so that a growing number of migrant people's bodies, piled up in morgues, funeral homes and shipping containers have yet to be traced or claimed, while countless others remain missing, presumed drowned. In some of the more privileged parts of the world (including New York), bodies piling up during the COVID-19 pandemic caused moral outrage, but the bodies of those whose lives (and therefore deaths) become de-realized are regarded as what Rees describes as an 'average atrocity', happening in plain sight and arising no such consternation. In the case of Hart Island, massed graves have been used over an extended period as a solution to an infrastructural problem (namely, that of what to do with a large volume of unclaimed bodies), in ways that reflect the negation of those involved. For Rees (2020: 13, emphasis added), memorialization has the potential to begin to undo some of the social death that made it possible for human life to be discarded in a mass grave in the first place; as she puts it, 're-connecting the dead with their living human kin serves to reconnect them with humanity and thus, *resuscitate them socially*'.

In a similar way to the HIP, Susan Ashley's (2015: 30) study of the Chattri Indian war memorial in Brighton, England shows how forms and practices of memorialization constitute value-laden organizing systems that perpetuate colonialism, but which also open up scope for future possibilities beyond it. Built in 1921, the Chattri honours the memories of Indian soldiers who fought in the First World War, but more than that, it provides a site on which the meaning and nature of those memories can be contested and reframed. As Ashley (2015: 42) puts it, memorializing can be seen as a complex combination of objects and practices 'that organize both meaning and value'. Ashley's (2015: 30) analysis of the rituals and modes of gathering that take place around the Chattri emphasizes how 'memorializing operates as an organizational process that constitutes and validates cultural significance', or of course, otherwise, showing how memorialization as a material form or sign, and as an embodied or felt practice, 'fundamentally organizes meaning-making and the shaping of values'.

Memorializing can be a phenomenon through which the marginalization and subjugation of the Other is affirmed; but as Ashley (2015: 43) and others show, it can also be 'a felt experience where embodied and intangible practices can confirm, modify or disrupt those authorized significations', resignifying meanings and associations in ways that open up scope for reclaiming spaces and narratives, and for embodying and enacting solidarity in and through vulnerability.

Concluding thoughts

Butler's phenomenal writing on dispossession, grievability and loss reminds us that 'one way of posing the question of who "we" are ... is by asking whose lives are considered valuable, whose lives are mourned, and whose lives are considered ungrievable' (Butler, 2009a: xx). This chapter has reflected on how the attribution of value shaping grievability and the degree to which a loss registers as a loss is the outcome of a process through which our desire for recognition comes to be organized in ways that, for some, result in national monuments or days of mourning, and for others, being stored indefinitely in a shipping container, or being buried in a mass grave, isolated from loved ones and communities, or being lost to the sea. And this process of organization is one that is shaped by both our primary vulnerability – our primordial, mutual interdependency, but also the way in which that vital aspect of the human condition comes to be socially situated and striated, including within caste- and class-based, racial, gendered, sexual and colonial relations that negate, and/or exploit, our shared interdependency.[23]

Their essay, 'Violence, mourning, politics', is perhaps Butler's fullest articulation, at least to date, of their thoughts on the relationship between liveability and who or what counts as grievable. Here, Butler outlines their views on how certain forms of grief become recognized and amplified, while others are rendered unthinkable and ungrievable. What Butler calls 'a disavowed mourning' involves the erasure from public representations of names, images and narratives of those deemed ungrievable. To put it simply,

> [S]ome lives are grievable, and others are not; the differential allocation of grievability that decides what kind of subject is and must be grieved, and which kind of subject must not, operates to produce and maintain certain exclusionary conceptions of who is normatively human: what counts as a livable life and a grievable death? (Butler, 2004a: xiv–xv)

Butler asks important questions about how our desire for recognition comes to be organized in and through social relations such as those shaping grievability: Who counts as human? Whose lives count as lives? What makes for a grieavable life? This chapter has sought to consider these questions as fundamentally organizational ones, specifically, as questions that require us to reflect on how our desire for recognition comes to be organized in ways that render vulnerability our shared but situated social condition. Hart Island may be populated entirely by those deemed unburiable but we are all, potentially, unburiable, if ungrievability is a failure of recognition, as Butler understands it. To this end, as a vital mode of recognition, grieving, mourning and registering loss becomes not only a (relational) ethical responsibility, but a political potential, bound up with outrage in the face of injustice; it becomes a vital way through which not simply to acknowledge but to narrate our shared, socially situated vulnerability.

Drawing on Levinas, Butler makes the case for expanding our understanding and recognition of who and what counts as liveable (and therefore grievable) as the premise of a more ethical life, arguing that

> certain faces must be admitted into public view, must be seen and heard for some keener sense of the value of life, all life, to take hold. So, it is not that mourning is the goal of politics, but that without the capacity to mourn, we lose that keener sense of life we need in order to oppose violence. (Butler, 2009a: xviii–xix)

It is to the theme of being seen and heard, and to the social relations of appearing as a counter to the de-realization discussed in this chapter and the previous one, that we now turn.

4

Enacting: The Social Relations of Appearing

> That visibility which makes us most vulnerable is that which also is the source of our greatest strength.
>
> Audre Lorde, *Sister Outsider*, 1984: 42

Introduction

As Blanche Dubois reminds us in Tennessee Williams's *A Streetcar Named Desire*, and as Lynne Segal (2023) cites in her book, *Lean on Me*, we all depend upon the kindness of strangers. But of course, this means that, in turn, we are all vulnerable to those same strangers' cruelty or are susceptible to their indifference to our's and others' suffering. In this chapter, we consider how this dynamic plays out in the ways in which social relations are enacted and embedded within, and are shaped by, processes of staring, looking and appearing in the context of what historian and critical theorist Martin Jay (1994) calls 'ocularcentrism' – a social landscape in which the visual senses have taken precedence.

Building on our discussions so far, we will interweave insights from Judith Butler (2020b), Adriana Cavarero (2000, 2016) and Hannah Arendt's writing (1998 [1958]) to consider the problem of interpersonal, or rather intersubjective violence, focusing specifically on the negation that follows from a failure to recognize a person, individual or group's right to appear. Our discussion will explore the ways in which, in this context, to borrow from Butler, violence occurs not only in the 'refusals and failures to recognize it as such' (Butler, 2020b: 190), but also in its widely pervasive and enduring effects. In this sense, throughout the chapter, our desire for recognition is understood, at least in part, as an appeal to the right to appear, to assume a presence, with co-appearing being what we might think of as a spectacular sociality – that is, as the ontological, ethical and political realm in which we appear not only to or with, but *for* one another, enabling us, in a very basic sense, to enact the ways in which our vulnerability is vital to our lived experience of what Arendt (1998 [1958]) called the human condition.

Taking issue with the limitations of philosophy and, instead, following Arendt's concern with the political sphere as the space in which we must find ways to interact that are ethically defensible, and in resonance with Butler's focus on relationality, in *Relating Narratives*, Adriana Cavarero (2000) emphasizes that the very nature of our existence means that we are mutually exposed throughout our lives, rendering us incapable of doing other than 'appearing' to one another. Also following Arendt, Cavarero's framing of this makes an important distinction between the philosophical question of *what* we are, and the ethico-political one of *who* we are in our lived, existential uniqueness. As Cavarero puts it:

> The ambiguity of these questions [of what and who we are] regarding the persistence of identity lies in fact in the confusion of the status of the *who* with the *what*. The *what* – that is, the qualities, the character, the roles, the outlooks of the self – changes and is inevitably multiple and may be judged or reinterpreted in many ways. The *who* on the other hand – as the uniqueness of the self in her concrete and *un-substitutable* existence – persists in continual self-exhibition, consisting in nothing else but this exposure, which cannot be transcended. (Cavarero, 2000: 72–73, original emphasis)

For Cavarero (2009), a violence that targets an individual or group's embodied uniqueness is an ontological crime, one that she describes as 'horrorism', fixing those who are subject to it in place not simply in a corporeal sense, but ontologically, politically and ethically so, rending those treated horrifically unable to be fully human, to act, or to relate to others. Drawing on Cavarero's writing, Valentina Moro (2022) reflects on the horror of George Floyd's murder on 25 May 2020 and the exercises in solidarity and protest that followed, considering the significance of appearing, or occupying public space, to the political processes involved:

> When [George] Floyd was murdered, thousands of people decided to show up in the streets, and in many other public spaces, to lament their outrage and to *reappropriate the right to visibility*, the right to walk safely in public while refusing to acknowledge the gaze that perceives them as the 'embodiment of terror'. ... Caverero argues that those protesters did more than enact a practice of care. ... By gathering in public, they also displayed their own embodied vulnerability. Not only did they protest and denounce structural racism and police violence, they were also able to initiate something, to inaugurate a new series of shared political experiences that required – and still require – taking care

> of each other while being in public: e.g., keeping a physical distance while marking together [during the COVID-19 pandemic]; wearing masks while chanting and screaming. The Black Lives Matter protesters and the supporters who demonstrated with them *enacted these practices of care precisely by recognizing the shared precarity* that characterizes Black lives, aiming to preserve each participant – and especially the most vulnerable ones – from the contagion but also from other risks that are always present when one exhibits one's own body for political reasons. (Moro, 2022: 52, emphasis added)

This chapter explores the social relations of 'the right to visibility', considering the dynamics of staring, looking and appearing in the context of an ocularcentric society, through insights from feminist theory and phenomenology, and considering the issues that Moro and Cavarero both raise in their discussion of Black Lives Matter and other appearance-based acts of resistance and affirmation. Building on discussions in earlier chapters, we will draw on Butler and others' writing on recognition and vulnerability to reflect, first, on staring as a process of objectification that reifies the Other's difference, and which, as a result, disavows agency.[1] We will also consider the dynamics of this process by exploring the scope for resistance that exists within and through the vulnerability engendered by staring, drawing particularly on Arendt's (1998 [1958]) notion of the space of appearance. In doing so, we will ask: What is staring, as a social process? What does it do? And what kinds of social relations and responses might it mobilize? And how does it relate to what we might think of as a liveable, grievable and workable life? In response to these questions, we will examine staring as a form of interpersonal, or rather intersubjective violence, one that arrests scope for mutual recognition and which in doing and being so, negates a person's most basic human dignity ('look at *that*!'). This is precisely because it takes away, in Arendt's terms, the opportunity to appear as an equal; hence the agentic capacity that appearing makes possible – to be part of something, and of the opportunity to take action – is disavowed.

Second, we will explore looking as a parallel or corollary form of ocular engagement in social relations, one that compels or commands attention in a way that also arrests opportunities for intersubjectivity ('look at *me*!'). As an alternative to the negativity of both phenomena, we will consider appearing, drawing on both Cavarero and Butler's reading of Arendt, as an ethical and political act, one that potentially mobilizes the conditions of possibility – or space – for social relationality, and for a re-cognition, or remembering, of the basic interdependency that underpins an ethics of relationality and a politics of solidarity. In this sense, the chapter explores how through appearing, the *organizing* capacity of vulnerability considered in earlier chapters, especially

Chapter 1, might be realized, at least more than it is currently, as Arendt, Cavarero, Butler and others urge us to consider.

In the eye of the beholder? Vulnerability, ocularcentricity and subjectivity

As we have already examined in previous chapters, understood phenomenologically, vulnerability is not simply a (arguably 'the') social condition; it is woven into the very structure of subjectivity, of what it means to be a living being open to the Other, and therefore inherently, albeit differentially, exposed. Vulnerability is relational in the sense that our intersubjective existence depends upon the mutual exposure that our necessary openness to others brings about[2], and in so far as the bonds formed through mutual recognition are themselves inherently vulnerable. Taken together, this means that 'vulnerability structures the subject's experience of the world' (Boublil, 2018: 184). As such, the term 'vulnerability' captures not simply a 'susceptibility' to being wounded rather than an actual failure or frailty, but the shared capacity to be so, a premise that underpins feminist writing on vulnerability. Cavarero, Butler, Segal and others have argued that it is only via particular philosophical and political discourses that the negative, and negating, connotations of vulnerability as a weakness or limitation to be 'overcome' have come to dominate our sense of what it means to be vulnerable. This means that, in neoliberal discourses and policies especially, a dependent life is often framed as a life that does not 'matter', as one that is not worth living, because it is deemed not to have the capacity to signify anything of value (namely, in the context of contemporary market societies – individualism, independence and productivity), or to thrive independently.

For Butler and Cavarero alike, we are bound up from the start – nascent, as Arendt (1998 [1958]) puts it, in our existential vulnerability. Our theoretical and political task therefore becomes how to recover the ethical potential invested, and embodied, in the ek-static condition that precedes the kind of ego-logical posturing that Cavarero (2016, 2021a, 2021b) traces in the history of western thought and symbolism as resolutely definitive of what it means to be a morally responsible living being. Butler reminds us that a person's violation depends upon their negation within and according to schemas of recognizability, intelligibility and normalization, schemas that 'not only *organize visual experience* but also generate specific ontologies of the subject' (Butler, 2009a: 3, emphasis added). Drawing on Butler's thinking on this point, we can understand social practices such as staring and other forms of reified social positioning as modes of address, or interpellations in the Althusserian sense, that have reificatory effects. The most negating forms of these, Butler emphasizes, are never generic modes of hate, but are always addressed specifically to someone, perhaps as a form of social display (as a performative speech act) – as an effort to exercise the power of interpellation: 'You are what I say you are; my speech defines you' (Butler, 2021a: 52). To push this further, we could say that the most negating forms of address are not simply always addressed to someone, but rather to repositioning someone as some*thing*, and further, through this process of address, one's desire for recognition comes to be organized in ways that 'fix' someone as something, as an object devoid of rights, resources and representation, and of the capacity to recognize and be recognized by others, and to signify value.[3]

As discussed in earlier chapters, crucial for Butler (2005: 45, original emphasis) is understanding the ways in which we are always outside ourselves, 'constituted in cultural norms that precede and exceed us, *given over* to a set of cultural norms and a field of power that condition us fundamentally'. In thinking through this scenario and the vulnerability it gives rise to, Butler (2005: 143) draws on Levinas (1969) to explain how forms of normative power operate through effacement, such that the public realm of appearance is constituted on the basis of exclusion. In this way, politics and power work through 'regulating what can appear', governing who and what can be seen, heard, known and so on. Referring to intelligibility, and recognizability, Butler goes on to argue that the de-realization that effacement brings about 'takes place neither inside nor outside the image, but *through the very framing by which the image is contained*' (Butler, 2005: 148, emphasis added).

In order to produce the public sphere in the way that Hannah Arendt understands it, it is necessary, Butler argues, to reimagine (and re-organize) the scope of how people see, how they hear, and what they see; the constraints, for Butler, 'are not only on content ... but on what "can" be heard, read, seen, felt, and known'. In this sense, Butler understands the public sphere as constituted in part 'by *what can appear*', and the regulation of the sphere of appearance 'is one way to establish what will count as reality, and what will not' (Butler, 2005: xx, emphasis added). This way of reading Arendt's (1998 [1958]) notion of the space of appearance, through a focus on how it is 'framed', leads Butler to ask, 'what are the cultural contours of the human at work here?' (Butler, 2005: 32); in other words, who is 'allowed' to occupy space in the public sphere, and on what/whose terms? Further, if de-realization takes place, at first, at the level of discourse, 'this level then gives rise to a physical violence that ... delivers the message', one that is already at work in culture (Butler, 2005: 34). Reasserting the capacity to appear, especially doing so collectively and collaboratively, as we will examine in due course, arguably reverses this logic and its negating effects, while staring and looking, as we will consider first, affirm it.

Staring: look at *that*!

As a form of intersubjective violence, staring situates those who are denied recognition, or who are recognized only on the basis of terms that are derogatory or negating, in ways that exclude or alienate them from the public sphere, relegating those who are subject to staring to the realm of the object, or abject. To borrow from Achille Mbembe (2019), actual and perceptual borders, material and symbolic barriers, shore up these exclusions, disavowing the possibility of occupying space, or at least doing so comfortably or even safely, for those denied access to the social and political realm of appearance. Staring, in this sense, can be understood as a mode of Other-orientated objectification, as a form of interpersonal, or more precisely intersubjective, violence. When a person is hailed through the phrase 'look at *that*!', their subjectivity or personhood is denied; they are de-realized, in Butler's terms, and their capacity for agency is, at best, diminished, if not entirely disavowed.

As a performative manifestation of dominance, staring perpetuates the hierarchy it enacts by 'paralysing' those subject to it, calling them to account and fixing them in (their) place, holding them under scrutiny and requiring them to give an account of themselves, as Butler might put it, as an ontological and semiotic process, asking 'who or rather what are you?', even 'why do you look like that?!'. Feminists have highlighted how this works in gendered power relations with reference to Laura Mulvey's (1975) critique of the 'male gaze'; Michel Foucault (1991) explained its historical evolution in medical science via the 'clinical gaze', and scholars and activists whose work focuses on disabled and/or trans people's experiences have foregrounded how staring positions those subject to it as objects, denied the right to an agentic mode of appearance while at the same time being rendered hyper-visible (Shakespeare et al, 2010).[4] John Berger (1972: 47) summed this up when he said, with reference to the disciplinary effects of the male gaze, 'men act, women appear', and this dichotomous, hierarchical organizing of agency in ocular-normative terms can be applied to many other aspects of social relations. Staring is part of a whole range of cultural forms laden with predation, intimidation and entitlement which take place (they literally 'take' place by dominating the landscape, seizing control of it) via a highly organized set of social practices and infrastructures that call us into being via acts of domination and exploitation.[5] As Franz Fanon (2007 [1967]: 109) also summed it up in *Black Skin, White Masks* in his description of racism as a visual framework for social relations, referring to a position of abjection: 'the glances of the Other fixed me there'.

Jean-Paul Sartre's writing on the staring encounter, exploring how when observed staring the starer is rendered (paradoxically) vulnerable to being 'caught out', offers interesting insights into the complex dynamic shaping staring as a site of social interaction, and as a setting on which power relations are organized and experienced. At the risk of oversimplification, for Sartre (1956: 235–236), when the person who stares is caught indulging in 'inappropriate looking', and the perversity of staring is revealed, the

Other who is stared at shifts from being the object of a dominating encounter to the witness to it. The risk of visually objectifying another therefore becomes that of being caught doing it, and of being subject to the shame that staring brings about. Read through Butler, Cavarero and others, however, the vulnerability that each party experiences within the staring encounter in Sartre's narrative is not mutual, but is always already socially organized, with the person who initiates the stare entering the encounter from a position of relative power and privilege (or 'recognizability' in Butler's terms [see Butler, 2021a, 2021b]), even if the outcome of the stare temporarily 'unsettles' that hierarchy. Further, a vulnerability lens – an approach to understanding staring as a way of framing or organizing the mutual interdependency that shapes social relations – foregrounds the question of the ethical burden that those subject to a staring encounter must bear. Again, this burden is not shared equally, or even recognized, as those subject to staring are fixed not only in an ocular sense (as staring implies), but in an ontological sense too, in so far as (even in Sartre's model) they are required to take on the moral responsibility of its 'revelation' or critique. When understood through these various threads, staring therefore becomes an important site on which social relations can be understood as organizing our desire for recognition, requiring careful, critical and reflexive consideration.

In her book, *Staring: How We Look*, feminist theorist and disability scholar Rosemarie Garland-Thomson (2009: 3, 49) examines the history and social relations of staring, framing the latter largely as an epistemic phenomenon – as she puts it, 'staring is an ocular response to what we don't expect to see', and therefore need to know or position relative to our more 'settled' ways of understanding the world around us. Garland-Thomson understands staring as a mode of social relationality: a kind of looking that is 'intense, focused and asymmetrical'.[6] For her, staring is an interrogative (and in this sense, predatory) gesture, not dissimilar to Butler's (1993, 2005) Althusserian notion of being hailed, or called to account, in so far as it is an encounter between the self and others that 'demands the story'. What is arguably distinct about staring is that those who are subject to it are the ones who are called upon to do the work of rendering what is otherwise illegible intelligible according to dominant, ocular norms governing recognition; in other words, they are called upon to 're-organize' themselves visually, and therefore ontologically and epistemically (to make themselves look 'right' in to order to 'be' knowable). What Sartre underplays most in his discussion of staring, in this sense, is the embodied labour, the ontological and ethical burden of Otherness that those who are de-realized by staring are called upon to enact. In the social relations that Garland-Thomson describes, it is those who are Othered by staring's negating effects who are required to render themselves legible according to prevailing modes of ocular social organization. As she puts it, emphasizing how staring is an encounter in which the struggle for recognition is played out, 'being stared at demands a response'.

Appearances are of course enactments of subjectivity; but more than that, they are appeals for the modes of embodiment that we enact in order to be recognized as subjectively viable. As Garland-Thomson (2009: 6) describes it, 'because we come to expect one another to have certain kinds of bodies and behaviours, stares flare up when we glimpse people who look or act in ways that contradict our expectations'. But staring also offers, she goes on to argue, scope for rethinking the status quo, as for her, our sense of who we are can shift into reflexive focus by 'staring at who we think we are not'. What this level of reflexive engagement would require, however, is a shift of the ethical burden from the other to the self, and in everyday forms of social interaction, this shift is rarely possible as the objectification that staring engenders (the organization of intersubjectivity that it brings about) generally precludes this, not least because staring encounters 'fix' or reify those who are stared at in narratives of their starers' own making; the terms of recognition are therefore negating, rendering the person who is stared at only able to contest their positioning within those terms. It is arguably on this latter point that Sartre's account most notably misses the mark, that is, in understanding staring as 'an uneasy fusion of curiosity and voyeurism' (Garland-Thomson, 2009: 14), the former a largely epistemic positioning, a 'calling to account', the latter a more ethical-ontological one, situating those who are subject to it as objects of visual intrusion and containment.[7]

What Garland-Thomson argues is that those who are stared at also embody the capacity to challenge these terms of reference, reframing the struggle for recognition in ways that expand scope for intelligibility. As she puts it,

> [W]hen people with stareable bodies ... enter into the public eye ... the visual landscape enlarges. Their presence can expand the range of bodies we expect to see and broaden the terrain where we expect to see such bodies. ... These encounters *work* to broaden collective expectations of who can and should be seen in the public sphere and help create a richer and more diverse human community. (Garland-Thomson, 2009: 9, emphasis added)

Here, Garland-Thomson acknowledges that such encounters – those that involve reversing the gaze – involve effort and effect; in other words, returning the stare requires an exercise in agency that transforms a position of relative vulnerability into the capacity to render one's self and potentially others, intelligible. This is what she describes as a staring encounter's 'hidden vitality', understanding staring not only as a social exchange that makes and remakes meaning, but as one that potentially reframes that meaning beyond an oppressive, suobrdinating disciplinary act. In this way, Garland-Thomson seeks to foreground staring's (re)generative potential, understanding staring as a psychologically fraught and socially charged encounter, one of intense interpersonal exchange, but also one pregnant with agentive potential. But as a struggle for recognition, there is much more at stake in staring – which we can understand as, simultaneously, an ethical and political organization of vulnerability.

Like many other writers and activists, Garland-Thomson (2009: 20) considers staring with reference to disability, arguing that historical practices of concealing disabilities and disabled people have served to shape perceptions of what it means to be disabled as unusual, or as a deviation from a norm, rather than understanding disability as fundamental to human embodiment, and as part of all life courses, albeit one that is experienced and embodied in different ways, and in different circumstances and stages of life. The result of normative perceptions of disability, she argues, is a scenario that involves staring at disabled people as the product of 'fascinated disbelief and uneasy identification' (see also Shakespeare et al, 2010). Shaped by the vulneraphobia that underpins a normative (imagined) independence as the human ideal, staring in this sense both negates our shared humanity and avows dominant, even eugenicist, perceptions of subjective viability. As Garland-Thomson and disability scholars and activists have described it, this perpetuates an ocular tyranny of 'normality' premised upon an ideal of inviolability.[8]

The ocular tyranny of normality

What Max Weber (1968 [1930]) called rationalization is the organizing process through which modern societies sought to control the rapidly expanding flows of information, processes, products and movement that industrialization brought about. Its effect has been to abstract us, through bureaucratic structures and systems, from social relations, dehumanizing us in the process. In a way that is not too dissimilar to Cavarero (2000) in *Relating Narratives*, what Weber argued was that rationalization does not actually reduce human variation or sever us from the lived complexity of our human existence; rather it eradicates the particularities of our lived sociality from our epistemological framing of who we are, and how we live, work and organize together. As Cavarero emphasizes, this homogenization of our human uniqueness then in turn shapes our perception of who we are, and how we can/should be; in other words, rationalization organizes us epistemologically and ontologically, but also normatively and ethically. It is in this context, Garland-Thomson (2009: 30–31, original emphasis) argues, that rationalization, and its articulation in medical science, has provided a prescription for 'normality', one that is largely ocularcentric in its orientation, so that '[t]he standard model of human form and function that has come to be called *normal* shapes our actual bodies and the way we imagine them.

The measure of the good, true, and healthy, normal also determines the status and value of people. ... "Normal" both describes and prescribes'.

This tyranny of 'normality' arguably makes it one of the most powerful ideologies framing perceptions and lived experiences of subjectivity in human history, coming to frame legibility in ways that are predicated on a pathological fear of vulnerability and, by implication, of bodily difference from an idealized notion of self-reliance, as 'the pathological shores up the normal' (Garland-Thomson, 2009: 31). Those who deviate, either out of choice or necessity, from ocular norms risk being relegated to a state of being 'beyond' recognition, not only rendered unintelligible, but reified or 'fixed' in their Otherness in ways that prop up normative ontologies and epistemologies shaping perceptions and experiences of shared and situated vulnerability. Both are, by default, understood negatively – through difference, and through a hierarchical organization of that difference that manifests in a wide range of intersubjective forms of violence, from eugenicist experimentation at one extreme, to charitable condescension at the other.[9]

So, while contemporary social and cultural landscapes provide (in theory) infinite variation, that variability (the vitality of each person's uniqueness) is policed by the conflicting need for conformity, not simply to embodied, aesthetic norms, but to a pretence of invulnerability. This is fundamentally an organizing process through which our desire for recognition is compelled and constrained in ways that ostensibly 'rationalize' away our interdependency, perpetuating learned preferences for invulnerability, and a pathological fear of anything other than idealized self-reliance. As Garland-Thomson (2009: 32) notes in this respect, contemporary culture 'prescribes our behaviour, appearance and relations with one another, even while we celebrate freedom and choice'; rhetorical commitments to valuing equality and inclusion in work organizations that perpetuate exploitation and marginalization being an obvious illustration of this, often in ways that render perceived vulnerability a repugnant affront to corporate values of resilience and achievement-orientated performative outputs. In this sense, the dynamics of staring and looking, to which we now turn, embody the fragile pretence of the bond between normality and invulnerability that shapes social relations, one that is not simply ocularcentric, but relentlessly, normatively so.[10] As well as staring, its corollary, looking, perpetuates an organization of recognition according to difference and hierarchy in ways that not only denigrate, but actively disavow, mutual vulnerability, the former orientated towards an objectification of those deemed Other, the latter much more towards the Self.

Looking: look at *me*!

As well as an ocular environment shaped by the objectification of those positioned as Other, we live in an era in which, for many of us, our cultural landscape is dominated by self-obsession; whether via personal or corporate social media accounts or more traditional forms of commercial visual culture, 'look at me!' seems to have become the dominant visual imperative shaping our everyday lives and social encounters.[11] In this context, the age of the selfie seems to be one in which the latter has become not simply a narcissistic photographic technique but an ethical orientation, a self-focused disposition in which egocentrism continually seeks to overshadow social relationality in a relentlessly performance-orientated environment in which we come to value the aspirational, individual, seemingly invulnerable, aesthetically ideal self as paramount. Perhaps most dispiriting is that this self-orientated objectification is often articulated through a highly stylized notion of 'sharing', masking reified social interaction as creative forms of self-expression and connection.

Reflecting on this situation in her final essay in *Surging Democracy*, 'Crowds with a cellphone', Adriana Cavarero (2021c: 92) describes the cult of the selfie and its relationship to narcissistic individualism as epitomizing a scenario in which online visibility has come to be so closely associated with social existence that the desire to continually put oneself on display has reduced notions of connection to the purely technological. Referring to gatherings attended by political leaders, Cavarero argues that 'selfie crowds' are crowds that are '[h]ighly individualistic and structurally unrelated. Their being together in the same space does not translate into a form of relationship and, much less, into an experience of plurality' in the way in which Arendt might understand the latter; rather, the selfie produces 'a subjectivity *folded back on itself*' (Cavarero, 2021c: 92, emphasis added).

Our contemporary world, at least in many parts of the globe, is ocularcentric in highly mediated and organized ways; our lifeworlds and social relationships are saturated with screens, and for many if not most of us, our mode of interaction is largely commercial and consumer orientated. Perpetually distracted by a bombardment of visual stimulations, we offer each other continuous partial attention at best, multi-tasking across devices and personas; what we see and how we look becomes our main – perhaps for many, our only – reference point for social interaction. Social media encounters in particular offer not the intense, focused scrutiny of staring that results in the other-orientated form of objectification discussed earlier, but rather a self-orientated visual demand. As a heavily mediated phenomenon, looking, in this sense, sits somewhere between *ennui* and enthrallment, we might say, demanding the aspirational engagement of others with a version of the self that can perhaps best be summed up with reference to what Siegfried Kracauer (Kracauer and Levin, 1995) called a 'mass ornament', attracting interest not by novelty (as Garland-Thomson argues is the case in staring encounters), but through an endless, uncanny repetition of sameness.

What staring and looking have in common, we might surmise, is that both are a form of intersubjective harassment, if not violence; a perverse, ocularcentric organization of our desire for recognition and a negation of our shared vulnerability. And we defend ourselves against the constant overstimulation of a cultural landscape that continually demands 'look at me!' by looking arguably not at but *through* one another, in a non-committal, uninvolved way, such is the effect of this continual demand for us to look.

Eyes down: anonymity and un/civil attention in a world of strangers

As Garland-Thomson's (2009) writing on staring emphasizes, anonymity is a relatively recent form of human relating; most human beings have historically lived together by knowing one another and being in relatively close social and physical proximity. Processes of industrialization and urbanization have of course meant that many of us are now surrounded by too many people to be acquainted with personally, and we find ourselves continually navigating social worlds populated by strangers in which, every day, we are seen by, and look at, large numbers of people who are unknown to us. As we noted at the start of this chapter, we each depend upon the kindness of these strangers; but by the same token, we are also exposed to their violence, hostility and/ or indifference to us, including to our suffering and that of others. The visual dynamic this creates means that most people (notably, for example, commuters) take refuge in being invisible to one another, especially to those who choose not to, or cannot, conform to dominant ocular-centric norms.

In an environment that precludes recognition because of the ways in which social relations come to be organized, we learn to expect and accord each other what Erving Goffman (1980: 83) calls 'civil inattention', getting through each day by means of what Garland-Thomson (2009: 35) describes as 'ocular complacency' – a tacit arrangement in which we come to expect, and accord others, only disengaged acknowledgement at best, and more commonly, total social indifference.[12] Achieving and maintaining a delicate balance between avoiding scrutiny and being accorded recognition in this way requires constant identity work, resources and organization, which for those who cannot or choose not to 'blend in' can be exhausting and depleting. As Butler's (1988, 1990, 1993) writing on performativity has of course emphasized, itself drawing on Hegel (1977 [1807]), our bodies act as the media through which we encounter one another and materialize our desire for recognition, even if that means that the recognition we desire is to be accorded discreet, respectful inattention that bestows the (relative) freedom not to be conspicuous (that is, not to be stared at). Yet what looking enacts, again through embodied encounters, is a self-orientated objectification that arrests the possibility for mutuality, or for civil inattention to be maintained; rather than expressing a desire for recognition, interactions premised upon an imperative to look, and be looked at, demand it, with 'likes' on social media providing evidence of an easily quantifiable, reified form of relating to one another in a (superficially) affirmative sense.

As we have already noted, not everyone can achieve discreet, civil inattention, however, or wants to, and of course as a mode of relationality in the form of, say, 'passing', looking away is not an unproblematic basis for social interaction, or *necessarily* a progressive alternative to staring. Some commentators on trans politics or on what we might understand or experience as invisible disabilities, for instance, have argued that passing is a privilege, one that is situated in social relations shaped by access to organizational infrastructures and resources, while others have raised concerns about its normalizing tendencies, framing the compulsion to pass in order to illicit inattention as a form of 'recognition policing', requiring those who appear different to blend in in order to function, or to remain safe – see Zhang (2022) for a discussion of trans people's experiences of the complex, ocular dynamics of 'passing'. In his book, *The Body Silent*, anthropologist Robert Murphy (1987: 93) reflects on his own experience of quadriplegia to make the point that looking away from people who make 'us' feel uncomfortable differs from granting those who desire it visual anonymity – the latter is recognition-based while the former, he argues, is an active disavowal, 'a deliberate obliteration of personhood' that can be 'visually brutal' in its negating effects. This shows us that while how we look seems to matter most in our self-orientated contemporary social landscape, but ethically, it is how we look away that arguably matters more. As Garland-Thomson (2009: 93) sums it up, 'as a block to mutuality, pity is repugnance refined into genteel condescension'. Empathy, on the other hand, 'bonds in a mutual recognition of shared humanity'.

Many social movements, artists and individuals have deliberately and consciously sought to challenge civil inattention in order not simply to exercise their right to appear, but in doing so, to develop a powerful, collective critique of the visual organization of social relations that leads, on the one hand, to staring as a form of other-orientated objectification, and to the demand to be looked at, as a more self-orientated imperative on the other, both of which arguably preclude mutual recognition of shared vulnerability, and negate the personhood of those who are 'fixed' in an ocularcentric hierarchy. The anonymity of pornographic imagery, or medical photographs, imposed on those whose bodies they depict prevents the person from staring back. But making eye contact, looking back at those who stare, is vital to recuperating the scope for mutual relationality and vulnerability within social relations; those who undertake it are arguably engaged in the (ocular) work of recognition, affirming shared but situated mutual vulnerability within social relations.

In contrast to both staring and looking as scenarios in which social relations play out human vulnerability in ways that are other- or self-objectifying respectively, appearing in this way can be understood, following Hannah Arendt (1998 [1958]) and others, as a more recognition-based sphere for social relations to emerge premised upon a shared, and reflexive awareness of mutual interdependency as the basis of the human (and more than human) condition. Appearance is, then, following points noted earlier, arguably a space marked by a refusal, on the one hand of hyper-ocularity, and on the other, to be visually inconspicuous. *Co-appearing*, understood in this way, becomes an alternative way in which to assume a collective, embodied presence. To explore this further, we now turn to insights from Butler and Cavarero who both draw, in slightly different ways, on Arendt's writing on the political importance of the 'space of appearance' as a sphere in which mutual vulnerability can be experienced and enacted.

Appearing: occupying spaces of/for solidarity

Drawing on Arendt, both Cavarero and Butler emphasize how appearing to one another creates political opportunities that are different from the social relations of staring and looking outlined earlier. For them, appearing affirms our shared but socially situated vulnerability in ways that open up scope for recognition-based social interaction and the transformation of vulnerability from a (negative) position of incapacity to agency and solidarity. Crucial for Arendt, and feminist writers who draw on her work, is that as an embodied assertion, co-appearing is not (simply) a plea for sympathy or politeness, but an agentic, assertive call for mutual recognition that can serve as a vital counter to visual exclusion. In contrast to the other- and self-orientated objectification underpinning staring and looking discussed so far, appearing can be understood as an engaged mode of relating to one another, and to the world we live in, in (to borrow from Arendt) the full, shared plurality of our unique, embodied existence.

The notion of the public sphere as a space of appearance has been most fully articulated by Arendt (1998 [1958]: 198–199, emphasis added) in her writing on the human condition. For her, the space of appearance is located within the *polis* – not the city-state in its physical location, but rather 'the *organization of people* as it arises out of acting and speaking together', emerging for the purpose of enabling people to live, work and act together. Located in the *polis*, the space of appearance is 'the space where I appear to others as others appear to me'; it is a collective, collaborative space holding within it the possibility of action, and of mutual recognition as a process through which we each appear to one another 'as' we are in our uniqueness. It is in this space that we appear to one another 'not merely like other living or inanimate things *but explicitly*'. Arendt acknowledges that not everyone has access to this space, and even those who do are not necessarily able to access it all of the time, or even on their own terms (as Butler reminds us), but for her it is a space that is at once ethical, political and ontological; to be able to occupy the space of appearance is ontologically (and hence ethically and politically) affirmative: 'to be deprived of it means to be deprived of reality' (Arendt, 1998 [1958]: 199) in a world in which co-appearance is synonymous with co-existence ('reality ... humanly and politically speaking, is the same as appearance', as she puts it). For Arendt, our existence is affirmed through the presence of others so that what or whoever lacks appearance remains ephemeral, 'passes away like a dream ... without reality'.

The space of appearance comes into being when we are co-present to, with and for one another, 'in the manner of speech and action', preceding the various forms through which the public realm has come to be organized. Its mode of existence is one of potentiality, its ontology being its capacity to bring other phenomena into being, occupying the public realm as a 'potential space ... between acting and speaking' (Arendt, 1998 [1958]: 200). It is in the space of appearance that, for Arendt, the uniqueness defining *who* rather than simply what we are, can come into being, and in which each person can be affirmed in their specific but shared speech and action. In essence, the space of appearance is 'a mode of being together' (Arendt, 1998 [1958]: 208), scope for which, not surprisingly, atrophies with the growth and normalization of alienating ways of organizing and of relating to one another within the public realm, while it flourishes in the context of plurality.

In *Relating Narratives*, Adriana Cavarero draws from Arendt's (1971: 19) notion that 'being and appearing coincide'. For Arendt, appearing has not simply a phenomenological, but an ontological, significance. The spectacular nature of sociality is crucial to her account of the human condition. Our mutual exposure is constitutive of who we are: through reciprocal exhibition a 'who' – a unique existent, in Arendt's terms – is shown to appear. Co-appearance, for Arendt, is how everyone shows who they are to others, as a unique existence, so that the exposed and relational nature of being are indistinguishable.[13] This is what Arendt means when she refers to the 'naked reality of our originary physical appearance'. First, we appear to each other reciprocally in all our 'corporeal materiality ... as creatures with sensory organs', effectively as matter, albeit 'uniquely and distinctly' so (Cavarero, 2000: 20–21). Our existence thus depends upon the presence of others, to whom we appear corporeally, in a scene of appearance in which 'we ourselves as appearances exist among other appearing creatures' (Cavarero, 2000: 21). But merely appearing as physical entities is different from actively showing others 'who' we are – this is not simply a difference (reflecting a post-Cartesian dualist ontology) between the body, and the mind or spirit. It is rather, as Caverero (2000: 21) sees it, 'a difference of scene'. What this means is that, in Arendt's account, the space in which human beings appear to one another is one that sees them acting, exercising agency, and in doing so, actively revealing their uniqueness. Crucial here is that for Arendt our capacity to take action is engendered by our occupation of the space of appearance, not vice versa.

Drawing from and developing Arendt, Cavarero (2000: 88) argues that the exhibitive nature of the self which is so central to the former's thinking 'is rendered even more explicit in the active and desiring practice of reciprocal storytelling'. Narrating, understood in this way, is 'the necessary aspect of an identity which, from beginning to end, is intertwined with others' lives', involving 'reciprocal exposures and innumerable gazes'. For Cavarero, following Arendt, the founding condition of what it means to be human is to be 'constituted by a being together ... within the plural space of appearance', enabling those who occupy the latter to reveal their uniqueness and to affirm their existence. The foundations of individualist philosophical and political doctrines, and social actions such as staring and looking discussed earlier, ignore precisely this co-constitutive relation of the self with and for the other.

In Arendtian thinking, it is within the space of appearance, and the sphere of the political, that the 'who' is exposed, finding themselves in constitution with the other; hence, 'the ontological status of the *who* as exposed, relational, altruistic – is totally *external*' (Cavarero, 2000: 89, original emphasis),[14] but never fixedly so, as Butler's Hegelian reading of Arendt emphasizes. For Cavarero (as for Arendt), the other is necessary to the self as a unique existence: 'In the light of a unique and unrepeatable identity – irredeemably exposed and contingent – the other is therefore a necessary presence. He or she [*sic*] is the one who consents to the very event of an appearance ... of *the existent*, which ... *is always a co-appearance*' (Cavarero, 2000: 89, emphasis added). The other is therefore ontologically, and hence ethically and politically, necessary to the status of the *who* which is 'always relational and contextual' (Cavarero, 2000: 90). Key to Cavarero's understanding of the relational significance of narrative is the ontological status of reciprocal appearance, as the space in which human beings can appear 'each one *for* and *with* another' (Cavarero, 2000: 90, emphasis added). In a context of co-constitutive, altruistic plurality, who we are – our unique existence – eludes categorization, and no collective identity can fully contain it; as unique existents, we are 'the inassimilable, the un-substitutable, the unrepeatable'. The 'I' that individualistic doctrines are preoccupied with ignores not only the 'us', but the 'you' as a vitally constitutive component of a collective we – of what it means to be a human, social being.

In narrative terms, what Cavarero (2000: 91, original emphasis) calls the 'empathetic trap' occurs via the constitution of a self (or collective identity) that 'metabolizes the story of the other', describing a scenario in which the narrative is such that the other's uniqueness disappears. In one of the few explicit discussions of recognition in *Relating Narratives*, Cavarero refers to the reciprocal appearance of uniqueness as the qualifying dynamic of 'recognition as an ethic', arguing that 'to recognize oneself *in* the other is indeed quite different from recognizing the irremediable uniqueness of the other'. For Cavarero, therefore, following Arendt, co-appearance is central to the politics and ethics of relationality, requiring the political to be a sphere in which all those who exist can appear, and persist, in both their uniqueness and (hence), plurality without the risk of being 'metabolized'.

Butler (2020b) too returns to Arendt (in *The Force of Nonviolence*) to emphasize that 'lives matter in the sense that they assume physical form within the sphere of appearance' (Butler, 2020b: 12). And through this discussion, Butler reminds us of the agentic capacity at the heart of vulnerability, as the essence of our very humanity, asking, what if the situation of those deemed vulnerable is, in fact, a constellation of vulnerability, rage, persistence and resistance? What if this constellation is articulated simply through asserting the right to appear (for example, by assembling)? In this instance, vulnerability cannot simply be identified with passivity, or a sense of helplessness, or lack of hope; rather, understood as an embodied set of social relations, vulnerability is a form of capacity, a capability (Butler, 2020b) – that of being able to withstand, together, the continual exposure of the open wound that mutual vulnerability brings about, once it becomes co-located in the space of appearance.

Understood in the way that Butler articulates it, drawing on Arendt, 'demonstration' has at least two meanings relevant to our discussion of how we might rethink vulnerability through a feminist, phenomenological focus on the dynamics of appearing, that is, as a shared, situated capacity for action and solidarity. First, it refers to that which is shown, enacted, incorporated bodily and second, to that which is opposed, or stood against. In Butler's (2020b: 196) words, this duality 'shows the knotted position of the subjugated subject by at once exposing and opposing its own subjugation'. And this dialectic, of simultaneous exposure and opposition, constitutes what Butler maps out as a politics of nonviolence (Butler, 2020b), or vulnerability in and *as* resistance (Butler, 2016), as a counter to reified social relations (that is, to ways of relating to one another that ostensibly 'forget' our mutual vulnerability, protecting and preserving the right to appear, and the resources attached to that right for some, but not all – as we discussed in Chapters 2 and 3). By staking a claim to the need and right to have access to the basic requirements to sustain a liveable life, a struggle for recognition is inaugurated, or reframed, enacted through a demand to be recognized as having the right to appear and not, reminding ourselves of points made earlier, to be stared at or 'made' to look. For subjugated individuals, groups and populations, this involves effectively articulating their desire for recognition within the public and media sphere – appearing and assembling (at once a coming together and a constituting) as a 'performative and embodied *persistence*' (Butler, 2020b: 196, emphasis added). What Butler seems to articulate here that is most important to our discussion, drawing from Arendt and developing insights from her writing in a slightly different way to Cavarero, is that appearing involves a radical re-orientation, or reclamation, of how the desire for recognition comes to be organized in ways that can be oppressive, negating and/or exploitative; in other words, it is via exercising and embodying not simply the right, but the *imperative* to appear, that vulnerability can be understood and enacted as a shared social condition, and hence as a form of resistance.

In the way in which Butler develops it, then, Arendt's (1998 [1958]) notion of the space of appearance becomes persistence (*contra* the more individualistic, neoliberal discourses of endurance and resilience that are currently in circulation, including within some activist spheres) as an assertion of the capacity to inhabit and embody a liveable life/grievable death. The body, in this sense, 'acts on its own *deixis*' (Butler, 2020b: 197, original emphasis) – it becomes a living sign that says 'Here! I am/we are here!', in so far as it constitutes '[a] pointing to, or enacting of, the body that implies its situation: *this* body, *these* bodies; *these* are the ones exposed to violence, resisting disappearance. These bodies exist still, which is to say that *they persist under conditions in which their very power to persist is systematically undermined*' (Butler, 2020b: 197, emphasis added). Understood in this way, that is, not as an assertion of the need to 'overcome' vulnerability, but as an appeal to mutual recognition of shared, socially situated interdependency and relationality, embodied assemblies – modes of occupying the space of appearance collectively and collaboratively – potentially act as a 'performative force in the public domain' (Butler and Athanasiou, 2013: 196), consisting of a collective bodily presence. This 'collective thereness' (Butler and Athanasiou, 2013: 197) enables bodies to 'enact a message, performatively' (Butler and Athanasiou, 2013: 197), articulating a radical, recognition-based vulnerability in ways that signal 'a defence of our collective precarity and persistence in ... *refusing to become disposable*' (Butler and Athanasiou, 2013: 197, emphasis added).

The feminist solidarity mobilized in support of Gisèle Pelicot throughout the trial in 2024 of the 51 men, including her husband, who were sentenced to over 400 combined years in prison for drugging and raping her over many years, provides a powerful illustration of what this might mean in practice. Pelicot took the decision to refuse the anonymity usually granted in rape trials, and attended the court sessions in Avignon, France throughout the more than three-month duration of the trial. Waiving her right to anonymity meant that the media and the general public had full access to all details of the trial, including the evidence presented. When gathering evidence, police found more than 20,000 videos and photographs on Gisèle Pelicot's husband's devices in a folder labelled 'Abuse' of Gisèle being drugged and raped by numerous men. In an unprecedented act, she insisted that some of these be shown in court in order to shift the burden of shame, as she put it, from victims to perpetrators. After the sentencing, she made a powerful statement in solidarity with those subject to sexual violence across the world, particularly 'the unrecognized victims, whose stories often remain in the shadows', saying 'we share the same fight'.

Of the many extraordinary aspects of this trial and the feminist action that it mobilized was Gisèle Pelicot's choice to appear – not only in person (as she did throughout the trial, and to the media – speaking in person, rather than as is more common, via her legal team), but also in the visual evidence that she asked to be shown in court. She did so precisely in order to open up urgent conversations in the media and public sphere on rape culture, misogyny and chemical submission, prompting a review of the legal definition of rape in France. In this sense, her actions interconnected in highly effective ways with those of other activist groups taking a stand against gendered violence and femicide, including the glue-based protests undertaken by Collage Femicides in France, and in other parts of the world, the impact of which emanates from their tactical use of the space of appearance as an act of resistance and solidarity. It also resonated with other groups such as trans activists in countries such as Turkey, persisting in gathering for Pride marches and other LGBTQA+ events in defiance of the criminalization of their right to exist and appear, and in the face of police brutality and state violence.[15]

In the final essay in *Dispossession*, 'Spaces of appearance, politics of exposure', Butler (Butler and Athanasiou, 2013) explores the importance of affective labour to critical agency in forging an alternative to the scenarios discussed here with reference to staring and looking, other- and self-objectifying, respectively. Their response develops a situated understanding of the affective politics of the performative that resonates with (and draws on) Arendt's (1998 [1958]) formulation of the 'space of appearance' that Gisèle Pelicot's actions embodied, and that those of other groups, movements and activists illustrate. In this essay, Butler returns to the idea of 'taking place' as a performative process (referring to both a 'happening' and a 'possessing', a becoming in/through space as the realm of the political), considering this process in relation to the theme of who and what 'counts' as subjectively viable. Here, Butler argues that 'it is through stabilizing norms of gender, sexuality, nationality, raciality, able-bodiedness, land and capital ownership that subjects are interpellated to fulfil the conditions of possibility for their appearance to be recognized' (Butler and Athanasiou, 2013: 195).

This point reminds us of the fundamental question (regarding the social conditions and consequences of the power relations governing the conferral or denial of recognition): How do particular forms of 'corporeal engagement' (Butler and Athanasiou, 2013: 195) become intelligible, sensible, liveable; in other words, how do they become organizationally viable within the ocularcentric contexts discussed in this chapter? And perhaps more importantly, how do we challenge and change those conditions in order to broaden the range of possibilities for how vulnerability might be lived, embodied and exercised beyond a 'resilience' narrative, in the way in which, for instance, Gisèle Pelicot enacted, and trans, indigenous and/or disabled people's rights groups continue to enact? Speaking to the political significance and capacity of appearing in (our) full precariousness, Butler argues that opposing de-realization opens up the radical possibility of a sense of ethical outrage, challenging us to think, exist and act 'at the limits of what we can know, what we can hear, what we can see, what we can sense' (Butler, 2005: 151), opening up possibilities for the 'instigation of *a sensate democracy*' (Butler, 2005: 151, emphasis added). But, to return to an earlier question, what ethical and political 'burden', we must ask, do those charged with the task of appearing bear? And perhaps more pressing: How can that burden be shared more equitably, and enacted as fairly, and effectively as possible?

Considering this very issue with reference to commemorative rituals and events that take place at the Chattri Indian war memorial near Brighton, England, discussed earlier (in Chapter 3), Susan Ashley (2015: 42, emphasis added) emphasizes the importance of undertaking shared activities such as mourning 'in public' as a condition of occupying 'a formal, imagined place out there that we enter and participate in symbolically and *in doing so, make an appearance*'.[16] This public appearance or visibility enables, she argues, a collectivity to be enacted in order to achieve solidarity with those taking part, by being 'adamant about the need to be seen in this space, to have a public presence *in relation to each other*'.[17] For Ashley, those who assemble at such sites engage in a form of spectacular sociality (to borrow from Arendt) that enables them, collectively, to reclaim the space and its meanings in much the same way as the feminist groups acting and appearing in solidarity with Gisèle Pelicot did. Reflecting on what takes place during commemorative assemblies at the Chattri, Ashley (2016: 42) describes the importance of solidarity and recognition to its capacity to assume a recolonizing presence:

> The audience, through its presence and solidarity in that remote location re-colonize what was once colonial, offering a public affirmation of value and a 'witnessing' that affirmed membership. They felt that the physical process of mutual witnessing and recognition led to cross-cultural negotiation and the transformation of human relations. … Their articulations of these values link the importance of this site to principles that underlie the nature of 'organizing'.[18]

A similar point can be made about Marc Quinn's statue, 'Alison Lapper Pregnant' (Figure 4.1), that was unveiled in London's Trafalgar Square in September 2005 and displayed there until the end of 2007. This statue was selected to occupy the Fourth Plinth, a platform used to display contemporary works of art that provide a counter to the more traditional militaristic statuary that dominates the space. Alison Lapper was born with no arms and shortened legs; she posed for Quinn's 13-ton work of art while she was eight months pregnant with her son. The sculpture remained in place for 18 months, prompting various responses to the work as 'indecent', 'confrontational', 'repellent', 'ugly' and 'beautiful' (see Garland-Thomson, 2009). Quinn's point was that the statue was 'vexingly visible',[19] forcing those who viewed it not to look away in its radical presentation of disability and maternity, juxtaposing the familiar female nude with the relatively rarely displayed disabled, pregnant woman's body in ways that invite recognition, bearing witness to variation and vulnerability as shared, human conditions.[20]

And more recently (since September 2024 and at the time of writing), also on the Fourth Plinth, Mexican artist Teresa Margolles's work, 'Mil Veces Un Instante' (A Thousand Times in an Instant) has depicted plaster casts of the faces of hundreds of transgender, non-binary and gender non-conforming people to powerful effect. The work, which was made collaboratively in the United Kingdom and Mexico, stands in tribute to Karla, a transgender woman who was murdered on 22 December 2016 in Ciudad Juárez, Mexico, raising awareness through its presence, and as a commemorative focal point, of the violence to which gender non-conforming people are subject globally. As a block of faces aligned together, in solidarity and in their embodied strength, 'Mil Veces Un Instante' contrasts markedly with the more traditional and obvious verticality (Cavarero, 2016) of Nelson's column in the middle of London's Trafalgar Square (see Figure 4.2), almost making the latter look feeble, fragile and isolated by comparison. Its depiction of multiple faces, together, looking upwards and outwards in unison also challenges the Othering effects of staring discussed earlier, via the substantial co-appearance that the statue embodies.

The resignification that is performed by these kinds of public artworks, and by those who appear and assemble in the spaces they occupy and others (including online), shows that we all too often encounter one another not as we are but as we are expected to be. This results in a misrecognition that disparages or ignores a person, group or community's distinctiveness; it shows that misrecognition is not only unjust but unviable as it disavows the mutual vulnerability that makes us not only what but *who* (to borrow from Cavarero's reading of Arendt) we are. And it also foregrounds the labour of appearing as a form of recognition work, with critical, feminist thinkers emphasizing that this is – and should be – a collective rather than individual endeavour, a collaborative insistence of a shared predicament, and an assertion of our most basic need to appear to, with and crucially for, one another (Segal, 2018, 2023; Butler, 2020b).

Figure 4.1: 'Alison Lapper Pregnant', Fourth Plinth, Trafalgar Square, London, September 2005

Source: Photograph courtesy of the artist, Marc Quinn and with Alison Lapper's permission

What we can draw from Arendt's understanding of the political potential attached to the space of appearance, then, and from the ways in which Butler and Cavarero have engaged with it, is an emphasis on the importance of the space (and time) involved in doing the work of politics and ethics, enabling us to connect in a more relational way precisely by being in the presence of others in ways that compel our full engagement. Such encounters can, as

Figure 4.2: 'Mil Veces Un Instante' (A Thousand Times in an Instant), Fourth Plinth, Trafalgar Square, London, July 2025

Source: Author's own photograph

Butler reminds us in their reading of Hegel, lead us into spaces (moments) of mutual understanding and affirmation that can be transformative, opening up scope for us to question and possibly reimagine not simply the ocular status quo, but the kind of ethical life that might we live. In some respects, this might require a kind of 'visual activism', changing the ways in which we read, for instance, depictions of 'vulnerable' people as living a diminished life, and instead see the 'raw' beauty of interconnection. And it involves working in solidarity to reframe the terms on which we can co-appear in order to live, work and act together.

In her classic book, *Black Looks*, bell hooks (1992) alludes to just this point in her discussion of the ethical and political potential of moments of recognition based upon visual interaction beyond the reifying, objectifying effects of staring and looking, as a conduit for social relations of mutuality. As she puts it, 'eye-to-eye contact, the direct, unmediated gaze of recognition ... affirms subjectivity', reinforcing solidarity. What hooks calls 'the look of recognition' co-constitutes us as equally legitimate, reciprocal participants in the public sphere.[21] This kind of engagement – appearing to one another – is of course an often deliberate and sometimes unavoidable strategy used by individuals and activists in response to the objectifying effects of staring and looking. In writing about what hooks (1992) calls the 'oppositional gaze', Garland-Thomson emphasizes how these are tactics that many people adopt every day in order simply to sustain their lives as liveable or, more collectively, to open up scope for others to do so, and to be liveable in the ways in which their unique existence is fully recognized as constitutive of the plurality of the human condition. How, we might ask, can this be enacted as a collaborative, collective endeavour, to sustain the oppositional gaze not as the work of individuals, but as a radical, relational form of solidarity? What work, and modes of organization, and organzing, are necessary for this to happen, and for vulnerability to be affirmed as the basis of solidary in this way?

Concluding thoughts

Responding to these kinds of questions, Butler (2020b: 201) notes that sometimes simply 'continuing to exist in the vexation of social relations is the ultimate defeat of violent power'. Interventions into the media and other contemporary permutations of the sphere of appearance can potentially open up ways of asserting – reassembling – we might say, that 'all lives ought to be able to persist in their living without being subject to violence, systematic abandonment, or military obliteration' (Butler, 2020b: 202). Among the many risks associated with this, however, is that of what we might call a 'hyper recognition' – a rhetorical rather than relational form that replaces an exploitation of vulnerability, and/or a reifying Othering of those deemed vulnerable, with a reification of 'value', as discussed in Chapter 1. Contemporary organizations are of course replete with the latter, articulated perhaps most obviously through 'manging diversity' discourses and initiatives that bear little resemblance to actual, meaningful commitments to social justice (see Hancock, 2008, 2024).

To counter the risks associated with reified, rhetorical forms of recognition, a new egalitarian imaginary is needed, Butler concludes, one that 'apprehends the interdependency of lives' and which 'does not rely on instrumental logics' (Butler, 2020b: 203). Two principles might shape this. First, 'in such a world, each life would deserve to be treated as the other's equal … would have an equal right to live and to flourish'. Second, each would be recognized, from the start, as 'given over to another', as mutually socially interdependent, so that the chance of persisting is underpinned by 'the desire for the other's desire to live' (Butler, 2020b: 203). Yet both logics require a radical commitment to recognition-based sociality that seems depressingly remote from, if not entirely at odds with, our current political and social landscape (Segal, 2023).

In the following, final, chapter we will respond to this dilemma, exploring what might make our lives more feasibly and sustainably workable, considering the relationship between vulnerability and organization in more depth, and drawing from feminist writing on liveability, relationality and care to explore how the ethical principles of a viable existence, one conditioned by mutual recognition of our shared, situated interdependency, might help us to tackle the extremes of exposure and precarity that contour our current ways of organizing.

5

Towards a Radical Vulnerability: Organizing for Workable Lives

> Interdependent, our persistence is relational, fragile, sometimes conflictual and unbearable, sometimes ecstatic and joyous.
> Judith Butler, *The Force of Nonviolence*, 2020: 64

Introduction

Imagine the scenario ... you board a crowded train and someone else is sitting in the seat that you have pre-booked. They ask if they can finish eating their food before they move and find somewhere else to sit, and you agree that this is fine, taking a free seat opposite them but seeing this as a temporary solution, as there is a risk that someone else will get on at a later stop and need the seat you are using. But a conversation strikes up, revealing shared interests and experiences. The person in 'your' booked seat shares with you their knowledge of the history, culture and language of the place you have just visited. You are fascinated by their insight, learning from them and laughing together at shared anecdotes. Through this process, you and the stranger become familiar, friends even, swapping details and hoping to meet again on the same train, as regular travellers; what began as an ostensibly hostile encounter becomes relational, harmonious and hopeful.[1]

Now imagine a situation in which we thought of all strangers as people we recognized but cannot quite 'place' or situate in our perceptual field, to borrow from Merleau-Ponty (2002 [1946]), and (at the risk of cliché) as fellow travellers. How might we relate to one another and to what we think of as our proprietary space if this were the case? But more importantly, what about the question of how we make time and space not for those we 'recognize' as having things in common with, but with those whose difference we experience as marked from us? How can we find ways not simply to organize our lives in ways that are liveable and workable, but in which we can relate to one another through our mutually shared, but socially situated, interdependency? If Achille Mbembe (2019) is right that 'the daily battle to survive … is won not in isolation but by people coming together', what might ways of co-organizing beyond isolation and proprietary values make possible for our lives to be not simply endurable (Butler and Worms, 2023) but 'workable' and active in the Arendtian (1998 [1958]) sense, moving – together – beyond daily struggles for existence, into scope for joy, hope and fulfilment?

As we have discussed in previous chapters, rejecting notions of vulnerability as an aberrative weakness that lead to paternalistic responses to reified dependency rather than mobilizations of solidarity, is vital to emphasizing, instead, the collective need and therefore responsibility that we all bear to care for, about and with one another, to borrow from Joan Tronto (2015).[2] Recognizing that vulnerability is existentially shared but also always socially situated foregrounds how it is inaugurally embedded in social relations.[3] Understanding this helps us to conceive of what we might think of as a radical vulnerability, one that constitutes a formative aspect of the human, social condition, as a site of collective agency from which collaborative ways of co-organizing might emerge. Recognition of our shared, situated mutual vulnerability as the basis of social justice in this way provides the starting point from which an ethics of relationality and a politics of solidarity might emerge. While feminists note that the latter might be the source of social transformation, giving rise to joy, hope and scope for what Lynne Segal (2018) has called 'radical happiness', they also recognize that realizing a politics and ethics based on mutual vulnerability requires struggle, and a considerable investment of time, energy, resources and infrastructure. Framed in this way, vulnerability becomes both the most basic way in which our sociality is organized – relationally, and as the basis for solidarity, community and action, *and* the site of struggle on which this takes place. What is needed, feminists argue, is a way to think of and through vulnerability as an affirmative way of being open to the world and to others, understanding what it means to be vulnerable as an agentic capacity for exposure and not as a weakness or limitation to be 'overcome' as liberal philosophical and political discourses would have it.

Arguably, then, what is needed to think this through and to respond to some of the questions posed here, and at the outset of this book, is a theoretical understanding of how our primordial interdependency could offer an ethical basis for the formation and sustenance of ways of living, working and organizing together that can provide the conditions for relationality and solidarity to flourish. Such an understanding would require a critical, reflexive appreciation of how mutual recognition of our shared but socially situated vulnerability might provide the basis for collaborative, collective agency in the way that Hannah Arendt (1998 [1958]) understands it, implying a relational co-appearance as the basis for political action. While the former sounds like a substantial task, even in the abstract, the latter seems to be nigh on impossible in the current geopolitical context in which, as Mbembe (2019), Butler (2020b, 2022) and others have argued, our social world is increasingly shaped by borderization instead of, or perhaps more precisely at the expense of, mutual recognition, care and solidarity, as we live in a world that seems increasingly contoured by a 'care deficit' (Segal, 2023). Yet as Adriana Cavarero has also emphasized, 'the endeavour of giving life to politics demands … empowering its relational condition and imagining the projection and proliferation of this very condition' (Cavarero, 2021b: 179). The question then becomes, especially when viewed through an organizational lens: How might we do this?

The themes examined in Chapters 2–4 point to the argument that a relational understanding of social justice, one premised upon recognition of our socially shared but situated vulnerability as an agentic capacity, can *only* emerge from a reimagined interdependency, enacted through modes of assembly organized within and through spaces of co-appearance that challenge dominant social arrangements and norms. As Butler (2020b, 2022) has argued, the task is not to overcome vulnerability, in this sense, but to recognize that it is our way of being, that is, that recognition of the mutual vulnerability engendered by our interdependency is perhaps *the* condition of possibility for a more ethical, sustainable world to emerge and flourish. A vital question for us to reflect on, especially when exploring ways in which a radical vulnerability might be the basis for collective, collaborative ways of reimagining how our desire for recognition might be organized, is why can we not see or sense our mutual interdependency even, perhaps most especially, in the wake of a global pandemic, and in the midst of an ongoing climate crisis and, instead, continue to shore up our time, spaces and resources? In other words, how has the recognition – and realization – of our most basic mutual interdependency become so far removed from our perceptual field, lived experience and sense of what is not only possible, but desirable?

Considering this question with reference to the theoretical and thematic content of previous chapters, this final chapter will explore how a radical understanding of vulnerability might provide a necessary recognition-based counter to discourses of resourcefulness and resilience, and to the imperatives and processes of borderization (Mbembe, 2019) that dominate our contemporary social and organizational lifeworlds. It will re-engage with theoretical material considered in Chapter 1 in light of the thematic content of Chapters 2–4. Via a discussion of breathing, grieving and appearing, the social relations of existing, enduring and enacting were considered in each of these three chapters, as examples or instances of how our desire for recognition comes to be organized in ways that exploit and/or accentuate vulnerability, at the same time as opening up scope for relationality and solidarity. In this chapter, we will reflect on how these three distinct but related sets of social relations constitute both political phenomena – modes of acting together, in solidary, where the latter is taken to refer to a recognition-based sense of vulnerability in/as resistance, and ethical imperatives – modes of relating to one another, underpinned by an ethic of relationality where the latter is taken to refer to a reflexive awareness of *both* the mutual vulnerability engendered by our interdependency and an understanding that while we are all therefore vulnerable, we are never equally so. Hence this final chapter will consider the implications of thinking about recognition-based, relational modes of organizing *as vulnerability* for more ethical, sustainable ways of living, working and acting together in the future.

By drawing together insights from earlier chapters focusing on the social (organizational) relations of breathing, grieving and appearing, the discussion will attempt to map out the forms of recognition that might be necessary to realizing some of the possibilities attached to dialogically affirmative modes of organization currently in evidence as pockets of activism across the public and media spheres (see Smolović Jones et al, 2021), including those directly concerned with respiratory poverty, grievability and precarity, and with 'mobilizing' vulnerability via collaborative efforts to reimagine what organizing might be. In doing so, it will revisit and develop ideas introduced in earlier chapters. It sets out to consider how public engagement for hopeful and solidary-orientated futures might be understood and enacted through more 'workable' forms of organizing embedded in and through vulnerability that are recognition-based in their grounding in relationality and reflexivity, contrasting these with the more reified, rhetorical modes of recognition currently dominating organizational life (Hancock, 2024) that we considered in Chapters 1 and 2.

One of the many challenges when considering vulnerability as the basis for ethics and politics is the issue of autonomy. Mackenzie et al argue that

> If human persons are both ontologically vulnerable but also autonomous agents, then we need an account of autonomy that is premised on recognition of human vulnerability *and* an analysis of vulnerability that explains why we have obligations not only to protect vulnerable persons from harm but also to do so in ways that promote, whenever possible, their capacities for autonomy. (Mackenzie et al, 2013: 16, emphasis added)

In other words, we need an account of vulnerability that connects it to agency and solidarity. For Mackenzie et al (2013) and other feminists, a relational approach helps us to reconcile autonomy with the ethical obligations arising from our shared, situated vulnerability, opening up scope to move beyond paternalistic responses, and to explore vulnerability as resistance (Butler, 2016) and as the basis of solidarity (Segal, 2018, 2023).[4]

Responding to the 'problem' of autonomy, the concept of relationality effectively reframes vulnerability as capacity, emphasizing both the need for infrastructural support to realize this shared potential, at the same time as foregrounding how exploitative and oppressive social arrangements appropriate and exploit it, notably via repressive institutions or unjust social arrangements, or simply diminishing infrastructures and/or their ideological bases. Such an understanding rests on mutual recognition of our fundamental interdependency within social relations and in our relationship with more than human beings, including the natural environment. Further, such an approach understands agency as collective and collaborative, rather than as a discrete individual capacity. It also frames paternalistic responses to vulnerability as pathogenic precisely because 'they entrench or exacerbate vulnerabilities rather than scaffold the development and exercise of autonomy' (Mackenzie et al, 2013: 6); the latter is understood throughout this chapter, as it has been throughout the whole book, via the Arendtian lens that Butler and Cavarero both develop, as our relational capacity for action.

Returning to her ongoing dialogue with Adorno, but also reflecting Arendt's influence, Butler argues that a good life will only ever be 'a life lived with others' (Butler, 2020b: 200), as the 'I' always requires a 'you' in order to survive and flourish. Beyond this, the 'I' and the 'you' need a sustaining world – a grounding for social relations to provide the necessary context for fulfilling the obligations we each bear towards one another. Yet in organizational terms, the risk becomes one of offering or accepting 'faux' recognition – a rhetorical rather than relational form that replaces a reification of vulnerability, a 'forgetting' of our shared, but situated mutual vulnerability in the process of designating some as 'vulnerable', and in need of protection, and others as invulnerable, with a reification of 'value', as is commonly articulated through 'managing diversity' discourses; again, we return to this during the course of this chapter.

Vulnerability and relationality

Feminists have emphasized how conceiving of human beings as relationally constituted allows for the idea of an agonistic solidarity, one that recognizes interdependency without presupposing reciprocity (Kenny and Fotaki, 2023). As Butler (2009a: 44) has put it in this respect, emphasizing the ontological necessity of relationality: 'If I seek to preserve your life, it is not only because I seek to preserve my own, but because who "I" am is nothing without your life, and life itself has to be rethought as this complex, passionate, antagonistic, and necessary set of relations to others.' This 'necessity' has been articulated via a range of feminist and other activist social movements. With reference to *Ni Una Menos*, Valentina Moro (2022: 66–67), for instance, describes how each person who enters into the movement embodies and performs it as a constitutive alliance, and in doing so, experiences 'a powerful expression of agency precisely in its interdependency'. Born as a response to a structural and pervasive violence that potentially reduces each life to its most precarious conditions, Ni Una Menos has created a global alliance. Every year, on 8 March, the movement performs the International Women's Strike against gender-based violence (*huelga feminista y transfeminista*). As Moro discusses it, the choice of a strike, as a very specific kind of struggle that is performed in a multiplicity of ways in many different parts of the world, has several meanings:

> It is a way of claiming that care work – notoriously feminized and mostly, but not exclusively, performed by women – is work and must be recognized as such. ... At the same time, it entails not just striking from traditional social roles and labour structures, but also from *gender* identities and the related social roles and expectations, which can lead to violence and discrimination. (Moro, 2022: 66, original emphasis)

On the one hand, Moro notes, this movement has fostered care by creating safe spaces – spaces of appearance, we might say – for women, LGBTQIA+ people, and all allied subjects and groups who fight against gender-based violence. On the other hand, it has re-articulated what it means to care in the context of assemblies and alliances in which collective agency is recognized and exercised. Moreover, the movement has created infrastructures of care, for example, by providing people with free legal and psychological support and finding housing for undocumented people and those escaping domestic violence. For Moro, this shows how, 'as a powerful and pervasively structured kind of "political kinship" and alliance', *Ni Una Menos* is itself 'an infrastructure of care'. While notoriously being forums for the dissemination of hate, social media platforms and technologies can also play a crucial role, Moro and others have argued, in making and sustaining movements such as *Ni Una Menos* on a global scale.

For Butler, the performative effectiveness of assemblies such as *Ni Una Menos* derives from their capacity to inaugurate spaces of appearance (Arendt, 1998 [1958]). In her book, *Surging Democracy*, Adriana Caverero (2021c) develops this line of argument further, drawing directly on Arendt's notion of politics to emphasize that the transformative capacity of such spaces lies in what is 'between' social actors and their shared actions.[5] This phenomenological emphasis on experiences of mutual recognition and belonging, through participating in a plurality of actions, involves what Cavarero describes as a democratic 'surging' (*sorgiva*). Etymologically, this term refers to the power of 'the source' as the origin of a concerted action, a springing forth as it were.[6] As Cavarero (2021c) notes, its connotations are radically different from the 'in-surgent' as an oppositional character that often has highly individualized, and often masculine, connotations.

Surging, Cavarero emphasizes, implies the bringing forth of something anew – a natality that requires participants to adopt a common dispositional tendency towards one another, foregrounding mutual interdependency and rejecting neoliberal notions of vulnerability as a weakness or limitation to be 'overcome'.[7] Hence, for Cavarero (as for Butler), again drawing on Arendt, the radical vulnerability that assembly inaugurates cannot be understood without reference to relationality.

For Cavarero, surging forms of democracy occur

> [w]herever people, by gathering in public spaces to protest or demonstrate, experience their ability to engender power – a diffuse, participatory, and relational power, shared equally, or better still, a power constituted by political actors who are unique and plural … allowing the human taste for *freedom* and emotional participation to surface. (Cavarero, 2021c: x, original emphasis)

Surging democracy is therefore (drawing this time on Butler), a 'performative type of politics that is enacted when people congregate, reclaiming a public space' (Cavarero, 2021c: xi), one that displays the protestors' corporeal plurality.

To develop her account of surging democracy, Cavarero (2021c: xv) draws both on Butler's reading of Arendt and her own, starting with Arendt's notion of what it means to be human as 'that ontological condition of plurality' that makes us unique and equal. She focuses on how this gives rise to a sense of political hope, exhibited through the embodied plurality of social movements and protests in public spaces of appearance in order to claim justice and equality. Crucial for Cavarero (2021c: xvi) is the political thrill that this engenders – the thrill of interacting with one another, speaking in a polyvocal plurality consistent with the collective emotion of participating in a nascent, democratic act – 'a germinal form of diffuse, equally shared and inclusive power'. For Arendt, it is this alone that deserves the name of politics and for Cavarero it is this understanding of politics, as a surging democracy, that provides the basis for an urgently needed imaginary of hope. To understand what Cavarero means by surging democracy, we can turn to her explanation that, in Arendt's language, it evokes 'a communal space of reciprocal appearance, where a plurality of unique beings acts in concert' (Cavarero, 2021c: 4).[8] Within Arendt's thinking, it is the exaltation of a certain type of political experience – one that in Cavarero's terms (see Cavarero, 2016) positions it as opposed to any hierarchical or vertical conception of power, and that is instead diffuse, participatory and relational, shared equally among a plurality of actors – that is at the heart of democracy.

For Arendt, the aim of politics is to enact a relationship between those who are fully present to one another, in so far as the latter enables them to 'mutually appear and remain distinct, unique human beings who do not melt into a uniform mass', as Cavarero (2021c: 7) sums it up. What is at stake, for Arendt, is precisely the meaning and experience of the human condition as a mode of interacting in a public space where people 'appear to each other' as unique beings, coming together in a plurality that neither exalts each individual, nor absorbs them into a mass, but instead sees them acting in concert as beings capable of 'beginning' something anew, together. As Arendt emphasizes, no human being can refrain from this appearance to others, 'and still be human'.[9] In this sense, and returning to themes considered in the previous chapter, the space of appearance, for Arendt, is essentially one of mutual visibility and, therefore, of constitutive exposure.

Her reading of Arendt's notion that while politics has all but disappeared from the sphere of governance, it remains as a 'hidden treasure' waiting to be rediscovered through plural interaction in public, shared space, leads Cavarero to argue that moments of resistance such as those that take place in and through protest movements provide hope for more communal alternatives to a politics modelled on hierarchical forms of control to emerge. In particular (as is the case for Butler [see Butler, 2020b]), it is Arendt's insistence on the plurality of power as nonviolent that provides an indispensable reference point for Cavarero's notion of a 'surging democracy', one that is fundamentally generative rather than oppositional. This latter point is precisely the case because, for Arendt, politics is a relational space that comes into being only through interaction, without which it disappears; for Arendt, politics is the experience of plurality, generated by human beings when and where they are able to act 'in concert'. This phenomenological view suggests that politics is germinal – it can 'spring up, surging anywhere' (Cavarero, 2021c: 26).[10] And in Cavarero's reading (see also Segal, 2018) it is joyful, in so far as it offers 'the assurance of being able to change things by one's own effort' (Arendt, 1998 [1958] 202). Mutual recognition of this capacity, one that is shared and situated in our uniqueness, is crucial to Arendt's notion of the political, and to Cavarero's (2021c: 34) understanding of the democratic 'surge' as a sphere of 'shared, diffuse, and horizontal power'.

Arendt's emphasis is expressly on the relational dimension of plurality, with the space of appearance being a common space in which those present can mutually appear to and for one another as actors, interacting on a horizontal plane. What Arendt understands as public happiness therefore occurs precisely when human beings act in concert, relationally, in the shared space of appearance, thus experiencing the 'natal', agentive capacity of acting together. To illustrate the affective power of such occurrences, Cavarero (2021c) refers to feminist marches and other protest events that involve, as she puts it, joyous participatory co-appearance in spaces of resistance and recognition (see also Segal, 2018; Tyler, 2019).

Cavarero does note, however, that Arendt's thought is largely (perhaps unfeasibly) utopian, articulated through a political vision that contains what are, arguably, unrealistic propositions, limiting its application to a climate dominated by populist agendas that generate, organize, intensify and disseminate hate. In contrast to the current scenario, Arendt's idea of politics, as Cavarero (2021c: 29) sums it up, opposes 'that affective pathology of negative egocentrism'. Yet perhaps more problematically for our purposes here, as Cavarero also notes, Arendt seems to have little interest in accounting for the conflict and struggle that inevitably accompany the social condition of plurality and mutual interdependency, interpreting the latter as simply a sign of alienation from the realm of politics. This may well be the case[11] but for Cavarero (2021c: 14), 'to declare, as Arendt does, that violence and political power are incompatible phenomena, and to deny that conflict and hostility are the foundation of politics, can only result in a theoretical gesture that is hardly realistic'.

And yet, the utopian impulse in Arendt's writing stands out for its critical potential and impetus, finding its articulation in a range of feminist ways of thinking about what the sphere of politics might be like if it were to be reimagined with hope (Segal, 2018). What Arendt's writing foregrounds, in this sense, is a way of thinking about politics as a realm in which we might co-appear to, with and for one another in our embodied plurality in nonviolent, affirmative terms (Butler, 2020b) in ways that help to open up scope for more workable modes of living, working and organizing together, ways that, collectively, we might think of as a radical vulnerability. A principal aspect of this vision, for Cavarero especially, is that it replaces the individualistic, atomizing ontology of modern politics with an embodied and relational subjectivity.[12]

Perhaps an even greater problem in Arendt's thinking on the space of appearance, one that Cavarero (2021c) develops further and that Butler (2015: 124) in particular has emphasized, is that the phenomenon of people gathering can refer equally well to extremist demonstrations, to military efforts to quell protests, and to populist movements and so on. To put it simply, not all 'assemblies' are radical or democratic, far from it. For Butler, the criterion for declaring which forms of assembly are desirable and which are not is the degree to which they are in the service of 'realizing greater ideals of justice and equality, even the realization of democracy itself'. Crucial for Butler are the motivations, the values and the ideas that assemblies express, as well as their modes of engagement (and on this latter point, Butler differs from Arendt). For Butler (2015: 183), it is the 'taking care' of bodily precarity through nonviolent resistance that is at the heart of the assembly as an embodied form of radical, relational vulnerability. As they put it, assembly in this sense takes place through 'a struggle to establish more sustaining conditions of liveability in the face of systematically induced precarity', the latter referring to what we might think of as organized vulnerability, or more precisely, vulnerability as the outcome of a process of organization.

Vulnerability, labour and workability

For Butler (2015) especially, it is through assembling in the space of appearance that bodies can display and affirm – mutually recognize – their essential condition of plurality and shared precarity (primordial vulnerability). An important aspect of Butler's reading of Arendt must be noted, however, one that is pertinent to our discussion here, and which rests on Arendt's distinction between the public and the private realm: between work and labour. Crucial to Arendt's (1998 [1958]) thinking is that labour is excluded from the space of appearance. For her, labour is merely the cyclical activity that sustains bodily life, focusing on meeting immediate needs – for example, for sustenance, whereas work involves the creation of lasting phenomena that transcend immediate, bodily needs. It is the latter that enables human beings to express their uniqueness and to leave their 'mark' on the world. 'Working', for Arendt, is a process that culminates in something lasting and tangible, creating value beyond more subsistence. As the highest form of activity, action, for Arendt, is what initiates change, enacted through participation in the public sphere, the space of appearance and in our plurality.

Arendt's critique of the reduction of work to mere labour, leading to a dehumanized existence in which individuals solely focus on survival and consumption, led her to emphasize the need to reclaim the importance of work and action to realizing the full potential of the human condition. Butler's (2015) critique of this view argues that this division is precisely what is called into question when bodies assemble in alliance in order to occupy the space of appearance, showing how the life of the body – its need for food, breathable air, shelter, protection from violence, reproductive rights and so on – belongs in the realm of the political. For Butler, it is not simply the phenomenon of people coming together that matters, but the reciprocal commitment they engender to a sociality in which the needs of bodies – all bodies – are recognized and met. In this sense, Butler also points to the labour *of* struggle – to the ongoing efforts made by those whose bodies undertake the 'work' of appearing in the public sphere as collective acts of resistance and, as Butler puts it, persistence. Yet Arendt's framing of politics cannot easily support this point, which is vital to Butler's thinking on the meaning and importance of assembly. As Cavarero (2021c: 51, emphasis added) notes, Butler acknowledges that, in this sense, to imagine a radical democracy through the lens of Arendt's writing means, in part, to 'think against her', and Butler does this by proposing an idea of politics – the assembly – that 'exalts the relationality *at work* within an embodied plurality'.

Cavarero's notion of an embodied plurality being 'at work' in Butler's concept of assembling is worth focusing on here in some detail, as it conveys the importance of what *workability* means – or might mean, *as the embodied, organized articulation of a radical vulnerability*. Understood through Arendt, the ability to engage in work means having the capacity to produce or contribute something of value that is lasting and substantial, beyond the merely cyclical outputs of labour. Read through the work of the Care Collective (2020), as well as Butler and Cavarero, we can reimagine this as the capacity not simply to produce tangible 'things', but to sustain networks of solidarity, relationality and mutual interdependency (see also Segal, 2018, 2023), so that vulnerability – as our shared but situated, embodied way of being – becomes our capacity to work, to be workable or, more precisely, to live workable lives and to enable those of others (on which we, in turn, depend) to flourish. This requires not simply an occupation of the same space, whether physical co-location or in digitally mediated ways, but being fully present, co-engaged with and for others, making both space and time to foster and sustain networks of solidarity and to act, with and for one another in mutual recognition of our shared but contoured interdependency. In this sense, read through Butler (*contra* Arendt), workability can be understood as having the shared but situated capacity to engage in relational modes of interaction and organization beyond mere subsistence, a capacity that is of course foreclosed to those whose lives – whose time, energy, resources, circumstances and space are entirely taken up by the cyclical work of survival. And it is only by recognizing our mutual vulnerability that we might begin to organize our lives and resources in ways that make 'workable' lives, understood in this way, more possible for more people, more of the time.

For both Cavarero (2021c) and Butler (2015), drawing on Arendt, understood in precisely this way, vulnerability is not a 'negative' or negating state of being – 'something *despite* which one acts' (Moro, 2022: 52, original emphasis); rather, it is the basis of the ethical choices we make and the political actions we take that render our lives, and those of others, more or less workable. Accepting this line of argument means shifting our understanding of vulnerability away from one of 'diminished' capacity, so that our theoretical approaches and political collaborations can lead not only to practices of care (Segal, 2023), but also to sustaining the organizational infrastructures that are needed to support them. This requires, as Moro (2022) emphasizes, a relational understanding of vulnerability and/as agency as the means through which to enact a radical vulnerability in and through solidarity to underpin the conditions necessary for more lives to be more workable, more of the time, and sustainably so. Recognition, to which we now turn, potentially provides a valuable but not entirely unproblematic starting point for such an endeavour.

Vulnerability and recognition

The relationship between vulnerability and recognition is somewhat vexed we might say, especially when viewed through an organizational lens, as organizations all too often exploit or co-opt our need for recognition (Hancock, 2024), reifying our mutual interdependency by framing vulnerability as a weakness or limitation to be 'overcome'. Butler (2004a: 4) sums up the consequences of this by noting how, 'I may feel that without some recognizability I cannot live. But I may also feel that the terms by which I am recognized make life unliveable'. This, for Butler, is an important juncture from which critique emerges, and it provides a vital and reflexive lens through which both to understand how vulnerability relates to the ways in which our desire for recognition comes to be organized, and to reimagine how it might be reorganized differently in order to make more lives more liveable, grievable and workable.[13]

Butler begins this task by arguing that the dominant social order means recognition plays a 'double' role – we desire to be recognized because the alternative is to be rendered ('organized' as) unintelligible, non-existent, and this prompts us to adhere to dominant social norms. Recognition then contributes to a belief in the 'naturalness' of the social order, shielding the latter from critique. Critical theorist and social philosopher Kristina Lepold (2021: 151) notes how this means that, for Butler, recognition is ambivalent because it 'actively participates in two different ways in the reproduction of a problematic social arrangement' – involving subjection, and a consequent naturalization. To this way of thinking about the 'double bind' of recognition, we might add a third dimension, one that is articulated most fully in Butler's more recent writing; namely the ethical responsibility/compulsion of those who are 'recognized' to change the terms of recognition (or the parameters of what they call 'recognizability' [see Butler, 2021a, 2021b, 2024]). Yet the second ambivalence associated with recognition noted earlier, the 'naturalization' of its terms, renders this problematic because it leads to a 'forgetting' (a reification) of shared vulnerability, resulting in a 'shoring up' of paternalistic/pastoral power relations that nullify opportunities, and arguably the will, to transform the terms of recognition that are on offer.

To fully understand this, it is important to return to Butler's engagement with Hegel's thinking, in which human beings are understood to be entirely dependent upon being recognized as viable social subjects – worthy of rights, resources, responsibilities, and so on. In this sense, recognition is not a social courtesy, but a basic human need, vital to our existential and social survival. Further, and crucial to Butler's reading of Hegel, is that our desire for recognition is embedded within social relations, and the struggle for recognition is enacted and experienced within social structures and normative frameworks in which power dynamics are played out. This means that, for Butler, recognition is an *ongoing* struggle – one that can never be fully 'resolved', as it is always enacted within the context of differential access to the resources necessary to meet its socially contextual and contoured terms, which are themselves continually evolving.

Yet contemporary recognition theorists have also argued that overemphasizing how our desire for recognition engenders political vulnerability (socially situated vulnerability, in Butler's terms) potentially leads to an 'incapacitation trap' in our thinking. For political philosopher Robin Celikates (2021), for instance, who makes precisely this point, the 'conditionality' claim (that is, the claim made by Butler and others that recognition is conditional upon meeting certain terms of recognizability) runs the risk of imposing a political incapacitation on those who are misrecognized/denied recognition, rendering them even more powerless. Further, when understood through an organizational lens, such an approach potentially provides the moral (even managerial) justification for a paternalistic relationship in which '"we" ... have to liberate "them"' (Celikates, 2021: 271). This is a risk that is taken when framing recognition as carrying with it the ethical burden of recitation; yet it also opens up important possibilities for reflexive critique of how the relationship between recognition and vulnerability is understood and enacted. For Celikates, the disavowal of agency as the basis of misrecognition not only further divests those who are misrecognized of their capacity for agency; in doing so, it also diverts attention away from the conditions on which recognition depends and shores up both scope for exploitation and domination, as well as rhetorical (paternalistic) forms of recognition that conflict with more reflexive forms. The latter, drawing on Butler and others, we might understand as premised upon mutual recognition of our primordial, existential or even 'pre-social' vulnerability, offering an alternative, more radical, reflexive form of recognition.

Through this line of argument – one that problematizes a disavowal of agency – we can potentially distinguish between three forms of recognition, revisiting ideas introduced in Chapters 1 and 2. The first, we might think of as a rhetorical form, or what Celikates calls 'minimal' (negative) recognition. In Butler's terms, this might involve a conferral of recognition according to terms that are beyond the subject's own sphere of reference, resulting (effectively) in a mode of recognition that one doesn't oneself 'recognize'. Second, we can identify what Celikates calls 'full' (affirmative) recognition. What is problematic in this latter mode, as noted in earlier chapters, is the disavowal of agency this implies – recognition is 'conferred' on those who are most recognizable. As such, the power relations in which struggles for recognition are already embedded are overlooked or at least played down.[14] But added to this, we can potentially begin to think about a more reflexive 'problematization' of the relations and terms of recognition, and of our differential investments in them, including of the norms that govern recognizability. This latter form involves 'recognizing' that claims to recognition are always already socially structured and situated and are, at the same time, grounded in a 'forgotten'/reified relation of mutual interdependence.

Hence, this more reflexive way of thinking about recognition potentially provides a starting point for understanding radical (recognition-based) vulnerability as an agentic capacity on both an individual and collective level, one that is grounded in our pre-social, yet socially situated, mutual interdependency. Crucially, this more reflexive, relational understanding of recognition rejects a foreclosure of vulnerability, emphasizing instead how the latter is, potentially, 'one of the most important resources from which we must take our bearings and find our way' (Butler, 2005: 30). To achieve, this, we might argue, requires a recognition-based theory of collective responsibility as the basis of a nonviolent politics and ethics.

Nonviolence and care as recognition-based solidarity

For Butler (2020b: 23), nonviolence is an embodied, performative endeavour – 'not an absolute principle, but ... an ongoing struggle'. Crucial to this is understanding and enacting nonviolence as a shared, agentic capacity, a 'nascency' in Arendt's (1998 [1958]) terms. In this sense, nonviolence is best understood as:

> The social and political power to establish existence *for those who have been conceptually nullified*, to achieve grievability and value for those who have been cast as dispensable, and to insist on the possibility of both judgment and justice within the terms of contemporary media and public policy that offer a bewildering and sometimes quite tactical vocabulary for naming and misnaming violence. (Butler, 2020b: 23, emphasis added)

Nonviolence is hence less a failure of agency or an acceptance of its disavowal and more 'a living assertion', a claim that is made 'by speech, gesture and action, through networks, encampments, and assemblies' (Butler, 2020b: 24). Nonviolence occurs when those who are most precarious, that is, situationally vulnerable, assert their persistence in order to defeat one of the aims of violent power, namely to cast those on the margins as dispensable, to push them beyond the sphere of appearance and the relations of recognition on which it depends, into 'a zone of non-being' to use Fanon's phrase. Nonviolence, hence, involves a persistent assertion of the right to appear (otherwise), or perhaps more importantly, to co-appear (Cavarero, 2021c), as discussed in the previous chapter. Moving beyond an ego-logical ethics and a politics of individualism, thinking about vulnerability and its relationship to nonviolence, recognition and appearance in this way opens up what Butler describes as 'a new consideration of social freedom *as defined in part by our constitutive interdependency*' (Butler, 2020b: 24, emphasis added). Seen in this way, violence against the other becomes violence against oneself, and nonviolence a reassertion (recognition) of our prior, primordial interconnectedness – of the vulnerability that we all share, 'something that becomes clear when we recognize that violence assaults the living interdependency *that is, or should be, our social world*' (Butler, 2020b: 25, emphasis added), shifting the ethical focus from living beings as discrete entities to living bonds as recognition-based networks or assemblages of solidarity on the basis of a radical (recognition-based) vulnerability.

The Care Collective's (2020: 3) *Care Manifesto* sums up what this might mean, and why it is stymied in a social context shaped by the 'near-ubiquitous positioning of profit-making as the organising principle of life', and in which the dominant model of social organization is one of competition rather than collaboration and cooperation. The Care Collective emphasize how what Arendt (1963) called systematic banality permeates our everyday carelessness, meaning that 'we are failing to challenge the limits being placed upon our caring capacities, practices and imaginations' (The Care Collective, 2020: 5), with potentially catastrophic consequences across the world. *Contra* to the borderizing impetus that currently dominates our social landscape (Mbembe, 2019), to put care centre stage would mean 'recognizing and embracing our interdependencies', acknowledging that '[c]are is our individual and common ability to provide the political, social, material, and emotional conditions that allow the vast majority of people and living creatures on this planet to thrive – along with the planet itself' (The Care Collective, 2020: 6).

Yet 'carewashing' is rampant – occurring when corporations try to increase their legitimacy by presenting themselves as socially responsible 'citizens' while actively and consciously, and/or unreflexively, contributing to social injustice and ecological destruction, capitalizing on the very crises that they have helped to create and perpetuate. And the global care deficit continues to grow with a voracity that appears to be as unchecked as it seems limitless; this is the case not only (and sadly, I would add) in opposition to feminist politics, but within it, as transphobia and gender exclusivity takes hold not only beyond feminism but, in many parts of the world and on global social media networks, within it. The solution, the Care Collective argue, lies in resourcing what they call promiscuous care (care beyond kinship), to provide care for each other and the environment by mobilizing and cultivating 'a radical, cosmopolitan conviviality'. The latter requires, first and foremost, recognizing our mutual interdependencies and the 'intrinsic value of all living creatures' (The Care Collective, 2020: 18, 21), cultivating a caring politics founded on a relational ethics. Yet, foreclosing this potential is the extent to which dependence on (and provision of) care has been pathologized, 'rather than recognized as part of our human condition' (The Care Collective, 2020: 23).

As the Care Collective also emphasize, in a way that Arendt possibly underplays (see Cavarero, 2021c), confronting the existential problem of our frailty, and that of the planet, 'can be both challenging and exhausting' (The Care Collective, 2020: 27), especially in the circumstances noted earlier. As such, and as noted earlier, the co-appearance that Arendt advocates must involve not simply a mutual occupation of space, but of time – creating opportunities for collective, collaborative moments of co-existence and fully engaged co-presence. This requires both labour – the expenditure of skill, time and energy in the generation of value – and a reflexive 'confrontation', or troubling in a more phenomenological sense, of norms that we take for granted as constitutive of contemporary social relations, even of what it means to be the subject of feminist care and politics. It also requires work in the way in which Arendt understands it, yet (*contra* Arendt's own emphasis on materiality), this work involves building something of lasting significance in the form of social relationality, shared vulnerability and connection as the basis of recognition-based solidarity. Further, and also in contrast to Arendt, this sense of existential confrontation, or troubling (to borrow from Butler), is entirely embodied, requiring us to fully engage with other ways of being and of living that we not only perceive as different to us, but which might be encountered as repellent. This requires putting effort into the cultivation of a reflexive form of recognition premised upon relationality of the kind discussed earlier, involving a facing up to our shared 'troubles'.[15]

Again, we can look to the Care Collective for insights into how we might respond to this challenge – one that is at once both ethical and political. Not surprisingly, the Care Collective (2020: 28) argue that we must work to provide and ensure the necessary social infrastructure that enables us to care for others, 'both proximate and distant'. As noted earlier, a key challenge is not simply how to do this in a geographical/spatial sense, but also in a political/philosophical one, working out how to care across distance when the distance between us is more than physical, but intersubjective, and hence social, political, cultural, religious, linguistic, and so on. In other words, a major concern for us – perhaps *the* key concern of our times, is that of how to care about, with and for one another in full recognition of the Otherness of the Other, to borrow from Levinas (1969), or across borders and in the context of the necropolitical, as Mbembe (2019) might put it. For the Care Collective (2020: 30), the most pressing issue is that of how we might create, and sustain, the conditions that make a caring disposition towards the Other, 'however distant', ever more possible. When distance and difference collide to shape our recognition of the Other, this makes care particularly 'troubling'. To move from a pathologization towards a recognition of care 'we need to break through the destructive linking of depending with pathology and recognise that we are all formed, albeit in diverse and uneven ways, through and by our interdependencies', as they put it. This viewpoint recasts difference by thinking through our sameness not in a sociological sense, but philosophically – we are all vulnerable and interdependent, just not to the same extent or in the same ways, as Butler of course emphasizes. For the Care Collective, recognizing the extent to which this is the case, and building an appropriate infrastructural response necessarily involves *working* to create and defend the commons: 'collectively owned, socialized forms of provision, space and infrastructure' (The Care Collective, 2020: 31); but it also requires investing the time, resources, and hence recognition, in order to do this.

Thinking about care beyond kinship, the Care Collective argue that it is only by multiplying our circles of care, by expanding our notion of who we desire to care for, that we can achieve the practical and psychic infrastructures necessary to building a society that has universal care at its heart. With this in mind, they advocate an ethics of care that would facilitate multiplicity and fluidity in the ways in which we connect to, and provide for, others. They look to models of care that proliferated during the AIDS/HIV crisis in the 1980s and 1990s as an example of how care might help to transform our notions of what constitutes caring kinship, as well as the more recent forms of care shared among trans people via digital and social networks. They note how sociologist Paul Byron's work on the latter illustrates how such opportunities can constitute vital spaces for marginalized communities to connect and provide care for one another based on mutual recognition of shared vulnerabilities, *including* of how these are experienced and situated in different ways. As a mechanism for sharing information, advice and support, they can potentially offer 'a space of organization, belonging and care' (The Care Collective, 2020: 38) – a space of appearance in the Arendtian sense, or of assembly, as Butler might think of it, we might say.

To return to points noted earlier, perhaps the most challenging issue for the Care Collective then is that of how we might imagine – and enact – radical models of care across difference within and through these spaces (and moments) of recognition. To respond to this, they turn specifically to academic and ACT UP activist, Douglas Crimp's (1987) writing on an ethics of promiscuity developed during the AIDS/HIV crisis, produced largely as a critical response to the idea (dominant at the time, including among some leaders of LGBTQIA+ activist groups) that the spread of the HIV/AIDS epidemic could be attributed largely to sexual promiscuity among gay men. Insisting that promiscuity resulted in the kind of experimental (safe) sex practices that could save lives, Crimp argued that rather than meaning 'casual' or 'indifferent' sex, promiscuity could change the way in which gay men are intimate, including how care is shared between and within gay communities.

For the Care Collective (2020: 41), borrowing from this idea, promiscuous care means caring not just more, but 'in ways that remain experimental and extensive', particularly if promiscuous also means 'indiscriminate'. This ethics of promiscuity, they argue, furnished with recognition and resources, could enhance our capacity to cultivate an orientation towards the Other – whether perceived as distant or proximate, different or the same – that is caring. To encourage promiscuous care means building institutions that can recognize and resource wider forms of care than 'our own', shaping our relationship to caring across every scale of life, from our families and communities, markets, states and transnational relations with humans and non-human life. In turn, this can lead us to think about what promiscuous care at work might mean, how it might be practised, what recognition and resources might be needed, and about what promiscuity might mean as a mode of organization, and as an organizational imperative.

Limiting our capacity, if not our desire, to reimage and organize social relations in the way that the Care Collective advocates is the extent to which the current era proliferates not connection, but borderization (Mbembe, 2019). Urgently needed, feminist organization theorist Marianna Fotaki argues (2022: 318), are 'public policies that reinforce ... our global interconnectedness, rather than individual identification' in order to promote the kind of solidarity that is needed by recognizing how we all depend upon each other for survival.[16] Across many parts of the world, our contemporary social and cultural landscapes are settings through which we are urged to feel and act like hyper-individualized, competitive subjects whose capacity and inclination to care extends only to ourselves and our immediate kin. But as the *Care Manifesto* reminds us, in order to thrive we need caring communities, or 'networks of belonging', and the organizational conditions that will enable these to flourish: 'We need localized environments in which we can ... support each other and generate networks of belonging [and] ... we need conditions that enable us to act collaboratively to create communities that both support our abilities and nurture our interdependencies' (The Care Collective, 2020: 45). For those of us who are interested in how our society, our goods, resources, rights and responsibilities, and, perhaps most notably, our desire for recognition, come to be organized, this raises the fundamental question of what role organizations might play in this. And further, what might it mean to pose or frame the question, 'How do we create the kind of caring communities that make our lives better, happier and even, in some cases, possible? *What kind of infrastructures are necessary to create communities that care*' (The Care Collective, 2020: 45, emphasis added), as an organizational one.

In responding to this issue, and to the questions posed at the outset of this chapter, it is important to think about what it might mean – and require – for radical vulnerabilities to be experienced and enacted through relational modes of organizing that provide the kinds of conditions that are necessary for safe, public spaces of co-appearance to exist, spaces that are egalitarian and accessible, both in the material realm and in the form of digitally mediated communities and networks. To be caring spaces and communities in the way in which the Care Collective advocate, such spaces of co-appearance and the moments of recognition they might facilitate would have to have the capacity to enable connection and collaboration based upon a recognition of our most basic, pre-social interdependencies and mutual vulnerabilities. They would also need to be based upon a reflexive appreciation of how these are situated in social relations and structures. They would have to be organizational contexts that could provide resources beyond extractive imperatives to support meaningful and sustainable relationality such as via a digital commons. For the Care Collective, this would require a shortening of working and commuting hours, free, open access to broadband and other digital infrastructures, and a substantial investment in safe, covered public places and shared resources. It would also require a substantial rethinking of how time is organized in order to make it possible for occupation of these spaces to be workable for as many people as possible.

Global disasters such as the COVID-19 pandemic and, perhaps most notably, the ongoing climate emergency and humanitarian crises across the world provide insight into both how interconnected we are, and of course, of how complex the nature and meaning of that interconnection is; but as Butler (2020b, 2022), Cavarero (2021c) and the Care Collective (2020) have all noted, such phenomena provide important glimpses – vital, in the sense in which Frédéric Worms (2015) has written about it, into how we could – and should – nurture the capacity, and desire, to create something better. For the Care Collective, this notion of 'something better' should be based on global alliances of caring, recognized and resourced across difference and distance and involving promiscuous care on a global scale, in order to move our caring imaginaries and capacities beyond narrowly defined kinship structures. Reflecting on how imperial dissolution has resulted not only in hostility towards Black people, immigrants and strangers, but also in the country's inability to value the 'ordinary, unruly multi-culturalism' that has evolved organically and unnoticed in Britain's urban centres, sociologist Paul Gilroy (2005) calls what is so urgently needed, alongside resources and infrastructure, a 'convivial culture'. Offering what she calls 'a love song to our mongrel selves', cultural theorist Mica Nava (2007) describes the same phenomenon as a 'visceral cosmopolitanism', evoking a being at ease with the sense of strangeness that makes recognition elusive when we encounter the Other across not simply distance, hostility or neglect, but perhaps most problematic of all – indifference.

COVID-19 provided what organizational sociologist Martin Parker (2020) called a 'critical moment' – one that 'laid bare the horrors of neoliberalism' (The Care Collective, 2020: 96). In being and doing so, it revitalized discussions about care, and about how we might recognize not just the work of those who care, but of our need to provide and receive care not simply as individuals, but as a social body. Yet, as noted in earlier chapters, this critical 'moment' was disappointingly fleeting. Nevertheless, the pandemic prompted critical thinkers such as Judith Butler (2022) to ask fundamental questions, such as 'What world is this?'. For Butler, this is at once a political and ethical question; but it is also a phenomenological one – what meaning, Butler asks, does the world have, what are the values, beliefs and practices through which it is made to mean, and to matter?[17] As the Care Collective (2020) note, 'moments' of profound rupture such as the pandemic, or at least as it was understood at the time or shortly afterwards, have historically paved the way for radical progress – they cite the role that the First World War played in bringing about women's suffrage in the United Kingdom, and the Second World War in the growth of the welfare state and birth of the National Health Service. But such ruptures in the established social fabric have also triggered a growth in nationalism, authoritarianism and a 'reboot' of capitalism, both historically and now. How, then, can both the interconnection and mutual interdependency that moments such as the pandemic revealed, and the opportunities for and necessity of, reflexive, relational modes of social interaction that periods of crisis foreground, be normalized and integrated into how we live, work and organize together – not just with, but for one another, especially in a climate in which the will and scope to do so seem increasingly remote?

Rethinking organization and recognition through relationality

Responding to this challenge through the lens of care, relationality and solidarity is one way to examine what kind of ethics and infrastructure might be necessary to reimagining organizational life beyond its contemporary pathologies. Reading the Care Collective's work, as well as Lynne Segal's (2023) book, *Lean on Me*, through Butler's writing on vulnerability and/as resistance and Cavarero's (2021c) work in *Surging Democracy*, the latter both drawing from Arendt's (1998 [1958]) writing on the space of appearance, had led me to think about how organizations might be more than instrumental assemblages of human and non-human resources and might become the basis for a realization of our mutual interdependencies, perhaps even spaces of and for co-appearance. Butler's work especially urges us to explore what radical potential 'assembly' (as a mode of organizing based on mutual recognition) might open up as an alternative to the current, vulneraphobic ways in which our desire for recognition is currently organized. But to understand why scope for this has waned rather than flourished in the wake of the COVID-19 pandemic and in the context of a climate emergency, ongoing geo-political conflict and humanitarian crises, it is helpful to return to Butler's theory of recognition, and their reading of Hegel (1977 [1807]), as well as Butler's response to Honneth's critique of this reading. As is often the case, via their discussion and critical interrogation of each other's work, Honneth and Butler set out important tenets in their thinking that help us to imagine what a radical vulnerability might be, especially when understood through the lens of Butler's writing on recognition and relationality.

In discussion with Honneth (2021a, 2021b), and developing earlier writing on intelligibility (Butler, 1990, 1993), Butler (2021a, 2021b) reaffirms their understanding of how two different forms of recognition are not simply conceptually distinct, but are dynamically interrelated, so that it is impossible to understand what recognition is or how it operates as a normative attribution in the way that Honneth describes it, without reference to recognizability (intelligibility). For Butler, recognition is always 'the consequence of an inequality that follows from hierarchies implied by *historically specific ideas of the human*' (Butler, 2021b: 62, emphasis added). The problem, then, is not simply that some individuals, groups or populations are attributed recognition while others are not, and hence 'are treated with normative status, esteem, and dignity', as is the case for Honneth. '*The problem, rather, is that there is a differential production of the human*' (Butler, 2021b: 62, emphasis added) that, crucially, *precedes* the struggle for recognition. This is important for our discussion here because the distinction – and relationship – between recognition and recognizability that Butler maps out provides a theoretical basis for understanding how vulnerability relates to recognition. As Butler puts it:

> When we ask who counts as human or even who counts as the subject, the very question points to the forms of inequality at work in the production of the human or the recognizable subject. *This is different from unequal treatment* which presumes that humans have already been constituted intelligibly within a social field. (Butler, 2021b: 62–63, original emphasis).

Butler therefore makes an analytical distinction 'between recognition and recognizability' (Butler, 2021b: 63) that is as crucial to their theory of recognition as was their earlier distinction between agency and subjectivity (see Butler, 1993); and Butler does so in a similar vein, that is, in a way that foregrounds how the two are distinct, *precisely* in order to show how they are related, and why this is politically significant. As Butler explains it, '[t]o understand the epistemological conditions under which the differential production of the human takes place, or the differential production of the subject, we have to first understand the nexus of power and knowledge that constitutes various fields of recognizability' (Butler, 2021b: 63).

The question of how recognition is organized then becomes one of giving 'an account of how the subject is produced within historical schemas' (Butler, 2021b: 63). As Butler has emphasized throughout pretty much their entire body of work, such epistemes can be displaced, 'though very often not without great risk' (Butler, 2021b: 64)[18] to those involved; engaging in/with displacement requires, first of all, a degree of workability in one's life. Understanding recognition without reference to recognizability as its precondition (as Honneth implies) is therefore problematic for Butler. As they put, referring to Honneth's writing on rights and recognition: 'Recourse to an ethic that obligates us to treat one another with dignity, though surely laudable, does not address the systematic differentials of power by which some are produced as recognizable beings worthy of such treatment and others not' (Butler, 2021b: 65). Understanding how recognizability and recognition are dynamically interrelated in this way enables Butler to develop a theory of how we perceive and treat each other that realizes the normative (and, by implication, political) potential of Hegel's (1977 [1807]) original narration of social relations as a struggle between two opposing entities. The way that Butler reads this has important implications for an organization theory of vulnerability:

> I worry ... that only those who manifest 'valuable human qualities' are worthy of recognition. But what about those who merely exist, or who manage to persist in stateless or precarious positions, and who want their lives to be recognized not because they have this or that feature, but because they are living creatures who deserve recognition for their struggle? (Butler, 2021b: 67)

In *What World is This?* Butler (2022) considers this dilemma further, starting from the premise that we urgently need to find better ways of living together, because our current arrangements are ethically indefensible and unsustainable. As Butler puts it:

> Implicit in the question, *how long can I live like this?* is an assumption that there must be other ways of living, and that we can – or, rather, must – distinguish between forms of life that are liveable and those that are unliveable. When the question *how can I live like this?* converts into a conviction – 'I will *not* continue to live like this' – we are in the midst of an urgent question both philosophical and social: What are the conditions that permit life to be lived in a way that affirms the continuation of life itself? And with whom shall I join my life in order to assert the values of our lives? These questions are different from

what is the good life? or even the older existential question, *what is the meaning of life?* (Butler, 2022: 30, original emphasis)

Creating a common world, one that we might broadly understand as a space of co-appearance in Arendt's (1998 [1958]) terms, positing 'the world itself as a site of belonging' (Butler, 2022: 3), is vitally different, Butler argues, from a struggle for recognition within the existing social coordinates and categories. The former – a common world, rather than a borderized one (Mbembe, 2019) – entails 'a fundamental transformation of *the understanding of value*' (Butler, 2022: 4, emphasis added). The kind of reflexive recognition this would require, one that would open up scope for vulnerability and relationality beyond existing social arrangements, necessitates 'a way of living life with the assumptions that one's life has value – a value beyond market value'. But we are, Butler reiterates, '*far from … a common world*'.

Again, evoking the spirit of Arendt's notion of the space of appearance, Butler emphasizes how a liveable life means, at least in part, to exist in a way that is to be part of a common:

> Part of what it means to live … in a way that is liveable, is to have a place to live, a part of the earth that can be inhabited without destroying it, to have shelter, and to be able to dwell as a body in a world that is sustained and safeguarded by the structures (and infrastructures) in which one lives – to be part of what is common, and share in a world in common. (Butler, 2022: 32)

What Butler calls 'the pandemic condition' denotes a relatively brief coincidence of circumstances in which precarity and poverty intensified but so too did possibilities for sociality and solidarity through the renewal of demands for networks of care and interdependency, as Segal (2023), Parker (2020) and others have also noted (see also Cavarero, 2021c). Crucially, in this moment, 'the definitive boundaries of the body presumed by most forms of individualism [were] called into question as the invariable porosity of the body – its openings, its mucosal linings, its windpipes – all bec[a]me salient matters of life and death' (Butler, 2022: 33). Here, Butler evokes how breathing, during a respiratory pandemic, functioned (or rather dysfunctioned) as a literal site on which bodily relations of liveability were played out, at the same time as it worked as a metaphor for understanding how social lives are deeply, mutually interdependent on a global scale, as we discussed in Chapter 2. A key question then becomes how might we 'rethink bodily relations of interdependency, intertwinement, and porosity' in light of what was experienced not just during the pandemic, but at other key moments of crisis (Butler, 2022: 33–34). Or perhaps rather, how do these times, and this world, 'offer a chance to reflect upon interdependency, intertwinement, and porosity?' (Butler, 2022: 34) *as our norm*, and as ways of being, living, working and acting together that potentially give us new possibilities for (or rather, new insight into) '*ways of organizing*' (Butler, 2022: 34, emphasis added), including of organizing our desire for recognition in ways that exploit or appropriate our primordial, fundamental vulnerability, but which also contain within them the potential for being and doing otherwise.

To advocate for the latter, Butler draws on Merleau-Ponty's (1964) writing on the dyadic scene of touch as one of intertwinement, so that 'my' body is never simply my own (in a 'proprietary' sense – just as the seat on the train and the space around it is never 'mine') but is enmeshed through what he calls the 'entrelac'. This latter term is often translated into English as 'entwinement', but as Butler notes, it also connotes a weaving or knotting together, an interlacing, in a way that helps us to understand the centrality of embodied intersubjectivity to Merleau-Ponty's thinking. Butler (2022: 39) draws directly from this notion to argue, simply, that 'our lives are knotted together', providing this as a way into a phenomenological critique of the kind of individualist, proprietary conceit that we discussed in earlier chapters. COVID-19, and other crises, 'undo' our pretensions, reminding us that we are all mutually interwoven: 'To be a body at all is to be bound up with others and with objects, with surfaces, and the elements, including the air that is breathed in and out, *air that belongs to no one and everyone*' (Butler, 2022: 37–38, emphasis added).

This way of thinking has important ethical and political implications, offering a way of understanding interdependency 'that moves beyond the ontology of isolated individuals encased in discrete bodies' (Butler, 2022: 38) which is crucial to phenomenological thought (and Merleau-Ponty in particular), and to a feminist relational ethics. As discussed in Chapter 2, Butler emphasizes how breathing illustrates being 'bound up' as our social condition, as we have to understand ourselves as being capable of communicating viruses, and so on, at the same time as being vulnerable to others' capacity to do the same to us, 'so potentially both acting and acted upon' (Butler, 2022: 40), a scenario – the human condition (Arendt, 1998 [1958]) – from which there is no escaping.

This condition – of being bound up with others through the possibility of causing or experiencing harm – underpins an ethical quandary, namely that 'my life and the lives of others depend upon a recognition of how our lives depend in part upon how each of us acts' (Butler, 2022: 40). For Butler, Segal and other feminists, interdependency, as the social relation or corollary of an ontology of 'intertwining' (Merleau-Ponty, 1964), constitutes an ethical paradigm in which we all (can only) exist in relation to each other, so that what Butler calls 'the liberal conceit' is haunted by 'a dependency that is imagined as if it could be overcome' (Butler, 2022: 42). In sum, if the pandemic and other ongoing crises have given us anything, not least in the form, as Butler puts it, of 'one rather large social and ethical lesson to learn', it is this: 'what makes a life liveable is a question that implicitly shows us that *the life we live is never exclusively our own*' (Butler, 2022: 43, emphasis added). This is at once an ontological, ethical and political predicament – the human condition, in Arendt's (1998 [1958]) terms – and it poses a key challenge for thinking through the relationship between recognition and vulnerability, namely that of how this relationship might be organized in order to make life more liveable and workable for more people.

What work is this? Organizing for workable lives

The more urgent the question of how we might mutually recognize shared but socially situated vulnerability as the basis of social relations the more vexed it seems to become, particularly in a context in which sociality seems so far removed from the dominant political discourses and power relations that shape our lives, and increasingly so. Butler urges us to 'link the interconnected character of our lives *to the obligation we have to organize the world* ... on principles of radical equality' (Butler, 2022: 47, emphasis added), as the current set of arrangements are clearly far from '*an equitable or life-supporting organization of common life*' (Butler, 2022: 48, emphasis added).

Working with the phenomenological concept of the lifeworld, and imagining its possible futures, provides Butler (2022) with a chance to bring two vital questions together: What makes a life liveable? And what constitutes an inhabitable world? In responding to these two questions, they connect three 'worlds' – the conceptual/phenomenal 'lifeworld', the market economy and the inhabitable ecosystem, each of which we might think of as organizational realms. To reimagine how each might be made more liveable, or workable in Arendt's terms, Butler draws further on Merleau-Ponty's (1968: 130) concept of the *entrelac* (perhaps most faithfully understood as our 'interlacing') through which he maps out how the porous boundaries of the body mark out paths of relationality, so that 'there is no clear way to distinguish activity and passivity as mutually exclusive' (Butler, 2022: 58). Butler works with Merleau-Ponty's notion of the social world as being composed of an interwoven nexus of self–others–things, illustrating this with reference to breathing as 'the social character of air', as discussed in Chapter 2, highlighting how the world is constituted by a set of social relationships, itself 'made, consumed, and distributed within socioeconomic organizations of life' (Butler, 2022: 59).

Understanding this world as a radical interdependency, or interlacing, might open up possibilities for an expansion of networks of support through collaboration, enacting not simply a new form of common life but also of 'collective values and desires', Butler (2022: 62) argues. For Butler, the effort to bring this about must be linked to the wider struggle to overcome profound global inequalities, and climate destruction premised, we might surmise, upon a collective desire for recognition. Making similar points to those of the Care Collective noted earlier, Butler argues: 'We must struggle for a world in which we defend the rights ... for the stranger on the far side of the world as fervently as we do for our neighbour or lover' (Butler, 2022: 62). In response to the question, 'what kind of world is this?', Butler therefore asks another: 'in what kind of world do we wish to live?'. For Butler, interdependency is 'the way out'; it is 'the possibility we may have for sensual ecstasy, for the support we need to live, and for radical equality and alliances committed to building and sustaining a liveable world in common' (Butler, 2022: 64).

However differently we may experience and register global crises such as the COVID-19 pandemic, the climate emergency, or deeply entrenched forms of exploitation and conflict, and however much the world continues to respond to interdependency through 'borderization' (Mbembe, 2019), it is also the case that we have come to understand one another and the crises that shape our lives as global; increasingly (reflexively) knowing that 'we are implicated in a shared world', as Butler (2022: 65) emphasizes. However strongly political leaders and powerful social media influencers may deny it, our interdependency *is* our way of being – a human condition, one that challenges notions of ourselves as 'isolated individuals encased in discrete bodies, bound by established borders' (Butler, 2022: 66).

For Butler (2022), it is Merleau-Ponty's notion of the *entrelac* that opens up scope to consider how vulnerability might become the basis for ethics and politics in a social and organizational lifeworld reimagined as relational. In particular, Butler cites Merleau-Ponty's understanding of social relations as chiasmic; that is, as embedded but situated differently within the sensory realm of reciprocity, so that the myriad sites on which our desire for recognition comes to be organized including those such as breathing, grieving and appearing, 'are *both what we share and what we share differently*' (Butler, 2022: 77, emphasis added). So, although realms such as these constitute the social worlds that are common between us, they are also (as we have considered in Chapters 2–4) sites of 'division, vexation and overlap'. In Butler's (2022: 78) view, Merleau-Ponty 'underestimates the rage that can emerge from unstable forms of differentiation', by which we might take Butler to mean those forms of difference that are bifurcated and then organized hierarchically. In this sense, his notion of interlacing is ultimately, for Butler, an idealistic notion of the social bond, one that is overly optimistic as a way of thinking about the intentional relations that shape our connections to others and the social world; his 'nexus' too harmonious in its portrayal of social relations in a way that rules out or minimizes the possibility of violence and of erecting both physical and psychic borders (Mbembe, 2019).

Yet as Butler and others who advocate for a feminist ethics of relationality also emphasize, while we may rail against this way of being and what it implies, interdependency is the inescapability of social relations, so that because we share a world (even if we do not share that world equally), we are obligated to find a way to live and work together. And while some may deny an ontology of shared vulnerability, or an ethics premised upon it, we cannot simply rule out or will away the embodied, existential vulnerability that we all have in common. But, again, the conditions that must be met for the continuation or persistence of life are '*always* socially organized' (Butler, 2022: 82, emphasis added), because (as noted earlier) they depend upon recognizability. In this sense, organization can be understood as a scene of 'mutual implication' (Butler, 2022: 82–83) that carries with it the weight of an ethical imperative, the task of which is to establish a reciprocal relationality that enables us to 'rethink ethical relationality as interlacing' (Butler, 2022: 83), within but also ultimately, beyond, the realm of what is possible, and in doing so, to reimagine organizing as a space of and for interdependency.

Towards a radical vulnerability

Important to enacting the ethics and politics that Butler and others whose work we have engaged with in this chapter map out is to find ways in which what it means to organize might be reimagined according to a radical vulnerability. As close as Butler (2022: 105, emphasis added) gets to outlining what this might entail is when they write, drawing inspiration from both Arendt and the *Care Manifesto*, that to keep 'the relationship between affect and action alive' we must set out to turn 'revulsion and outrage into the collective potential and revolutionary promise' of transformation, including through recognizing the value of '*the cumulative power of small acts of labour*'.

Butler notes that the *Care Manifesto* articulates a feminist ideal of interdependence 'that moves beyond the dyadic model to a cross-weaving of intersubjectivity itself' (Butler, 2022: 106), insisting on critical reflexivity as a political necessity and on the importance of finding space for that to emerge. The normative principles for this movement include interdependency, social solidarity and radical critique, 'seeking to provide *the conditions for life, for living on, for living together*' (Butler, 2022: 107, emphasis added).

And yet the liberal conceit of 'righteous entitlement' (Butler, 2022: 108) remains steadfast, gaining not only popularity but credence in many places and spheres across the world. For Butler, this cannot continue to co-exist alongside our social ontology; yet not only does it do so, it flourishes. Following Arendt, Merleau-Ponty and of course Hegel, Butler is resolute that the reality of our social condition is such that '[w]e cannot ... live without each other, without finding ourselves inside another's pores, or without letting another in. For that is where we live, *outside of this bounded self and its conceits*' (Butler, 2022: 109, original emphasis).

To understand the hold that this juxtaposition has over our lives and the extent to which, as a result, we cannot see or sense our interdependency, it is of course important not to fall into the trap of romanticizing social relationality, and Butler's writing published just before the pandemic helps us to think this through. In *The Force of Nonviolence* Butler (2020b) recognizes that hostility is part of our psychic constitution so that the field of social relationality is a fraught one; characterized by negativity, our relationality is not simply 'a good thing', a sign of love or interconnectedness, but is rather 'a vexed and ambivalent field in which the question of ethical obligation *has to be worked out*' (Butler, 2020b: 10, emphasis added). Of course, recognition is easier to comprehend with reference to those we identify with, wish to protect, and so on, but more complex when applied to those we are hostile towards, including those whose beliefs, ways of life, and so on, we might find ourselves objecting to. The dialectical and socially situated nature of relationality means that this working out is a process of struggle, one played out through the body – as the social relations of breathing, grieving and appearing illustrate. Further, while our way of being is one situated in interconnection, as noted earlier, we continue to live and work under not only the fantasy of autonomy, but its idealization to the point of vulneraphobia, relating to one another through a frame of reference that posits dependency as negativity and which, in doing so, erases our basic and ongoing mutual vulnerability. An example of the result of this is the perception that a dependent life is not a 'real' life, or a life lived fully.

So, what can we do? It seems that the concerted actions of our bodies, assembled physically and virtually in whatever way we can to resist and protest against precarity, the destruction of the conditions of liveability, and the impossibility of leading 'workable' lives for the world's most precarious people and populations, must be combined with an assemblage of resources so that a liveable, workable life becomes more possible for more living beings, in more places and more of the time.

Showing how recognizability and recognition are dialectically related (we might even say, 'organized') enables us to understand the epistemological conditions governing what it means to be accorded recognition, and its normative consequences. Butler's non-teleological reading of Hegel has important implications, or possibilities for responding to the kinds of questions we have considered in this book, in so far as it highlights that our desire for recognition renders us socially (organizationally) vulnerable in at least two important ways. First, often, our only choice is to be recognized in ways and according to terms that are 'beyond us' and which therefore can lead to our subordination, or at least our constraint, or not being recognized at all (of course, this may happen to us unreflexively, or sometimes more 'tactically'). Hence, our vulnerability becomes reified. Second, even when we achieve recognition that might be liveable or 'workable' for us, the meaning of the terms we are subject to is never fixed or stable, *and* 'there is ... no recognition of all that a person is *or may be*' (Butler, 2021a: 34, emphasis added), hence we are perpetually vulnerable, or as we have noted in earlier chapters, we are vulnerable 'in perpetuity' and organizations are important social contexts in which these dynamics are played out.

But this vulnerability also opens up important possibilities that might be transformative, and which raise important questions for thinking about the kinds of work, and organizational forms and relations involved. If, for example, 'norms are "resignified" by bodies that are not supposed to embody them, and that can change the way we think about embodiment, norms and social transformation' (Butler, 2021a: 40–41) what kind of *work* do such bodies do? Do they embody a radical vulnerability, but only do so in spaces of co-appearance that enable mutual recognition and relationality to flourish? If so, what kinds of organizational infrastructures or relations might enable such bodies to enact, individually and collectively, transformative ways of being and of relating to one another, in more places, more often, with more impact?

Butler's view has long been that recitation constitutes a possible source of emancipatory change from the outside, from the domain of non-intelligibility, and at stake here is the question of an 'alter agency' as it were – action and appearance based on the agentic capacity of vulnerability. Lynne Segal (2023), the Care Collective (2020) and others have argued for the importance of a promiscuous mode of care, and for the resources necessary to enable such a principle to emerge and flourish, while Adriana Cavarero (2016) makes the case for a more inclined ethic as the basis of social relations. Perhaps another way in which the Hegelian narrative might be extended to our current sphere of interest (that is, in understanding and advocating for modes of organizing premised upon a relational, reflexive recognition of mutual, but socially situated vulnerability) is by combining political and philosophical lines of argument that connect post-recognition solidarity and pre-recognition vulnerability, as discussed in earlier chapters. Doing so might enable us to develop a reflexive, relational understanding of recognition and (its) organization that has the potential to form the basis of a critical, reflexive, ethically and politically orientated theory of our encounters with one another (in other words, a response to the question of why we don't see/sense our mutual vulnerability, even/especially when we all breathe, grieve and appear together).

Returning to the different forms of recognition considered earlier in this chapter to flesh this out a little more, we might conclude that a rhetorical, largely (negative) ideological form that is not simply cognitive or classificatory in Honneth's terms, but which establishes the terms of intelligibility or recognizability in Butler's cannot provide the basis for a radical vulnerability. An example of the form this takes might be employee recognition schemes. As discussed in Chapter 2, Philip Hancock (2024: 381) has argued that such programmes, replete with pathological tendencies towards reification, disrespect and compelled identification, effectively undermine 'the ontological conditions necessary for recognition to flourish'. Restricting expressions of evaluation solely, or even primarily, to the level of the symbolic means that so-called employee recognition schemes provide little beyond a 'cheap and instrumentally effective ... *normative* grounding for organizational life' constituting a form of recognition that is 'all too easily appropriated' (Hancock, 2024: 390, emphasis added). This way of thinking about recognition as reification is illustrated in the discourses and practices that hailed health and social care workers as heroes during the COVID-19 pandemic.[19] Such practices 'constitute recognition less as a process of mutual attentiveness – as an associative, intersubjective outcome – and *more as an object or property to be individually coveted and possessed*' (Hancock, 2024: 393, emphasis added), reifying the subjectivities, labour and social relations of mutual interdependency involved. Taken together, this results in a false or alienating form of recognition that undermines the conditions necessary to its own realization, reducing recognition and vulnerability alike to a reified, 'thing-like status' (Hancock, 2024: 396). While Hancock refers to organizational recognition schemes as an example of reified forms of recognition, other forms of organizing our desire for recognition can be thought of that have the same reificatory effects. In her memoir, disabled artist Alison Lapper describes a form of 'recognition' to which she was subject as a young art college student that provides an arresting example:

> When I began my degree course some of the male tutors had problems with me being there. They couldn't cope with a disabled art student, and they dealt with my presence by just never speaking to me. One of them had been particularly distant and always passed me by in the corridors without a word, so I was surprised when he came into the studio one day to look at my work [based on casts made of Lapper's own body]. He walked slowly up and down the rows of casts assessing each one. Then he stopped, turned around and looked at me, 'You've got really nice tits', he said. I was flabbergasted and confused. They were the only words he'd said to me in a year and a half. It was an outrageously sexist thing to say. But at the same time ... I'd never been told before that I had nice breasts. (Lapper, 2005: 187)

Second, what for Honneth (2021a, 2021b) is a 'full' (affirmative/normative) version of recognition is one that reinstates our social bond and is, hence, to a degree transformative but which carries with it two interrelated risks. First, it similarly involves a paternalistic shoring up; second, in doing so it risks failing to fully recognize the ambivalence engendered by the terms of recognition (that is, the normative effects of what Butler calls 'recognizability') as pre-established, which, as Butler's work has emphasized, can have a normalizing, disciplinary effect.

The third, more reflexive, non-teleological or dialectical version of recognition introduced earlier (see Chapter 2) involves participation in a reflexive 'problematization' of the relations and terms of recognition and of our differential investments in them, including of the norms that govern recognizability, recognizing that claims to recognition are always already normatively embedded and are grounded in a 'forgotten', reified relation of mutual interdependence. This is a kind of recognition that links to contemporary feminist work on solidarity, foregrounding the importance of relationality and mutual recognition of our shared but always socially situated vulnerability as the basis of ethics and politics. Drawing on Frantz Fanon (2007 [1967]), Achille Mbembe (2019: 141) argues that this kind of reflexive recognition, one marked by individual and collective refusal as organized struggle, is the kind that aims to bring about a new set of relations between people, things and planetary resources, engaging in the sort of struggle that involves organized, collective *work* and the reinstatement of a commitment to care premised upon recognition of our mutual yet socially situated vulnerability as our most basic, and vital human condition.

An interesting and important example of this latter approach can be found in Kate Kenny's (2024, 2025) work on whistleblower activism. In a recent response to Trump's rapid assaults on civil servants' rights during the first few months of his second administration, Kenny cites the appearance of Trump's then adviser Elon Musk on stage in February 2025 brandishing a red chainsaw, shouting about a 'chainsaw for bureaucracy',[20] arguing that 'this is exactly the kind of chaotic, performative scene that stokes fascist passions, but leaves critics frozen'. But Kenny injects a good deal of hope into her critique, emphasizing how whistleblower activists and their supporters are able to mobilize in order to counter what could otherwise be a very paralysing geo-political scenario, showing how civil society groups work together to collaboratively reaffirm workers' rights, challenging threats to whistleblower protections through legal means, and by raising public awareness.

In a similar vein, Judith Butler (2025) has warned that all too easily people can be stunned into inaction by the rapidity of events such as the succession of executive orders brought into effect by Trump in the first days and weeks of his second terms in office in early 2025, designed specifically to stop people seeing how interconnected they are in the ways in which they undermine rights, resources, legal protections and representation. Butler emphasizes, in response, the vitality of not being immobilized by outrage, a point that Kenny reiterates by showing how whistleblower activists and their supporters are able to organize in order to act, collectively. Butler writes of the shameless sadism of Trump 2.0, and of the 'exhilarated hatred' parading as freedom that it fuels ('parading' here seems quite deliberate – as the counter to assembling). And Butler is clear – while Trump was the global figurehead of this, at stake is a much wider erosion of hard-won rights enacted via 'a communal and contagious celebration of cruelty'.[21] Butler's point is that much like in the midst of COVID-19, we are at another crucial 'moment', and that it is time to find passions of our own, namely, to articulate, organize and mobilize:

> The desire for a freedom equally shared; for an equality that makes good on democratic promises; to repair and regenerate the earth's living processes; to accept and affirm the complexity of our embodied lives; to imagine a world in which government supports health and education for all, where we all live without fear, knowing that our interconnected lives are equally valuable.[22]

Drawing on Butler (2025), Kenny points to the work of bodies like the Whistleblowing International Network and the United Nations Convention Against Corruption (UNCAC) as crucial to maintaining democratic accountability, organized via online events and forums to sustain momentum. In her book, *Regulators of Last Resort*, Kenny (2024) shows how this collective activism is not easy – organizations such as these operate on limited funding; and in the face of disinformation on social media, defending truth can be challenging. Yet, as she also emphasizes, finding and occupying critical spaces in which to collaborate can help to counter aggressive opposition. As Kenny (2025) sums it up, 'a shared commitment to democratic rights is what keeps coalitions of whistleblower activists going – they demonstrate passions for equality and the right to live without fear'. As Butler and Kenny both illustrate, the paralysing effects of relentless attempts to erode workers' and citizens' rights seem to foreclose sustainable, organized opposition; yet 'through their dedication, mutual support and celebration of even small wins, international collectives of whistleblower activists remind us that there is a way forward and why it's vital to keep going' (Kenny, 2025: np).

In a similar vein, with reference to community initiatives organized by non-governmetnal organization (NGO) volunteers with homeless people in France, Lucie Cortambert and Karen Dale (2025: 17) highlight not only the centrality of vulnerability to social relations, but also its radical capacity to challenge and shift established assumptions about precarious individuals and groups labelled as 'vulnerable'. Drawing on Bakhtin and Levinas, they show how vulnerability is not fixed or static but is co-created in interaction in ways that allow openness between one another. In particular, they show how the 'mutual recognition of the possibility of being wounded, reflected in the etymology of "vulnerable", implies a reciprocal relationality between volunteers and homeless people and helps build relations of solidarity'. And with reference to communal gardening projects, Emmanouela Mandalaki and Marianna Fotaki (2020) have shown how commoning has the potential to open up scope for alternative forms of organizing, by offering the ethical and political possibility of countering forms of economic competition based on recognition of shared corporeal vulnerabilities as the basis of reciprocity and embodied relationality. All of these vital interventions into exploring, and showing, how lives might be made more workable, of which these are but a few examples, emphasize what feminist organization theorist Sheena Vachhani (2020: 755) has called the 'promise ... of vulnerability' to bring about embodied and generous ethical relations that prioritize co-organizing as an openness to, with *and for* one another.

Concluding thoughts

However we organize in, through and for our shared by socially situated vulnerability, a simple premise holds true: 'simply being together strengthens us' (Segal, 2018: 267). On that note, I realize that what I am about to write is not a traditional 'conclusive' section – a reiteration of key points and lines of argument – and it runs the risk of being a considerable overshare, and for that I apologise. I am also sorry for the irony of writing about my own experience in a book that has been at pains to think beyond the individual, and to deflect the self-orientation discussed in Chapter 4 especially. But I hope that my reflections will not only illustrate some of the ideas and values discussed throughout earlier chapters but also provide a moment of recognition for anyone reading it who has experienced anything similar.

While I was working on this book, a member of my family became very unwell and had to be my priority. Midway through a busy academic year I struggled with my workload, sleep patterns and ability to keep on top of everything. There were things I simply couldn't do, events I could not attend. I found myself telling senior colleagues that I had research commitments if I couldn't be at a meeting, something I have had to do during school holidays and on non-pupil days, or if my children became ill, since becoming a working parent over two decades ago. But this was different. I told some trusted friends and colleagues about my situation, but not others who I was aware were already over-burdened themselves, or who I knew less well. I began to rack up debts that I knew I wouldn't be able to repay as generous and thoughtful colleagues did more than their share of collaborative work. It was the group of feminist friends and colleagues that I am fortunate to be able to work with who got me through, always keeping me involved but asking nothing of me until I was ready and able to give it. Around me (and others in similar circumstances), and without realizing the significance of what they were offering, they formed a site and space of radical vulnerability premised upon a reflexive, recognition-based mode of relationality. In this way, not only did they show me that they understood and fully recognized my predicament (and that of others in similar circumstances); they enabled me to carry on collaborating with them in and through my relative vulnerability, making mine and other people's lives during this period 'workable' in a way that they might not otherwise have been. Some of those involved are close friends, while others are people I barely know, and some are people I have never met in person, yet our shared but socially contoured circumstances provided a much-needed point of connection. I entrusted my wellbeing to them, and I hope that they would do the same if the situation had been different, or may be in the future, enabling us to exist as a collective assemblage of resources, solidarity and care. We shared time, energy, expertise, experience and skill, bringing varying amounts of capacity to the work we did together. I will always be grateful to them for this in ways that are hard to express (especially in an ostensibly academic book), not only for their kindness but also for showing me what a workable life means and needs at a very basic level – to live in and through vulnerability as a source of strength and as a carefully crafted and nurtured site of solidarity and compassion, care and relational capacity.

And it was during this period that I got in touch with a good friend and colleague who I hadn't spoken to for a while to suggest that we have a 'catch up'. Even if only online, being in her company is always a pleasure and we arranged a time to meet, as we normally do to discuss family and mutual friends, our current work and plans. She said something that I have been thinking about since, and as I continued to work on this chapter, namely that if all we have the time and energy to do with those who matter to us is 'catch up' we never have the chance to make new memories, and to nurture the relationships – be they with those close to us, or with an extended network of people we may never know personally, but whose lives are important to us – that sustain us. I was immersed in Adriana Cavarero's writing at the time and, influenced by her characteristic practice of tracing etymons, began to think more about the origins and implications of what it means to 'catch' up, rather than to make new memories, or create new beginnings in the ways in which we relate to one another, as Arendt might lead us to put it. And what I learnt is this: the word 'catch' has a fascinating history, originating from the Middle English terms, *'cacchen'* (to take or capture), which itself derives from the Anglo-Norman and Old French word, *'cachier'*, or *'chacier'* (again, to capture, with connotations of hunting, pursuing or driving animals). The latter takes its origins from the Late Latin *'captiare'* (to seize), and the vulgar Latin, *'captare'*, meaning to take or to hold in place. Hence, my friend's point makes a lot of sense – if all we do is 'catch' up, we fail to make the time and space – to assemble – in ways that are open to one another, and to the possibilities that being fully co-present to and for each other, in 'moments' of recognition, might open up.

Reflecting on the implications of these experiences and associations, and about themes and ideas explored in earlier chapters in this book, I began to think more about the extremities of social relations that render some lives not only more liveable and grievable, but also more or less workable than others. And this led me to conclude that, borrowing from Cavarero and Butler's reading of Arendt, we might think of workability as a situation in which we are able, intercorporeally, to bring about new beginnings, and to (co-)invest in something lasting in ways that sustain not only ourselves but others, some of whom might be very close to us – our own family, friends or kinship networks; others we will never know at all – the 'strangers at our door' (Bauman, 2016), those who are in our seats, arriving on our shores or appearing on our screens.

In her book, *Radical Happiness*, Lynne Segal (2018: 267) opens up vital lines of thought that help us to imagine what this might involve. Drawing from Lauren Berlant's (Arendtian) argument that the political is that which 'magnetises a desire for intimacy, sociality, affective solidarity, and happiness' (Berlant, 2011: 252), Segal replaces Berlant's point about the cruelty of optimism with a characteristic reaffirmation of the possibilities attached to a hope-infused solidarity. This leads her to conclude that even in what might seem like the most hopeless of circumstances, in which our capacity for shared action appears to be increasingly diminished, simply trying to envisage how we might work and act together to create 'a more equitable, peaceful and fairer world brings a certain audacity and energy to life' (Segal, 2018: 268). And this, she reassures us, might be the best we can do, at least for now. The process of sharing such imaginings – recognizing in one another the audacity to be and to think 'otherwise', assembling to explore these imaginings, and to share time, energy, resources, and whatever capacity we can muster, at least holds onto the beginnings of a world in which we might live, work and organize for and with one another in and through our shared, socially situated vulnerability.

Notes

Introduction

1. With this in mind, one of the book's aims is to examine vulnerability as a source of agentic strength, through which ethical bonds that challenge individualization and the essentialization of difference (Johansson and Wickström, 2023: 318), enabling us to 'capture and theorize the sense and recognition of corporeal connectedness', based on which an other-oriented ethical agency of care might emerge and affect change.
2. Perhaps one of the most poignant accounts of what we might call disinclination is Primo Levi's *If This is a Man*, which is not simply (as Simona Forti puts it), an exercise in thanatopolitics, but also an account of relations of complacent smiles and deference, 'of unaware signatures and shrugs' (Forti, 2021: 148).
3. Regionality is clearly of vital importance here. As Achille Mbembe has put it (2020), 'the right to exist is meaningless unless it is accompanied by its corollary, the right to subsist'. For most people, 'food can only be acquired by leaving the house' and, for some, 'often, travelling long distances at increasingly great expense (unreliable transport, interminable journeys on foot, all sorts of permits and authorizations)'. For the world's most vulnerable populations, 'the hunt for food is an endless cycle of walking, hustling, haggling, bargaining, moving on, using all means possible, even illegal ones'.
4. In this sense, Mackenzie et al's (2013) understanding of some vulnerabilities as pathological overlaps with Turner's (2006: 32) argument that human rights legislation responds to the 'dynamic and dialectical relationship between institutional precariousness and ontological vulnerability'. As Mackenzie et al note, this argument conveys how, on the one hand, human rights protections are a response to ontological vulnerability, yet on the other hand, institutional structures are often themselves fragile and precarious, and state power can equally be the cause of human rights abuses.
5. Here and throughout this book, I use the term 'organization' in its broadest sense, to refer to an aspect of social life that is much more significant and ubiquitous than the purposeful, predominantly profit-orientated co-ordination of goods and services that Organizational Behaviour textbooks often narrowly refer to as their subject matter. Instead, my understand of 'organization' is based on the premise that, as sociologist Amitai Etzione put it, 'ours is an organizational society' (Etzioni, 1970: 1), one which our most fundamental human need and everything on which it is based comes to be organized (categorized, classified, ordered hierarchically and resourced), in ways that can be exploitative and oppressive but which also contain the possibility of more relational ways of structuring and experiencing social relations, namely our desire for recognition.
6. A similar point is also made by feminist theorist Rosi Braidotti (2020: 465), who argues that in moments of crisis 'we are together, but we are not the same'. Thank you to Daniela Pianezzi for reminding me of this connection.

NOTES

7   Here Butler concurs with Adriana Cavarero's (2016: 30–31) distinction between vulnerability as a lifelong human condition, and helplessness, which is more dependent upon circumstances. For an insightful illustration of what this means in organizational life, see Shepherd et al's (2022) account of Mumbai-based ragpickers who describe their situation with reference to the work they do, to where they work and how they live, and to their circumstances within a caste-based system of social stratification.

8   By the 'necropolitical', Mbembe (2019: 39–40) refers to the subjugation of life to the constant threat of death, involving both a 'generalized instrumentalization of human existence and the material destruction of human bodies and populations', as well as wider threats from historical and contemporary forms of colonialism, occupation and destruction of the natural world.

9   The etymology of the term 'consignment' is important and interesting here, having connotations of being both contained and delivered (conveying a state of being 'given over' to one another as our default way of being).

10 Please note that here and throughout this book, plural pronouns (they/their, and not she/her) are used when referring to Judith Butler.

11 This is what Hannah Arendt referred to, in her eulogy to her friend, W.H. Auden, as the 'curse of vulnerability' to and for the human condition (cited in Stonebridge, 2025: 234).

12 Arguably, recognition of our mutual vulnerability requires the kind of dramatic phenomenological, ethical shift that even the COVID-19 pandemic couldn't bring about (Segal, 2023). A clear illustration of this is the extent to which, rather than solidarity and compassion, migrant travellers are often met with indifference or outright hostility (Fotaki, 2022), even in the immediate wake of the pandemic and increasingly so in the years since.

13 Butler also acknowledges of course that while our ecstatic way of being renders us beside ourselves, 'undone' and at the same time constituted by our loss as a condition of our very formation, essential to many social and political movements is their claim to bodily integrity, even autonomy, as the basis of certain rights and modes of recourse.

14 Butler explains this via a Hegelian reading of Freud, noting how 'one mourns when one accepts that by the loss one undergoes one will be changed, possibly for ever' (Butler, 2004a: 21).

Chapter 1

1   As Daniela Pianezzi (2025: 2) has phrased it, 'the vulnerability of bodies seems to be a common condition that holds us together, but some bodies are more fragile than others'.

2   Referring to the devastating loss of human lives deemed to lack value, Achille Mbembe (2020) argues (citing Karl Polányi, 2001 [1944]) that what is needed is a 'great transition' from one state of existence to another, one that strikes at the roots of a social, political and economic system of extraction and predation, rejecting the notion that prosperity equates to, or requires, the indefinite depletion of living beings and other natural resources. On the contrary, he argues, a world that flourishes is one that is (or should be) marked by the quality of its social ties, its sharing of resources, and its commitment to simplicity and restraint, meeting basic needs that restore and recognize the value of dignity for all. These are signals of strength, not weakness in any given social context, he emphasizes. See Robin Wall Kimmerer's (2024) *The Serviceberry* for a further development of this line of thought.

3   Recent feminist writing, adopting an embodied understanding of vulnerability as the basis of a relational ethics, has emphasized, for instance, how vulnerability in organizational life can emerge from a constant sense of being different, and of being compared to dominant organizational norms governing intelligibility (Johansson and Wickström, 2023).

See also Shoaib Ahmed's (2024: 883) account of how de-realization reifies the relative positioning of women and child workers as 'excessively vulnerable' in the Bangladeshi garment factory he studied, disavowing their agency and therefore capacity to resist the dehumanization, dispossession and displacement that the chronic wage theft to which they are subject perpetuates.

4 This is Judith Butler's (2021a) view in their essay, 'Recognition and the social bond', which implicitly frames vulnerability as a power effect of our desire for recognition, one that shapes our more or less reflexive acceptance of normative positions within the social order, binding us to our own subjugation.

5 By the same token, organizational processes and protocols are often designed to minimize exposure to risk, rendering organizations themselves as 'invulnerable' as possible, often with reference to financial and/or legal compliance or profitability. In these circumstances, that shape the nature, meaning and experience of vulnerability and its relationship to organization, these two phenomena are framed not just as distinct but opposed forces.

6 Critics of Adriana Cavarero (2016) have raised concerns about the essentializing implications of her advocacy of inclination, relating notably to her equation of the latter with femininity (or specifically, the maternal feminine), and by implication, to both a reaffirmation and inversion of precisely the types of normative views on gender that she ostensibly sets out to critique. It strikes me that this is a problematic aspect of Cavarero's writing, one that makes it challenging for feminists committed to relationality and solidarity to draw from her otherwise insightful work.

7 Here Cavarero (2016: 34) draws on Simone Beauvoir's (2011 [1949]: 25) point that 'a man is in his right by virtue of being … an absolute vertical', an observation that she develops into her critique of the geometry of verticality in which 'upright' signifies both a postural disposition and a moral claim 'on the same perpendicular line' (Cavarero, 2016: 35, 38–39) so that the opposition between, for example, straight and crooked or 'bent' embodies an ethical division between right and wrong. Aside from the political connotations of this etymology, Cavarero (2016: 41, emphasis added) notes its ontological consequences for ethics, emphasizing how in philosophical terms, leaning towards inclination means that (in Beauvoirian terms), '*the woman is never for herself, but always for the other* … [imposing on her] as natural – typical and stereotypical – an inclined posture'. Because they have become so embedded in our symbolic landscape, Cavarero argues, essentialist idealizations that frame inclined feminine subjects as existing by and for others, and vertical masculinity as by and for the self, have become extremely difficult to dismantle, or even think beyond. Drawing from this, we could argue that the scenography of subjectivity that western philosophy and art has so firmly established has taken on simultaneously ethical, ontological and epistemological qualities so that dominant conceptions of what we 'know' to exist, and believe to be right, cannot be thought or lived outside of this frame of reference without risking significant wounding to oneself and others. This is a key component, we might suggest, of the fear of vulnerability that our societies have normalized, both now and historically.

8 Links between sexual categories that equate heteronormative sexualities with being 'straight' and (pejoratively) being gay or queer with (in English) being 'bent' are not lost on Cavarero (2016), who cites Foucault and Bernini, as well as the etymology of the term 'queer' to emphasize that normative heterosexuality ('straightness') is traditionally associated with moral rectitude.

9 Olivia Guaraldo (2012) goes further, emphasizing that vulnerability is the shared dimension that makes human life *thinkable*, insofar as it expresses the crucial nexus between corporeality and relationality that defines what it means to be human. It is this epistemic perspective on vulnerability that Cavarero (2016) arguably develops, mapping out not only

a relational ontology of vulnerability as the basis of a feminist ethics and politics but also, in doing so, developing a critique of how we come to know what vulnerability is, and what it means to be a 'vulnerable' subject, most notably with reference to the maternal feminine, and its depiction in western philosophy and art (see note 6, this chapter).

10. For Achille Mbembe, vulnerability is the very essence of life, shared among all living (and once living) things. Yet his work emphasizes how, as he puts it, 'a whole constellation of forces … are busy weaving a lattice of fractures between every part of the world', shattering belief and hope in the inter-dependency that this engenders (Mbembe, 2020: np). Making a similar point, Butler (2021c: 57) reflects that 'self-preservation is overrated as a moral ideal'.

11. The neoliberal equation of care with dependency and its articulation within an 'overcoming' discourse of resilience has its origins, as Joan Tronto (2015: 1) reminds us, in the Aristotelean narrative that first a person is cared for, then they are ready to enter politics in order to wield power as a political actor.

12. At the risk of oversimplification, while Butler establishes an ontology of vulnerability and writers like Cavarero help us to map out its epistemology, it could be said that Lynne Segal situates vulnerability more sociologically, framing our need for care as ubiquitous but socially structured and striated.

13. See Riach (2025) for a much more developed discussion of ageing, fear, vulnerability and recognition.

14. See also Robin Wall Kimmerer's (2013) *Braiding Sweetgrass*.

15. In her book, *Corporeal Ethics for Feminist Work*, Daniela Pianezzi (2025: 103) develops this point, arguing for the importance of feminists resisting what she calls 'the logic of victimization' for two reasons: first, because of its individualizing tendencies, and second, because it risks promoting 'solutions that reinforce … paternalism', both of which undermine scope for political agency.

16. In this respect, we might say that although Butler and Cavarero mutually influence each other's work, both drawing on Arendt (1998 [1958]) and developing similar lines of argument about the ontological, ethical and political significance of vulnerability, Butler develops a largely critical reading of Cavarero (2016), at least on this precise point about inclination being a maternal, feminist posture.

17. Drawing on Sophocles' *Antigone* and Euripides' *The Bacchae*, Bonnie Honig (2021) expands on Cavarero's (2016) analysis of inclination, foregrounding sorority rather than maternity as its locus.

18. While acknowledging that Cavarero's (2021a, 2021c) postural perspective has been 'enormously useful for theorizing ethics and politics', Honig (2021: 63, 64), like Butler and several others, is rightly critical of her framing of inclination as a specifically material 'gesture of care'. Christine Battersby also finds Cavarero's relative neglect of bonds of care and friendship based on relations between individuals, states and other social groupings as the potential basis for inclination problematic, while Lorenzo Bernini (2021) draws from antisocial queer theories to offer a complementary interpretation of inclination to Cavarero's, foregrounding alternative views of exposure that also problematizes Cavarero's equation of an inclined care ethic with the maternal feminine.

19. Mark Devenney (2021: 131, 134, emphasis added) argues that Cavarero's (2016, 2021c, 2021c) writing is '*haunted by what it tries to expel*', so that her analysis does 'a hermeneutic violence' to the complex, dialectical relationship between verticality and inclination, closing down the ethical possibilities she sets out to open up and failing to work with the 'messy' nature of the relations she maps out, staying suspended 'inside the conventional family structure with no obvious way out' (Woodford, 2021: 172; see also Battersby, 2021; Bernini, 2021; Butler, 2021**c**; Honig, 2021).

20 See Ikäheimo et al (2021) who examine the status of 'non-personhood' brought about by the objectifying effects of conditional recognition.
21 Stahl (2021: 177, emphasis added) understands the political vulnerability engendered by the ambivalent nature of recognition as a 'constitutive domination'. By this, he means that 'a state of dependence on others in the subject's very constitution, where either the socio-ontological conditions for becoming a subject, or the normative, motivational, or epistemic implications of this dependence, form a limit to the subject's capacities to contest the norms regulating its recognizability, *thus making it vulnerable to the arbitrary power of others*'.
22 For Axel Honneth (2021a, 2021b), it is only the interrelationship between recognition as a cognitive and ethical process that constitutes recognition in the way in which Hegel understood it, for it '*demands from the giver a self-constraint*' with regard to how to act or behave' (Honneth, 2021a: 27, emphasis added). In other words, for Honneth following Hegel, recognition is a transformative process that establishes future conditions of possibility for vulnerability's worst extremes to be mitigated or avoided.
23 See also Butler's (2009a: 192, emphasis added) earlier point that 'it is important to remember that the "no" delineates and animates a new set of positions for the subject; it is inventive and, in that sense, *operates as a determinate negation*'.
24 This view is articulated perhaps most clearly in Levinas's notion that the subjectivity of a subject *is* vulnerability.
25 See Butler (2020a).
26 In their introduction, Arto Charpentier and Laure Barillas (2023: 2) note how Worms' critical vitalism resonates with Butler's notion of a social ontology of the living body (see their 'Postscript' to *The Force of Nonviolence* [Butler, 2020b]). Both Worms and Butler, they argue, do not go as far as Simone Weil in proposing a list of the body and soul's essential needs, but they do nonetheless present us with 'a normative aspiration that can serve as a guide for politics: the aspiration to ensure each and every living human the conditions of a liveable life (but without prescribing in advance what this life must be)'. This is arguably the challenge for work and organization studies, and for feminist thinking, that Butler's recent writing on the relationship between precarity and politics presents.
27 On this latter point, Charpentier and Barillas emphasize that Butler's phrasing must be understood not simply in a biological sense (for example, in terms of life span), but with reference to the more Arendtian-inspired ability to project a sense of self into the future, living life with hope and 'an enduring sense' that one's life will persist (Butler, 2015: 20). See also Didier Fassin's (2018) *Life: A Critical User's Manual*, which makes a similar point about how life expectancy reflects the unequal social value placed upon human lives (as well as Riach, 2025 for a more developed discussion).
28 In *Frames of War* Butler (2009a) distinguishes between *precariousness* as a shared, human condition, and *precarity* as socially contoured, situated vulnerability. While the language they use evolves, this distinction remains fundamental to Butler's writing on mutual recognition of our shared but situated vulnerability as the basis of ethics and politics.
29 Crucial for Butler, of course, is the related question of how networks of solidarity, governance mechanisms and organizational infrastructures might be implemented, 'without the predictable forms of paternalism' (Butler and Worms, 2023: 69).
30 On this point, Butler reminds us that because all social relations are in part characterized by negativity, relationality is not simply 'a good thing', a sign of love or interconnectedness; it is rather 'a vexed and ambivalent field in which the question of ethical obligation *has to be worked out*' (Butler, 2020b: 10).
31 In this sense Butler effectively inverts the state of nature thesis animated in the figure of the 'lucky man', showing how rather than being unencumbered from the start we are, throughout our lives, mutually interdependent.

³² In its critique of this discourse through a foregrounding of the meaning and value of embodied relationality, a feminist understanding runs counter to a normative view of vulnerability as a condition that must be 'overcome' in order to reassert the 'I' as a self-reliant, self-contained subject. At its worst, this neoliberal individualistic subject is 'constituted through, and inhabited by, processes of de-subjectifying others, rendering them usable, employable, but then eventually into waste matter, or of no use: always available, always expendable' (Butler and Athanasiou, 2013: 27, cited in Kenny and Fotaki, 2023: 346).

³³ Kaasila-Pakanen et al (2024: 268) use the French term '*colligere*' (to gather, collate) to convey their sense of producing feminist knowledge as a relational effort to hold together ontological and epistemic space with openness, vulnerability and struggle. Vulnerable ways of knowing, they suggest, offer new possibilities for understanding one another and of knowledge creation by embracing paradigmatic plurality and embodied relationality. Such an approach embraces vulnerability 'not only as an existential condition but also as an epistemic attitude', rendering the self open to unknowing and/or to never fully knowing as a precondition for reflexive, relational understanding and interaction.

³⁴ This way of positioning 'the vulnerable' is therefore, in sociological and political terms, quite different to that of the 'precariat' in Guy Standing's (2014) account, particularly as the latter are imbued with the characteristics of a class and, by implication, the capacity to exercise agency. 'The vulnerable', by contrast, are implicitly divest of agency either because of the extreme circumstances in which they find themselves (for example, as 'victims') or because their capacity to act is undermined by a particular attribute (for example, their age, physicality or mental health status).

³⁵ In Hegelian (1977 [1807]) terms, we might think of what Scully (2013) calls 'ascribed global vulnerabilities' simply as a form of misrecognition on the basis of organizing norms underpinned by a 'non-disabled' ontological and embodied ideal.

³⁶ A notable exponent of this view is Alistair MacIntyre (2013: 1), who says that the 'dependence on particular others for protection and sustenance is most obvious in early childhood and old age. But between these first and last stages our lives are characteristically marked by longer or shorter periods of injury, illness or other disablement, and some among us are disabled for their entire lives', implying that that there are long stretches in many people's lives during which a person is independent, not in need of care and, relatively speaking, invulnerable. This is quite different from the view, as articulated by Eva Feder Kittay (2019: xii) in her book, *Love's Labour*, that 'we are all interdependent', a perspective that challenges the erroneous assumption that vulnerability is 'a characteristic of, and limited to, disabled persons or the very young, old, or ill' (Scully, 2013: 215).

Chapter 2

¹ Thinking about the centrality of breathing to embodied existence through an etymological lens reminds us of the common Greek origins of the term 'pneuma' (to 'breathe' or 'blow'), and the same term's Latin connotations that include 'spirit' and 'soul'. Breathing is vital to our existence, and our essence.

² This scenario is one that Franco Berardi (2018: 71) describes as 'bodily conspiration' (a 'breathing together'), a philosophical diagnosis of what society is or could/should be that, he argues, is becoming increasing untenable in our current circumstances, particularly in a context (post-AIDS, post-COVID-19) in which contact with others' bodies is regarded as dangerous. As he puts it, referring to the decline of opportunities and desires for bodily conspiration, 'since meaning emerges in the dimension of affective conjunction, the possibility of meaningful exchange rapidly dissolves when the community of bodies disaggregates' (Berardi, 2018: 72).

3 A parallel point is made by James Dutton (2022) in his recent discussion of Sloterdijk's (2009, 2011) writing on atmospheric mediation. In a similar vein to Merleau-Ponty, Dutton draws attention to how airborne transmission is a consequence of breathing the same air, but he goes on to emphasize that air conditioning, by attempting to reproduce identical atmospheres across the globe, increases viral and bacterial spread. As a manifestation of our efforts to make air 'objective' – in both senses of attempting to define it according to its material properties *and* believing in the possibility of a uniform version of it – air conditioning, he argues, not only harms the planet; it eradicates the possibility of vital differences. This unreflexive, instrumental commitment to replicable sameness props up contemporary globalized cultures and modes of exchange depending on them, he argues, so that (ironically) populations become far more susceptible to the rapid spread of respiratory epidemics. To put it simply, his view is that virality is increased by the 'sameness' of objective air conditioning, and that vitality is depleted by it.

4 https://breathelife2030.org/the-issue/who-it-affects/

5 Robin Wall Kimmerer (2013: 238) also acknowledges, however, that a philosophy of reciprocity is 'beautiful in the abstract, but the practical is much harder'.

6 A notable example of this is Hindmarsh and Pilnick's (2007) study of the coordination work undertaken by anaesthetic teams responsible for managing others' respiratory vulnerability, a study that highlights the importance of intercorporeal, dialogically enacted knowing in the real-time coordination of embodied labour.

7 Another notable text that has focused on the relationship between precarity and respiration is Barbara Ellen Smith's (1981) work on the West Virginian 'black lung' movement in the 1960s. Ellen Smith raised awareness of interacting socio-political perspectives within this movement, namely opposing medical, occupational and cultural forces that sought to define the 'black lung' illness and how it should be recognized, treated and responded to.

8 Here Pérezts et al (2024) draw on Abram's (2005: 174) point that breathing opens up scope to recognize and affirm 'our corporeal immersion in the depths of a body much larger than our own'.

9 See also Adriana Cavarero's (2016) critique of rectitude in *Inclinations* (as discussed in Chapter 1, and later).

10 The body in this sense, as Daniela Pianezzi (2025: 114) notes, serves as an ethically significant reminder (literally a 're-membering') 'not to overlook the condition of vulnerability that unifies and connects us'.

11 This indicates that the problem is less one of a persistent dualism between verticality and inclination, as mapped out by Cavarero (2016), but that of *disinclination* – a scenario depicted by Scottish painter, Peter Howson, in his 1992 work, *The Age of Apathy*, which conveys the embodied violence underpinning and ensuing from a scenario in which we simply don't care.

12 In making sense of the relationship between recognition and recognizability, Butler draws on Fanon's (2007 [1967]: 91) notion (reflected in their earlier writing on the heterosexual matrix) of a 'historical-racial schema' that functions as a perception and projection of what is viable, as '*an interpretive casing*' (Butler, 2020b: 113, emphasis added). This, Butler notes, bears a direct relationship to Merleau-Ponty's notion of the 'bodily schema' – '*the organization of tacit and structuring bodily relations within the world*' as well as the act of 'constituting oneself within the terms made available by that world' (Butler, 2020b: 113, emphasis added). In making this link, Butler poses a series of important questions about how this framing works to establish relative values for different lives, asking: 'How do we account for the differential ways in which lives and deaths matter or fail to matter? … How do such differentiated modes of perception … operate, as a set of uncritically

accepted presuppositions' (Butler, 2020b: 114–115)? Questions such as these are always, Butler maintains, '*bound up with ... recognition*' (Butler, 2020b: 116, emphasis added).

13 We might even go as far as to say that Butler reads Hegel first, politically, tracing the power relations shaping recognizability, and second, sociologically, situating the Hegelian struggle for recognition in social relations, structures and inequalities.

14 This is a particularly gendered problem as personal protective equipment (PPE) is normally designed to fit men's bodies so that safety clothing and footwear, armoured body wear, eye and face masks, protective head gear and so on leave women more physically exposed than men.

15 A similar post-dualist ontology underpins recent work by Nancy Harding and colleagues (Harding et al, 2022: 650), which, drawing on both Karan Barad and Judith Butler, emphasizes how the body is 'constituted through performative acts in which material flesh and discourses of bodies are intertwined' in ways that open up embodiment as agency – a theme we return to in later chapters.

Chapter 3

1 *In Memoriam A.H.H.* was completed by Tennyson in 1849 as a requiem for Arthur Henry Hallam. The less often quoted preceding line, 'I feel it, when I sorrow most' resonates with Butler's emphasis on the affirmative potential of ek-static loss.

2 In characteristic fashion, Butler seems to evoke several meanings of the term 'managed' here, denoting both a state of being controlled, categorized, ordered and contained, and of enacting a performative achievement demonstrative of the capacity to act and to engage in struggle.

3 I use the term 'endurance' here and throughout this chapter to refer not to the capacity for resilience or performance (for example, in the often highly individualized sense in which the word might be used in relation to extreme sports or profit accumulation), but borrowing from Butler (who, in turn, draws from Arendt), in reference to the ability to persist; that is, to elicit recognition in an affirmative, intersubjective sense of 'mattering' in the sphere of appearance. In the case of social relations of enduring, the latter refers in simple terms to being remembered, recollected, commemorated and/or grieved – to having 'grievable' capacity, as Butler puts it.

4 To recap, ek-statis is the term Butler uses, drawing from Hegel (1977 [1807]), to refer to the ethical state attached to living a life characterized by 'standing outside of oneself' (Butler, 2004a: 258).

5 Moya Lloyd (2007: 144) sums this up when she notes that 'the point is that Hegel fails to acknowledge the fact that the scene of recognition itself assumes a set of cultural norms – or a normative horizon – that conditions who is recognizable as human'. Arguably, what Lloyd describes here, and what Butler adds to Hegel, is an understanding of recognizability as the *organizing* condition of recognition.

6 This is an argument that Butler develops in *Frames of War: When is Life Grievable?* (Butler, 2009a), which examines the marking off of categories of personhood in the context of the US military's attacks in the Middle East, focusing particularly on the mainstream media's role in portraying Muslim people as deserving targets. Butler's point here is that the media 'frames' war in such a way that we do not recognize as fully human all of those who are harmed by it, in order to justify the actions of aggressors.

7 For Butler, being dispossessed means to be subject to 'processes and ideologies by which persons are disowned and abjected by normative and normalizing power that define cultural intelligibility and that *regulate the distribution of vulnerability*' (Butler and Athanasiou, 2013: 2, emphasis added). In other words, dispossession helps us to understand the relationship between shared, existential (ontological) and ascribed (social) forms of precarity as an

organizational one, in which the latter is an exploitation of the former, rendering us *all* vulnerable, but not homogeneously so – a line of argument that recurs throughout this book.

8 As a reminder, Butler (1993) uses the term 'matter' to refer both to having value (to being of significance) and to having a material substance or presence that is imbued with the capacity to signify something of value.

9 This question raises the radical potential that emerges from loss, foreclosure and normative exclusion in a way that connects to Butler's (2008) engagement with Honneth (1995), positing a relational enactment of struggle as one possible outcome of communities that are collectively negated (see Butler and Athanasiou, 2013: 36–37).

10 Responses to the mass shooting that took place on a Latino LGBTQIA+ night at the Pulse nightclub in Orlando, Florida in June 2016 illustrate this, with the tragedy engendering, on the one hand, racist trans- and homophobia, and on the other (fuelled largely by social media), what some commentators described at the time as a kind of mass 'grieving hysteria', elements of which involved an insidious co-optation of grief and loss (see Segal, 2018; Tyler, 2019).

11 Raudon (2022: 84) makes an important point when she notes that the dead are largely interred on Hart Island in three deep plots, each holding approximately 150 adults or 1,000 babies. While the island is commonly referred to as a mass grave, this term is not strictly accurate, as the term 'mass grave' suggests a pit where bodies are piled together. Rather, the island is better understood as consisting of a series of randomly positioned *massed* graves, where the dead are communally, if predominantly anonymously, interred in individual pine boxes (or in the case of those known to have died from AIDS-related illnesses, lead coffins). Most accounts suggest that official records are somewhat vague, and where they are precise, they are often contradictory, but some also suggest that full details of burials are kept so that graves can be identified, and bodies can be disinterred when necessary.

12 On 1 July 2021, the administration and management of Hart Island transferred from the New York City Department of Corrections to the City's Department of Parks and Recreation, thus (formally) ending an association with incarceration that had been in place since the island's first use in the 1860s. While for some (see Brouwer and Morris, 2021) this transfer is not enough to eradicate the complex legacy of this historical association, and its grounding in racialized and class-based systems of oppression, others (for example, Byers, 2022: 2–3, emphasis added) are more optimistic, noting how 'if lingering social stigma and practical obstacles can be addressed, this could be an incredible opportunity to transform Hart Island into a multifunctional, modern burial site … *to create a space that offers genuine healing, reconciliation, connection and community* for the living'. Yet for Byers (2022: 6), 'a damaging, one-dimensional public perception of the island as a deeply shameful and degrading site' represents a substantial obstacle to the island being re-imagined in this way, noting how this reputation has served to create an additional 'layer of suffering' for the communities of those interred there. Therefore, 'without unpicking the historic threads of this legacy and the ways in which cultural attitudes to pauper burial have endured, any real transformation … will be hindered by this powerful public perception, and the enduring social stigma associated with being buried there'.

13 Byers outlines how the COVID-19 pandemic represents one of those rare historical moments when New Yorkers from across a wider social spectrum than are normally interred there were temporarily or permanently buried on Hart Island as the City authorities struggled to cope with rapidly rising mortality rates and a much larger number of unclaimed dead bodies than usual in ways that were as humane as possible (see also Raudon, 2022). For Byers (2022: 8), this scenario potentially offered an opportunity,

a 'critical moment' as it were, to reconsider how we recognize people when they are dead, and to explore the possibility of how we might rethink an anonymous burial 'as an inherently shameful endeavour' and to explore the relational possibilities attached to reconceptualizing burial sites as playing a multi-faceted role within a community, as well as offering both individual and mass burial within the same geographic space (see Pianezzi and Tyler, 2025).

14 A small stone pillar marks the only individually identified grave on the island, of the first child known to have died from AIDS-related causes in the United States, who was buried with the inscription 'SC-B1, 1985' (an abbreviation of Special Child, Baby), but (at least at the time of writing), no proper AIDS memorial exists there, despite Hart Island playing a major role in the history of the AIDS epidemic in New York. Rees (2020: 9) notes that more people who died of AIDS-related causes are believed to buried on Hart Island than in any other place in the United States, perhaps even the world.

15 Keene (2019: 40) contrasts this anonymity and detachment with the City's National September 11 Memorial, which contains a secure repository in which unidentified fragments of human remains are stored behind a blue tile inscribed with a quote from the Roman poet, Virgil: 'No day shall erase you from the memory of time.'

16 In this aspect of her work and elsewhere, Adriana Cavarero draws on Arendt's argument that the question of 'who' somebody is in their uniqueness can only be understood through the ways in which their lives are narrated. For Arendt (1998 [1958]: 97), a recognizable, liveable life (*bios*) is one which is 'narratable', constituting 'a story with enough coherence to be told'.

17 On this point, and unlike Butler (2005), Cavarero does not develop an extended critical analysis of the terms or conditions of narratability. In her writing, narrative is framed largely in affirmative terms, rather than in relation to a discussion of the normative compulsions or constraints attached to recognizability, as it is in Butler's (see Butler, 2021a, 2021b).

18 Cavarero (2000: 37, emphasis added) goes on to emphasize that it is unity (a shared sense of familiarity) that stories told about us ideally confer. In this sense, Cavarero is determined to appreciate the Arendtian emphasis on the uniqueness of each person; yet she is equally concerned not to neglect the desire for unity, as she claims Arendt does, noting the shared etymological root that these two terms have in common as a good indication of the importance of understanding the narratable self as desiring both uniqueness and unity: 'from the beginning, *uniqueness* announces and promises to identity a *unity* that the self is not likely to renounce'. Cavarero (2000: 72) is also at pains to point out, however, that 'this unity does not have to be understood as a homogeneity'.

19 In a recent essay, Butler notes, for instance: 'I take very seriously the Hegelian claim that we are the sorts of creatures who desire recognition, and who come to understand ourselves in the social relations by which recognition is conferred and received' (Butler, 2021a: 44).

20 Here Butler develops their critique of Honneth's (1995) typology of recognition, arguing that the latter presupposes 'an existing subject who attributes intelligibility (or value) to another' (Butler, 2021a: 46). This strikes Butler as an insufficiently dialectical position in so far as it fails to reflexively interrogate the conditions of possibility governing the formation of the subject. *Contra* Honneth and drawing explicitly from Hegel, Butler's theory of recognition emerges, in this sense, as a critique of recognizability. For Butler, when we ask who emerges as an intelligible life, as a recognizable subject, 'we are asking about the matrices of subject formation, the fields of intelligibility and recognizability into which and by which any of us emerge. They make some of us very recognizable and cast some of us as nearly unrecognizable, depending on the terms of recognition themselves' (Butler, 2021a: 46).

21. It is worth noting in this respect that until public condemnation put an end to the policy in 2015, bodies due for burial on Hart Island were automatically made available for unconsented dissection (Keene, 2019). As Raudon (2022: 92) puts it, this practice was significant as it was not only an ethical violation; it 'clearly signalled the deceased's value to the City, classifying them as a physical resource [matter] rather than a person'.
22. Presumably because of Hart Island's continuing stigma, other narratives, however, refer to family members' desire to exhume bodies buried there and to have them re-interred in marked graves (for example, in their home towns), although the cost-prohibitive nature of this is also noted.
23. In his critique of the performative act of Queen Elizabeth II's funeral being 'declared' a day of national mourning in so many parts of the world, author and academic Clint Burnham (2022) makes the point that asking about grievability means confronting uncomfortable truths about the kind of society such acts perpetuate, especially when we are made to understand, via declarations of public holidays as national days of mourning, for instance, that individuals such as a monarch are somehow, inherently, more grievable than others (effectively rendering invisible, or naturalizing, the organizing processes involved).

Chapter 4

1. My focus here is not on staring as such (as a physiological or pathological phenomenon), but rather on staring encounters in social interactions. Although there are many instances when a stare might be intended or experienced affirmatively (for example, during a romantic or erotic encounter, or in instances of intense engagement), sociologists and philosophers tend to understand staring as a largely negating experience, one that induces feelings of guilt, shame, fear or panic, producing a traumatizing sense of being under a process of scrutiny from which one is unable to escape, as Sartre (1968) describes it in his novel, *The Reprieve*.
2. See Philip Hancock's (2008) work on feminist writer, Rosalyn Diprose for a more developed discussion of the relationship between ethics, generosity and openness to the Other..
3. Sartre (1968: 315) emphasizes this in his allusion to the paradox of being stared at: 'he who sees me causes me to be; I am as he sees me'.
4. In her account of growing up in a care home for disabled children, artist Alison Lapper (2005: 25–26, emphasis added) recalls in her memoir, *My Life in My Hands*, her memories of being subject to the objectifying effects of the clinical gaze. As she describes it: 'In the early years before I started going to school, my life had two aspects. First, there was the domestic side of things: eating, sleeping, washing and socializing. And then there was the medical side where we would be examined, looked at, photographed and appraised by a continual visitation of various groups of doctors. A nurse would come to the dorm, consult the list on her clipboard, and call out the names. The chosen group would toddle outside where a kind of handcart was waiting. It was a bit like a small cattle truck with very high sides and no roof. It was impossible to see anything once you were in and the tailgate was pulled up. Of course, there were no seat belts or safety devices, and we just rolled from side to side in a jumble of bodies. … Once there, a nurse would help me up on to an examining table, where I would like naked or sometimes with just my knickers on while a group of ten to fifteen older medical professionals would make a circle around me. They would then poke this or that part or pull that part or rotate another part, all the while conversing in that detached medic-speak which is impossible to understand if you are not a doctor yourself. And sometimes they took photographs. They rarely addressed me, and I could tell that I was just an object of curiosity for them, nothing more. … Of course, there was no question of anyone asking our permission. *We somehow weren't quite*

human enough to be asked if we were happy to be sprawled naked on the table for examination by the medical profession.'

5. In this context it is perhaps not surprising that fashion modelling, stripping and pornography are among the very few areas of work in which the gender pay gap is inverted and men, on average, tend to earn less than women – see Mears and Connell's (2015) analysis of the gender politics of display work for a detailed account.

6. See also Garland-Thomson (2006).

7. In her book, *Anatomizing Embodiment and Organization Theory*, Karen Dale (2000) highlights the enduring and organizing power of the conviction that visual observation is the source of truth, showing how this epistemological faith underpins the history of modern science and its anatomizing impetus, including within the field of organization studies. And as Michel Foucault (1991) documented in his writing on the clinical gaze, scientific observation and medical diagnosis require sustained ocular scrutiny, imagined to be 'untainted' by the medical or scientific professional's subjectivity. The microscope, stethoscope and so on, and later technologies such as X-rays and sonography, all act as powerful conduits for objectification, in both an epistemic and ontological sense, positioning the observer and the observed through the anatomizing effects of scientific scrutiny, rendering those who are subject to it as 'matter'. As Foucault emphasized it, while the growing dominance of medical science eased disease, pain and suffering, it also extended its notion of human pathology into the social world in disciplinary ways, exposing the body to scientific authority, for example, via the invasive stare of the medical expert (as described by Alison Lapper).

8. In this sense, staring arguably acts as a 'excessive' reminder of embodiment, as the denial of death and vulnerability depends upon the negation of our shared, embodied existence and the disappearance of 'our' bodies to ourselves, resulting in the 'dys-appearance' (simultaneous invisibility and hyper-invisibility) of injured, ill, disabled or older bodies. Staring therefore 'jolts' us out of the reification of our purportedly disembodied, invulnerable ways of being, dependent as these are upon a 'forgetting' of our mutually vulnerable intercorporeality, disturbing the taken-for-grantedness of our bodies and revealing the myth of independent, self-sufficient individualism for what it is – a pretentious conceit.

9. See the documentary film, *Liebe Perla*, for an account of Nazi doctor Josef Mengele's treatment of the seven Ovitz siblings at Auschwitz where, it seemed, their dwarfism protected them from immediate extermination, as happened to many people with disabilities sent there and to other camps, not because of any recognition of their human rights, but because of their value as entertainers and/or specimens, according them a precarious 'safety' as a result of the objectifying gaze to which they were subject. In *Liebe Perla*, the eldest sibling, Perla Ovitz, reflects on her ambivalent 'gratitude' for her and her brothers and sisters' status as novelties that effectively enabled them to survive from their arrival at Auschwitz in May 1944 until the camp's liberation in January 1945.

10. A notable illustration of this can be found in sociologist Jessica Gerrard's (2019) study of the embodied labour carried out by homeless people, in which she shows how the way people look carries value in ways that conflate the commercial and affective in economies of exchange that are underpinned by moral judgements of deservingness, and worth. Drawing on a multi-city (Melbourne, London, San Francisco) study of homeless street press sellers (selling *The Big Issue* and *Street Sheet* direct to the public) to explore the ways in which contemporary practices of charity and care are carried out through individualized marketplace exchanges, Gerrard's research foregrounds the importance of street sellers embodying the right 'look', revealing how smiling and being (or looking) happy is a performative expectation that must be managed in the face of poverty and precarity at

the same time as vendors are required not to look 'too clean' or well-nourished so as to appear as 'undeserving'. To be able to sustain themselves, even at a basic level, Gerrard found that homeless street vendors have to look vulnerable, but not overly so, in order to appear as worthy but not hopeless causes.

[11] See Christopher Lasch (1980) for a critique of what he calls our 'culture of narcissism', in which we relate to ourselves and one another as preening, anxiety-ridden, self-obsessed individuals.

[12] Staring of course interrupts this arrangement, exposing those who are subject to it to what, drawing from Goffman's (1986) writing on stigmatization, we might term 'uncivil attention' (in the way that Sartre evokes).

[13] Jean-Luc Nancy (1991: 1–43) has put it similarly – 'the un-exposable is the non-existent'; in other words, everyone exists by 'disclosing' themselves to one another within a scene in which, by appearing to one another, everyone is shown to be a unique existent.

[14] Here Cavarero's argument is not dissimilar to Butler's (Hegelian) insistence on the ek-static nature of the subject.

[15] An example of the inverse of this can perhaps be found in the 'visual social cleansing' of urban spaces that takes place ahead of major civic events. In the run up to the Olympic Games in Paris 2024 for instance, thousands of homeless people were reportedly removed from the streets, including from temporary shelters. Those moved on included asylum seekers, sex workers and drug addicts, as well as families and children who were already living in highly precarious circumstances, making life impossible for those affected, and for the networks of support that they needed access to (for example, food and clothing banks, and shelters, community healthcare provision and so on) in order to continue to function at a basic, subsistence level.

[16] Here Susan Ashley reminds us of a key point that Lynne Segal (2018: 265–266, emphasis added) makes in her book, *Radical Happiness* – namely that public spaces in which to assemble and realize democratic potential are vital to opening up possibilities for new publics to come into being 'by means of concerted actions, *whether of resistance, celebration or mourning*'. Ashley's example of the Chattri Indian war memorial brings each of these three elements together, enacting and materializing resistance in and through a commemorative space in which both mourning and celebration 'takes place', as Butler (2005) might put it.

[17] In contrast to the modes of solidarity that Ashley (2015) describes, another example of negation relating to themes explored in Chapter 3 is discussed by Rohit Varman and Nidhi Srinivas (2025) in their work on what they describe, drawing on Mbembe (2019), as the 'necroptics' of colonial power relations. They document how over 14 million Indian deaths from influenza in 1918 came to be erased from visual memory via media reporting that not only rendered these deaths invisible, but also occluded the profits extracted from this huge, but largely undocumented, loss of life. By developing the concept of 'necroptics', Varman and Srinivas draw critical attention to how visual violence, through practices of mediated erasure, organizes the contours of vulnerability to create untraceable lives in racially contoured and caste-based deathscapes.

[18] Returning to themes considered in the previous chapter, what Ashley (2015) highlights is a commemorative mode of appearing enacted in the interests of postcolonial justice, collective healing and social transformation. In this sense, what she describes is not dissimilar to the activities of the Hart Island Project discussed in Chapter 3, or the efforts of the Israeli-Palestinian group, Zochrot, to show how Israel's redemption narrative is inseparable from Palestinian dispossession. All of these modes of appearing, saying 'See, here!' as Butler puts it, illustrate the political potential of the collective, collaborative work of mourning when it is reflexive and immersed in mutual recognition of shared histories and circumstances of vulnerability. Movements such as Zochrot, Naomi Klein (2024) has

argued, are our best hope of exiting endless loops of genocidal histories, reclaiming spaces for intersubjectivity and carving out scope for remembering as a form of reconnecting as a body politic via spaces of co-appearance.

19   While Quinn's statue clearly had a very material form as a public artwork, British Iranian artist Anahita Harding's recent digital collaboration with Tate Modern, London, 'Are You Comfortable Yet?', has a similar effect. See https://www.waiwav.org/artists/anahita-harding

20   For Alison Lapper's (2005: 236, 247, emphasis added) own account of the Fourth Plinth project, and her collaboration with Marc Quinn, see her book *Alison Lapper: My Life in My Hands* in which she reflects on her initial misgivings about the work, asking: 'statues are created and exhibited to give pleasure, to be admired. Would anybody be able to admire the statue of a naked, pregnant, disabled woman?', and on her later sense of its recognitive potential: 'in many ways, I think it makes the ultimate statement about disability: that *it can be as beautiful and as valid a form of being as any other.*'

21   hooks (1992) goes on to emphasize how separating people off through segregation or being shut away, or covering up devalued human differences, arrests opportunities for mutual recognition, so that being seen is both an ethical and political imperative. To put it simply, to be recognized, one has to appear.

Chapter 5

1   Thank you to Daniela Pianezzi for sharing and recollecting this incident with me.

2   Tronto (1993) discerns four elements of care as constitutive features of a 'good society': attentiveness to others' needs; taking responsibility for caring about those needs; having competence to give care according to those needs; and responsiveness between care-taker and care-receiver. Valuable though this framing is, it arguably underplays the significance of recognition of our mutual but socially situated vulnerability to relationality, and hence ethical social relations.

3   This view is of course resonant of Levinas's contention that vulnerability is an ontological aspect of human life, ambivalently connected both to the perpetual risk of being exposed to violence, and to the ethical responsibility not to engender violence.

4   This way of thinking about vulnerability *as* resistance is indebted to Hannah Arendt's notion that resistance 'always begins with those who cannot live with themselves and suffer violence towards others – *whatever* the circumstances and however powerless they are' (Stonebridge, 2025: 231).

5   For Cavarero (2021c: x) it is the 'plural, horizontal, nonviolent, generative and affirmative' forms of interaction that can be found in social movements that, drawing on the Arendtian notion of politics, can be described as 'surging democracy'.

6   In characteristic style, Caverero (2021c: 12) turns to the etymon *surgere* (a 'springing fourth') to explain her Arendtian understanding of politics, denoting an emergent pouring out. As Cavarero puts it, 'in revisiting the Arendtian idea of politics, the term surging is intended to express these various connotations, accentuating the experience of democracy in its germinal, birthing state … generative, incipient and spontaneous'; in other words, nascent in the Arendtian sense. For Cavarero, the democratic surge is what takes place when a democracy is experienced 'precisely at its incipient moment' (Cavarero, 2021c: 47). Developing this, she reminds us that for Butler (2015), when bodies assemble they assert the right to appear and to exercise freedom, to demand a liveable life.

7   Unfortunately, on these points, Cavarero once again veers close to the essentialism that has been noted by others in their critiques of her writing, and in earlier chapters. My sense is that, despite beautiful prose and insightful work which reflects a rich body of knowledge acquired through a lifetime of philosophical reading and writing, Cavarero's thinking on gendered subjectivity lacks dialectical nuance and this leads her simply (and

frustratingly) to invert the hierarchies she sets out to critique rather than problematize them in the way that Butler's and Segal's more meticulous analyses do.

8   Important to note here is that for Arendt, Butler and Cavarero alike, acting 'in concert' does not mean acting harmoniously and certainly not homogeneously; rather, it evokes a sense of exercising agency, collectively, in order to work towards a common struggle. What Caverero calls 'democracy' in this sense corresponds, in Arendt's terminology, to her understanding of what constitutes the political.

9   Cavarero (2021c: 7, emphasis added) notes that on this point, Arendt can come across as somewhat 'overemphatic', but she also reminds us of the context in which her work took shape, in response to the totalitarian catastrophe which Arendt sets out to make sense of, and with it, to reimagine the human condition, reconceiving of politics (and thereby ethics) in terms of a participatory experience of plurality that, as Cavarero puts it, is 'completely *incompatible with a model of vertical, hierarchical organization*'.

10 Cavarero (2021c: 26) is explicit here that what Arendt (1998 [1958]) calls the 'space of appearance' is for her (and for this reason), a 'surging democracy' – 'always in the making', its nascent status 'is produced and reproduced, every time anew, by the interactions of different concrete pluralities'.

11 See Karen Lee Ashcraft's book, *Wronged and Dangerous* (2022), for a fascinating discussion of the relationship between what she calls 'viral masculinity', populism and political disaffection.

12 It is interesting that Italian feminist, Simona Forti (2021), discerns in Arendt's writing a 'pure concept of what constitutes the political'; understood through a feminist lens, we could say much the same about vulnerability – namely, that it provides us with a fundamental, foundational starting point for ethics.

13 I use the term 'workable' here and throughout this chapter to refer not to some pragmatic notion of functionality in a practical or even performative sense, but rather, drawing on Butler (2015) and Cavarero (2021c) and, in turn, Arendt (1998 [1958]), to understand the quality of being recognized as having the capacity to contribute to social relations in ways that have meaning and value. For some, workability might involve the expenditure of substantial effort, time and skill; for others, it might mean simply existing – asserting or persisting as a presence, enduring, and in doing so, occupying a vital space of co-appearance. In this sense, as Arendt explains it (and as Butler has developed with reference to Beauvoir [see Tyler, 2019]), 'the accomplishment lies in the performance itself' (Arendt, 1993 [1961]: 154).

14 See Philip Hancock's (2024) work on organizational recognition schemes for a critique of the reificatory effects of both of these forms of recognition that Celikates (2021) describes, and Chapter 2 for a more detailed discussion of his critique.

15 As the Care Collective (2020) note, the effort required here is perhaps better captured via the French term, '*travails*', meaning simultaneously our labours and our troubles.

16 In her discussion of Europe's migration crisis, Marianna Fotaki draws on sociologist Zygmunt Bauman's (2016: 19) point that we are currently faced with 'a crisis of humanity', and the only exit from this crisis is to recognize our interdependence, and to find new ways to live together in solidarity and cooperation, amidst strangers who may hold opinions and preferences, or lead lives according to values and in circumstances, that may be very different from, or in conflict with, our own.

17 In *What World is This?* Butler (2022: 12–13) writes about the pandemic as a moment in which the world was 'exhibited or disclosed' as an object of critical, reflexive scrutiny. The book considers the question, 'in what kind of world could the COVID pandemic happen?', framing this question as a phenomenological one, by asking 'what *kind of* world is this?'. Butler then proceeds to examine this via a related ethical and political question, 'how are

we to live in this world?'. From these, a further set of questions follow (or are referred back to): 'What makes for a liveable life? And what makes an inhabitable world?' Butler concludes that the pandemic was a moment of reflexive recognition, because through it (albeit for a brief period), we came to know that 'if we ask the question *what makes a liveable life?* we do so precisely because we know that under some conditions it surely is not – for example, under unliveable conditions of poverty, incarceration, destitution, or social and sexual violence' (Butler, 2022: 29, original emphasis).

[18] Titus Stahl (2021: 187, n. 18) notes how, in the extended German version of *Giving an Account of Oneself*, Butler emphasizes how questioning the norms of recognition carries with it the risk of no longer being a recognizable subject according to the terms established by, and practised within, current regimes. The 'radical ambivalent' view that Stahl works with, to explore the emancipatory potential in Hegel's narrative, sees emancipation in the taking of this risk anyway, an approach that opens up the possibility of connecting this political-ontological risk (*post*-recognition, or as a second order process, in Stahl's terms) alongside mutual recognition of the shared ethical-ontological risk brought about by our primordial (*pre*-recognition) vulnerability, engendered by our mutual interdependence.

[19] Different from my own reading, for a more affirmative view of this scenario, emphasizing applause for healthcare workers in Italy during the pandemic as an act of 'solidarity and gratitude', see Cavarero (2021c: xiv).

[20] Trump's senior advisor, Elon Musk, appeared on stage at a Conservative Political Action Conference in Washington, DC in February 2025, brandishing a red chainsaw gifted to him by Argentina's ultraconservative President Javier Milei (see Kenny, 2025).

[21] Antithetical to the scenario in Butler's commentary is what Lynne Segal (2018: 206–207) has described as 'radical happiness' – the capacity for transformative, collective experiences of joy. For Segal, radical happiness emerges in and through experiences of resistance and renewal, affirmative interaction, and the generation of socially transformative energy such as that found in feminist and other political forms of activism in the 1960s and 1970s, and more recent assemblies such as the feminist demonstrations that took place across the world following Trump's (first) inauguration as US president in January 2017 (see also Tyler, 2019). For Segal, radical happiness embodies 'the significance of a politics of hope', one that (in Arendtian terms, as a rediscovery of the hidden treasures of collective optimism) springs forth from a 'revival of revolutionary imagination'. See also Olivia Guaraldo's (2018) discussion of the re-cognition of public happiness as a collective 'remembering' of forgotten emotion.

[22] https://www.theguardian.com/commentisfree/2025/feb/06/trump-sadism-judith-butler

References

Abram, D. (2005) 'Between the body and the breathing earth: A reply to Ted Toadvine', *Environmental Ethics* 27(2): 171–190.

Agamben, G. (1998) *Homo Sacer: Sovereign Power and Bare Life*. Stanford University Press.

Ahmed, S. (2000) *Strange Encounters*. Routledge.

Ahmed, S. (2024) 'Wage theft, secrecy, and derealization of "ideal workers" in the Bangladesh garment industry', *Organization Studies* 45(6): 881–901.

Allen, I. (2020) 'Thinking with a feminist political ecology of air-and-breathing-bodies', *Body and Society* 26(2): 79–105.

Arendt, H. (1963) *Eichmann in Jerusalem: A Report on the Banality of Evil*. Penguin Classics.

Arendt, H. (1971) *The Life of the Mind*. Harcourt Brace.

Arendt, H. (1993 [1961]) *Between Past and Future: Eight Exercises in Political Thought*. Penguin.

Arendt, H. (1998 [1958]) *The Human Condition*. University of Chicago Press.

Ashcraft, K.L. (2022) *Wronged and Dangerous: Viral Masculinity and the Populist Pandemic*. Bristol University Press.

Ashley, S. (2015) 'Re-colonizing spaces of memorializing: The case of the Chattri Indian Memorial, UK', *Organization* 23(1): 29–46.

Baines, E. (2004) *Vulnerable Bodies*. Ashgate.

Battersby, C. (2021) 'Cavarero, Kant and the arcs of friendship', in T. Huzar and C. Woodford (eds) *Towards a Feminist Ethics of Nonviolence: Adriana Cavarero with Judith Butler, Bonnie Honig and Other Voices*. Fordham University Press, pp 109–120.

Bauman, Z. (2016) *Strangers at Our Door*. Polity.

Beauvoir, S. (2011 [1949]) *The Second Sex*. Trans by C. Borde and S. Maldvany-Chavallier. Vintage.

Berardi, F. (2018) *Breathing: Chaos and Poetry*. Semiotext(e).

Berger, J. (1972) *Ways of Seeing*. Penguin/BBC Books.

Berlant, L. (2011) *Cruel Optimism*. Duke University Press.

Bernini, L. (2021) 'Bad inclinations: Cavarero, queer theories and the drive', in T. Huzar and C. Woodford (eds) *Towards a Feminist Ethics of Nonviolence: Adriana Cavarero with Judith Butler, Bonnie Honig and Other Voices*. Fordham University Press, pp 121–130.

Boublil, E. (2018) 'The ethics of vulnerability and the phenomenology of interdependency', *Journal of the British Society for Phenomenology* 49(3): 183–192.

Bowring, J. (2011) 'Containing marginal memories: The melancholy landscapes of Hart Island (New York), Cockatoo Island (Sydney), and Ripapa Island (Christchurch)', *Memory Connection* 1(1): 251–270.

Boys, J. (ed) (2017) *Disability, Space, Architecture: A Reader*. Routledge.

Braidotti, R. (2020) 'We are in this together, but we are not one and the same', *Journal of Bioethical Inquiry* 17(4): 465–469.

Brouwer, D. and Morris, C. (2021) 'Decentring whiteness in AIDS memory: Indigent rhetorical criticism and the dead of Hart Island', *Quarterly Journal of Speech* 107(2): 160–184.

Brown, N. (2017). 'Anatomospheres: A "respiratory politics" of buildings and breath'. Discover Society, https://archive.discoversociety.org/2017/08/02/anatomospheres-a-respiratory-politics-of-buildings-and-breath/

Burnham, C. (2022) 'Decolonize the Queen's funeral: Why it shouldn't be a national holiday in Canada', *The Conversation*, 15 September.

Butler, J. (1987) *Subjects of Desire: Hegelian Reflections in Twentieth-Century France*. Columbia University Press.

Butler, J. (1988) 'Performative acts and gender constitution: An essay in phenomenology and feminist theory', *Theater Journal* 40(4): 519–531.

Butler, J. (1990) *Gender Trouble: Feminism and the Subversion of Identity*. Routledge.

Butler, J. (1993) *Bodies That Matter: On The Discursive Limits of 'Sex'*. Routledge.

Butler, J. (1997a) *Excitable Speech: A Politics of the Performative*. Routledge.

Butler, J. (1997b) *The Psychic Life of Power: Theories in Subjection*. Stanford University Press.

Butler, J. (2004a) *Precarious Life: The Powers of Mourning and Violence*. Verso.

Butler, J. (2004b) *Undoing Gender*. Routledge.

Butler, J. (2005) *Giving an Account of Oneself*. Fordham University Press.

Butler, J. (2008) 'Taking another's view: ambivalent implications', in A. Honneth (ed.) *Reification: A New Look at an Old Idea*. Oxford University Press, pp. 97–119.

Butler, J. (2009a) *Frames of War: When is Life Grievable?* Verso.

Butler, J. (2009b) 'Critique, dissent, disciplinarity', *Critical Inquiry* 35(4): 773–797.

Butler, J. (2015) *Notes Toward a Performative Theory of Assembly*. Harvard University Press.

Butler, J. (2016) 'Rethinking vulnerability and resistance', in J. Butler, Z. Gambetti and L. Sabsay (eds) *Vulnerability in Resistance*. Duke University Press, pp 12–27.

Butler, J. (2020a) 'On COVID-19, the politics of non-violence, necropolitics, and social inquality', Verso/British Library lecture, 29 July.

Butler, J. (2020b) *The Force of Nonviolence: An Ethico-Political Bind*. Verso.

Butler, J. (2021a) 'Recognition and the social bond: A response to Axel Honneth', in J. Butler, A. Honneth, A. Allen, R. Celikates, J.-P. Deranty, H. Ikäheimo, et al, *Recognition and Ambivalence*. Columbia University Press, pp 31–53.

Butler, J. (2021b) 'Recognition and mediation: A second reply to Axel Honneth', in J. Butler, A. Honneth, A. Allen, R. Celikates, J.-P. Deranty, H. Ikäheimo, et al, *Recognition and Ambivalence*. Columbia University Press, pp 61–68.

Butler, J. (2021c) 'Leaning out, caught in the fall: Interdependency and ethics in Cavarero', in T. Huzar and C. Woodford (eds) *Towards a Feminist Ethics of Nonviolence: Adriana Cavarero with Judith Butler, Bonnie Honig and Other Voices*. Fordham University Press, pp 46–62.

Butler, J. (2022) *What World is This? A Pandemic Phenomenology*. Columbia University Press.

Butler, J. (2024) *Who's Afraid of Gender?* Allen Lane.

Butler, J. (2025) 'Trump is unleashing sadism upon the world. But we cannot get overwhelmed', *The Guardian*, 6 February.

Butler, J. and Athanasiou, A. (2013) *Dispossession: The Performative in the Political*. Polity.

Butler, J. and Worms, F. (2023) *The Liveable and the Unliveable*. Trans by Z. Hanafi. Fordham University Press.

Byers, C. (2022) 'Rethinking New York's "dark shadow": Managing the unclaimed dead on Hart Island, 1869 to the present day', *Architecture MPS* 23(1): 1–18.

Byron, P. (2020) *Digital Media, Friendship and Cultures of Care*. Routledge.

The Care Collective (2020) *The Care Manifesto*. Verso.

Cavarero, A. (2000) *Relating Narratives: Storytelling and Selfhood*. Trans by P. Kottman. Routledge.

Cavarero, A. (2009) *Horrorism: Naming Contemporary Violence*. Trans by W. McCuaig. Columbia University Press.

Cavarero, A. (2016) *Inclinations: A Critique of Rectitude*. Trans by A. Minervini and A. Sitze. University of Stanford Press.

Cavarero, A. (2021a) 'Scenes of Inclination', in T. Huzar and C. Woodford (eds) *Towards a Feminist Ethics of Nonviolence: Adriana Cavarero with Judith Butler, Bonnie Honig and Other Voices*. Fordham University Press, pp 33–45.

Cavarero, A. (2021b) 'Coda', in T. Huzar and C. Woodford (eds) *Towards a Feminist Ethics of Nonviolence: Adriana Cavarero with Judith Butler, Bonnie Honig and Other Voices*. Fordham University Press, pp 177–186.

Cavarero, A. (2021c) *Surging Democracy: Notes on Hannah Arendt's Political Thought*. Trans by M. Gervase. University of Stanford Press.

Celikates, R. (2021) 'Beyond needs: Recognition, conflict and the limits of institutionalization', in J. Butler, A. Honneth, A. Allen, R. Celikates, J.-P. Deranty, H. Ikäheimo, et al, *Recognition and Ambivalence*. Columbia University Press, pp 257–291.

Charpentier, A. and Barillas, L. (2023) 'Introduction', in J. Butler and F. Worms, *The Liveable and the Unliveable*. Trans by Z. Hanafi. Fordham University Press, pp 1–10.

Cole, A. (2016) 'All of us are vulnerable, but some are more vulnerable than others: The political ambiguity of vulnerability studies – an ambivalent critique', *Critical Horizons* 17(2): 260–277.

Cortambert, L. and Dale, K. (2025) 'Relational solidarity on the streets: Shared vulnerability in face-to-face encounters', *Organization Studies* (online early).

Crimp, D. (1987) 'How to have promiscuity in an epidemic', *October* 43: 237–271.

Cutcher, L., Hardy, C., Riach, K. and Thomas, R. (2020) 'Reflections on reflexive theorizing: The need for a little more conversation', *Organization Theory* 1(3). https://journals.sagepub.com/doi/10.1177/2631787720944183

Dale, K. (2000) *Anatomizing Embodiment and Organization Theory*. Palgrave.

Dartington, T. (2010) *Managing Vulnerability: The Underlying Dynamics of Systems of Care*. Routledge.

Devenney, M. (2021) 'Querying Cavarero's rectitude', in T. Huzar and C. Woodford (eds) *Towards a Feminist Ethics of Nonviolence: Adriana Cavarero with Judith Butler, Bonnie Honig and Other Voices*. Fordham University Press, pp 131–140.

Dutton, J. (2022) 'Objective breathing: Peter Sloterdijk's atmospheric mediation', *Cultural Politics* 18(2): 151–172.

Etzioni, A. (1970) *Modern Organizations*, 2nd edn. Prentice Hall.

Fanon, F. (1967) *Black Skin, White Masks*. Routledge.

Fassin, D. (2018) *Life: A Critical User's Manual*. Polity.

Fineman, M. (2008) 'The vulnerable subject: Anchoring equality in the human condition', *Yale Journal of Law & Feminism* 20(1): 8–40.

Fisher, B. and Tronto, J. (1990) 'Toward a feminist theory of caring', in E. Abel and M. Nelson (eds) *Circles of Care*. SUNY Press, pp 35–62.

Forti, S. (2021) 'From horrorism to the gray zone', in T. Huzar and C. Woodford (eds) *Towards a Feminist Ethics of Nonviolence: Adriana Cavarero with Judith Butler, Bonnie Honig and Other Voices*. Fordham University Press, pp 141–150.

Fotaki, M. (2022) 'Solidarity in crisis? Community responses to refugees and forced migrants in the Greek islands', *Organization* 29(2): 295–323.

Foucault, M. (1991) *Discipline and Punish: The Birth of the Prison*. Trans by A. Sheridan. Penguin.

Foucault, M. (2004) *Society Must be Defended: Lectures at the Collège de France 1975–76*. Penguin.

Freud, S. (2001 [1917]) *The Complete Works of Sigmund Freud, Volume 17*. Vintage.

Fromm, E. (1977) *To Have or To Be?* Continuum.

Garland-Thomson, R. (2006) 'Ways of staring', *Journal of Visual Culture* 5(2): 173–192.

Garland-Thomson, R. (2009) *Staring: How We Look*. Oxford University Press.

Gerrard, J. (2019) 'The economy of smiles: Affect, labour and the contemporary deserving poor', *The British Journal of Sociology* 70(2): 424–441.

Gilroy, P. (2005) *After Empire: Melancholia or Convivial Culture?* Routledge.

Gilson, E. (2014) *The Ethics of Vulnerability: A Feminist Analysis of Social Life and Practice*. Routledge.

Goffman, E. (1980) *Behaviour in Public Places: Notes on the Social Organization of Gatherings*. Greenwood Press.

Goffman, E. (1986) *Stigma: Notes on the Management of Spoiled Identity*. Penguin.

Górska, M. (2016) *Breathing Matters: Feminist Intersectional Politics of Vulnerability*. PhD thesis, Linkoping University Press, Sweden.

Guaraldo, O. (2012) 'Thinkers that matter: On the thought of Judith Butler and Adriana Cavarero', *International Journal of Gender Studies* 1(1): 92–117.

Guaraldo, O. (2018) 'Public happiness: Revisiting an Arendtian hypothesis', *Philosophy Today* 62(2): 397–418.

Guenther, L. (2013) *Solitary Confinement: Social Death and Its Afterlives*. University of Minnesota Press.

Gullette, M.M. (2024) *American Eldercide*. University of Chicago Press.

Hancock, P. (2008) 'Embodied generosity and an ethics of organization', *Organization Studies* 29(10): 1357–1373.

Hancock, P. (2024) 'Employee recognition programmes: An immanent critique', *Organization* 31(2): 381–401.

Harding, N., Gilmore, S. and Ford, J. (2022) 'Matters that embodies: Agentive flesh and working bodies/selves', *Organization Studies* 43(5): 649–668.

Hegel, G.W.F. (1977 [1807]) *Phenomenology of Spirit*. Oxford University Press.

Hindmarsh, J. and Pilnick, A. (2007) 'Knowing bodies at work: Embodiment and ephemeral teamwork in anaesthesia', *Organization Studies* 28(9): 1395–1416.

Honig, B. (2021) 'How to do things with inclination: Antigones, with Cavarero', in T. Huzar and C. Woodford (eds) *Towards a Feminist Ethics of Nonviolence: Adriana Cavarero with Judith Butler, Bonnie Honig and Other Voices*. Fordham University Press, pp 63–89.

Honneth, A. (1995) *The Struggle for Recognition*. Trans by J. Anderson. Polity.

Honneth, A. (2008) *Disrespect: The Normative Foundations of Critical Theory*. Polity.

Honneth, A. (2021a) 'Recognition between power and normativity: A Hegelian critique of Judith Butler', in J. Butler, A. Honneth, A. Allen, R. Celikates, J.-P. Deranty, H. Ikäheimo, et al, *Recognition and Ambivalence*. Columbia University Press, pp 21–30.

Honneth, A. (2021b) 'Intelligibility and authority in recognition: A reply', in J. Butler, A. Honneth, A. Allen, R. Celikates, J.-P. Deranty, H. Ikäheimo, et al, *Recognition and Ambivalence*. Columbia University Press, pp 55–60.

hooks, b. (1992) *Black Looks: Race and Representation*. Turnaround.

Howard, N. (2020) 'A world of care', in M. Parker (ed) *Life after COVID-19: The Other Side of the Crisis*. Bristol University Press, pp 21–30.

Ikäheimo, H., Lepold, K. and Stahl, T. (2021) 'Introduction', in J. Butler, A. Honneth, A. Allen, R. Celikates, J.-P. Deranty, H. Ikäheimo, et al, *Recognition and Ambivalence*. Columbia University Press, pp 1–20.

Ingold, T. (2020) 'On breath and breathing: A concluding comment', *Body and Society* 26(2): 158–167.

Jagannathan, S. and Rai, R. (2022) 'The necropolitics of neoliberal state response to the Covid-19 pandemic in India', *Organization* 29(3): 426–448.

Jay, M. (1994) *Downcast Eyes: The Denigration of Vision in Twentieth Century French Thought*. University of California Press.

Johansson, J. and Wickström, A. (2023) 'Constructing a "different" strength: A feminist exploration of vulnerability, ethical agency, and care', *Journal of Business Ethics* 184: 317–331.

Jokela-Pansini, M. and Militz, E. (2022) 'Breathing new futures in polluted environments (Taranto, Italy)', *Transactions of the Institute of British Geographers*, https://rgs-ibg.onlinelibrary.wiley.com/doi/pdf/10.1111/tran.12532

Kaasila-Pakanen, A.-L., Jääskeläinen, P., Gao, G., Mandalaki, E., Zhang, L.E., Einola, K., et al (2024) 'Writing touch, writing (epistemic) vulnerability', *Gender, Work and Organization* 31(1): 264–283.

Karpf, A. (2021) *How Women Can Save the Planet*. Hurst.

Keene, M. (2019). *New York City's Hart Island: A Cemetery of Strangers*. The History Press.

Kenny, K. (2024) *Regulators of Last Resort: Whistleblowers, the Limits of the Law and the Power of Partnerships*. Cambridge University Press.

Kenny, K. (2025) 'After months of Trump's shock tactics, whistleblower groups are pushing back against attached on workers' rights', *The Conversation*, 25 March.

Kenny, K. and Fotaki, M. (2023) 'The costs and labour of whistleblowing: Bodily vulnerability and post-disclosure survival', *Journal of Business Ethics* 182: 341–364.

Kittay, E.F. (2019) *Love's Labour: Essays on Women, Equality, and Dependency*, 2nd edn. Routledge.

Klein, N. (2024) 'We need an exodus from Zionism', *The Guardian*, 24 April.

Kottman, P. (2000) 'Translator's introduction', in A. Cavarero, *Relating Narratives: Storytelling and Selfhood*. Routledge, pp vii–xxxi.

Kracauer, S. and Levin, T.Y. (1995) *The Mass Ornament: Weimer Essays*. Harvard University Press.

Lapper, A. (2005) *Alison Lapper: My Life in My Hands*. Simon & Schuster.

Lasch, C. (1980) *The Culture of Narcissism: American Life in an Age of Diminishing Expectations*. Warner Books.

Leogrande, S., Alessandrini, E., Stafoggia, M., Morabito, A., Nocioni, A. and Ancona, C. (2019) 'Industrial air pollution and mortality in the Taranto area, southern Italy: A difference-in-differences approach', *Environment International* 132: 105–130.

Lepold, K. (2021) 'How should we understand the ambivalence of recognition? Revisiting the link between recognition and subjection in the works of Althusser and Butler', in J. Butler, A. Honneth, A. Allen, R. Celikates, J.-P. Deranty, H. Ikäheimo, et al, *Recognition and Ambivalence*. Columbia University Press, pp 129–159.

Levi, P. (1987 [1947]) *If This Is a Man*. Penguin.

Lévinas, E. (1969) *Totality and Infinity: An Essay on Exteriority*. Duquesne University Press.

Lloyd, M. (2007) *Judith Butler*. Polity.

Lora-Wainwright, A. (2021) *Resigned Activism: Living with Pollution in Rural China*. MIT Press.

Lorde, A. (1984) *Sister Outsider: Essays and Speeches*. Crossing Press.

MacIntyre, A. (2013) *Dependent Rational Animals: Why Human Beings Need the Virtues*. Bloomsbury.

Mackenzie, C., Rogers, W. and Dodds, S. (eds) (2013) *Vulnerability: New Essays in Ethics and Feminist Philosophy*. Oxford University Press.

Mahalingam, R., Jagannathan, S. and Selvaraj, P. (2019) 'Decasticization, dignity, and "dirty work" at the intersections of caste, memory, and disaster', *Business Ethics Quarterly* 29(2): 213–239.

Mandalaki, E. and Fotaki, M. (2020) 'The bodies of the commons: Towards a relational embodied ethics of the commons', *Journal of Business Ethics* 166: 745–760.

Mbembe, A. (2019) *Necropolitics*. Trans by S. Corcoran. Duke University Press.

Mbembe, A. (2020) 'The weight of life: On the economy of human lives', *Eurozine*, 6 July, https://www.eurozine.com/the-weight-of-life/

Mears, A. and Connell, C. (2015) 'The paradoxical value of deviant cases: Toward a gendered theory of display work', *Signs: Journal of Women in Culture and Society* 41(2): 334–359.

Merleau-Ponty, M. (1964) *The Primacy of Perception and Other Essays on Phenomenological Psychology, the Philosophy of Art, History and Politics*. Trans by C. Dallery. Northwestern University Press.

Merleau-Ponty, M. (1968) *The Visible and the Invisible*. Trans by A. Lingis. Northwestern University Press.

Merleau-Ponty, M. (2002 [1946]) *The Phenomenology of Perception*. Routledge.

Moro, V. (2022) 'Feminist archives: Narrating embodied vulnerabilities and practices of care', *Biblioteca della libertà* LVII, September–December, 235: 39–71.

Mulvey, L. (1975) 'Visual pleasure and narrative cinema', *Screen* 16(3): 6–18.

Murphy, R. (1987) *The Body Silent*. W.W. Norton.

Nancy, J.L. (1991) 'Introduction', in E. Cadava, P. Connor and J.L. Nancy (eds) *Who Comes After the Subject?* Routledge, pp 4–7.

Nava, M. (2007) *Visceral Cosmopolitanism: Gender, Culture and the Normalisation of Difference*. Berg.

Oxley, R. and Russell, A. (2020) 'Interdisciplinary perspectives on breath, body and world', *Body and Society* 26(2): 3–29.

Parker, M. (2020) 'Beginning, again', in M. Parker (ed) *Life After COVID-19: The Other Side of the Crisis*. Bristol University Press, pp 1–10.

Pateman, C. (1988) *The Sexual Contract*. Cambridge: Polity Press.

Pérezts, M., Fotaki, M., Shymko. Y. and Islam, G. (2024) 'Breathe and let breathe: Breathing as a political model of organizing', *Organization*: 1–18.

Pianezzi, D. (2025) *Corporeal Ethics for Feminist Work: (Dis)Organized Bodies*. Bristol University Press.

Pianezzi, D. and Tyler, M. (2025) 'Who's grave's this, sir? An ethico-political critique of burial sites as organizational settings', *Business Ethics Quarterly*.

Polányi, K. (2001 [1944]) *The Great Transformation: The Political and Economic Origins of Our Time*. Beacon Press.

Priestley, J.B. (2000 [1947]) *An Inspector Calls*. Penguin.

Pullen A. and Vachhani, S. (2020) 'Feminist ethics and women leaders: From difference to intercorporeality', *Journal of Business Ethics* 173: 233–243.

Raudon, S. (2022) 'Huddled masses: The shock of Hart Island, New York', *Human Remains and Violence* 8(1): 84–101.

Rees, A. (2020) 'Unclaimed and unknown: Examining Hart Island', *Relics, Remnants, and Religion* 5(1): 1–17.

Riach, K. (2025) *Working Through Ageing: Experiencing Growing Up and Older at Work*. Bristol University Press.

Ricoeur, P. (1983) 'On interpretation', in A. Montefiore (ed) *Philosophy in France Today*. Cambridge University Press, pp 175–197.

Sartre, J.-P. (1956) *Being and Nothingness: An Essay on Phenomenological Ontology*. Philosophical Library.

Sartre, J.-P. (1968) *The Reprieve*. Penguin.

Scheibmayr, I. (2024) 'Organizing vulnerability exploring Judith Butler's conceptualization of vulnerability to study organizations', *Gender, Work and Organization* 31(4): 1385–1408.

Scully, J.L. (2013) 'Disability and vulnerability: On bodies, dependence and power', in C. Mackenzie, W. Rogers and S. Dodds (eds) *Vulnerability: New Essays in Ethics and Feminist Philosophy*. Oxford University Press, pp 204–221.

Segal, L. (2018) *Radical Happiness: Moments of Collective Joy*. Verso.

Segal, L. (2023) *Lean on Me: A Politics of Radical Care*. Verso.

Shakespeare, T., Thompson, S., and Wright, M. (2010) 'No laughing matter: Medical and social experiences of restricted growth', *Scandinavian Journal of Disability Research* 12(1): 19–31.

Shepherd, D., Maitlis, S., Parida, V., Wincent, J. and Lawrence, T. (2022) 'Intersectionality in intractable dirty work: How Mumbai ragpickers make meaning of their work and lives', *Academy of Management Journal* 65(5): 1680–1708.

Shildrick, M. (2009) *Dangerous Discourses of Disability, Subjectivity and Sexuality*. Palgrave Macmillan.

Sloterdijk, P. (2009) *Terror from the Air*. Semiotext(e).

Sloterdijk, P. (2011) *Spheres, Volume 1: Microspherology*. Semiotext(e).

Smith, B.E. (1981) 'Black lung: The social production of disease', *International Journal of Health Services* 11(3): 343–359.

Smolović Jones, S. (2023) 'Gaslighting and dispelling: Experiences of non-governmental organization workers in navigating gendered corruption', *Human Relations* 76(6): 901–925.

Smolović Jones, S., Winchester, N. and Clarke, C. (2021) 'Feminist solidarity building as embodied agonism: An ethnographic account of a protest movement', *Gender, Work and Organization* 28(3): 917–934.

Stahl, T. (2021) 'Recognition, constitutive domination, and emancipation', in J. Butler, A. Honneth, A. Allen, R. Celikates, J.-P. Deranty, H. Ikäheimo, et al, *Recognition and Ambivalence*. Columbia University Press, pp 161–190.

Standing, G. (2014) *The Precariat: The Dangerous New Class*. Bloomsbury.

Stonebridge, L. (2025) *We are Free to Change the World: Hannah Arendt's Lessons in Love and Disobedience*. Vintage.

TallBear, K. (2019) 'Caretaking relations, not American dreaming', *Kalfou* 6(1).

Tronto, J. (1993) *Moral Boundaries: A Political Argument for an Ethic of Care*. Routledge.

Tronto, J. (2015) *Who Cares? How to Reshape a Democratic Politics*. Cornell University Press.

Turner, B.S. (2006) *Vulnerability and Human Rights*. Pennsylvania State University Press.

Tyler, M. (2019) 'Reassembling difference? Rethinking inclusion through/as embodied ethics', *Human Relations* 72(1): 48–68.

Vachhani, S. (2020) 'Envisioning a democratic culture of difference: Feminist ethics and the politics of dissent in social movements', *Journal of Business Ethics* 164: 745–757.

Vachhani, S. and Pullen, A. (2019) 'Ethics, politics and feminist organizing: Writing feminist infrapolitics and affective solidarity into everyday sexism', *Human Relations* 72(1): 23–47.

Varman, R. and Srinivas, N. (2025) 'Theorizing necroptics: Invisibilization of violence and death-worlds', *Organization* 32(1): 30–52.

Wall Kimmerer, R. (2013) *Braiding Sweetgrass: Indigenous Wisdom, Scientific Knowledge and the Teachings of Plants*. Penguin.

Wall Kimmerer, R. (2024) *The Serviceberry: An Economy of Gifts and Abundance*. Allen Lane.

Weber, M. (1968 [1930]) *The Protestant Ethic and the Spirit of Capitalism*. Unwin.

Woodford, C. (2021) 'Queer madonnas: In love and friendship', in T. Huzar and C. Woodford (eds) *Towards a Feminist Ethics of Nonviolence: Adriana Cavarero with Judith Butler, Bonnie Honig and Other Voices*. Fordham University Press, pp 161–176.

Worms, F. (2015) 'Pour un vitalisme critique', *Esprit* January (1): 15–29.

Young, I.M. (1997) 'Asymmetrical reciprocity: On moral respect, wonder and enlarged thought', in I.M. Young (ed) *Intersecting Voices: Dilemmas of Gender, Political Philosophy and Policy*. Princeton University Press, pp 38–59.

Zhang, E. (2022) '"I don't just want to look female; I want to be beautiful": Theorizing passing as labour in the transition vlogs of Gigi Gorgeous and Natalie Wynn', *Feminist Media Studies* 23(4): 1376–1391.

Index

References to figures appear in *italic* type. References to endnotes show both the page number and the note number (156n7).

A

abjection 36, 43
Adorno, T. 42, 119
Agamben, Giorgio 43
age, and breathing 52, 57
agency 4, 11, 17, 26, 42, 43, 45–46, 71, 92, 95, 97, 103, 118, 135
 collective 66, 116, 119, 120
 disabled people's 45, 46
 disavowal of 10, 92, 127–128
Ahmed, Sara 67
Ahmed, Shoaib 152n3
AIDS/HIV epidemic
 care models 131
 Hart Island interments 77, 82, 83, 84, 85
air pollution 8, 50, 52, 53, 55, 156n7
 see also breathing (existing)
'Alison Lapper Pregnant' statue (Marc Quinn) 109–110, *111*
Althusser, L. 61, 75, 81, 93, 96
anonymity 100–103
appearing (enacting) 9–11, 14, 90–93, 113–114, 117–118, 142
 anonymity and un/civil attention 100–103
 co-appearance 104, 105, 106, 110, 116–117, 122, 130, 133, 134, 137, 143
 looking 9–10, 11, 14, 90, 92, 99–101, 102–103, 108, 113
 normality, tyranny of 98–99
 spaces of appearance 10, 20, 92, 94, 103–105, 106, 107, 108, 111, 122, 123, 124, 131, 134, 137, 164n10
 spaces of/for solidarity 103–113
 staring 4, 9–10, 11, 14, 90, 92, 94–98, 99, 100–101, 102–103, 108, 113
 vulnerability, ocularity and subjectivity 93–94
Arendt, Hannah 15, 68, 73, 84, 93, 116, 148, 151n10
 appearing (enacting) 10–11, 14, 90, 103–105, 106, 107, 108, 111–112
 spaces of appearance 10, 20, 92, 94, 103–105, 106, 107, 108, 111, 122, 123, 124, 131, 134, 137, 164n10
 breathing (existing) 68–69
 and Butler 5, 10, 19, 28, 72, 92, 94, 103, 105, 106–107, 108, 111, 119, 120, 121, 123, 124, 125, 128, 134, 137, 139, 141, 149, 153n16, 154n27
 and Cavarero 19, 20, 21, 22, 70–71, 79, 80–81, 91, 92, 103, 104–106, 108, 111, 119, 120–122, 123, 124–125, 134, 149, 159n16, 159n18, 163n5, 163n6, 164n9, 164n10
 grieving (enduring) 70–71, 73, 79, 80–81
 'human condition' 1–4, 10, 43, 44, 69, 71, 73, 91, 122, 124, 138, 139, 151n11
 on labour 124–125
 nascent vulnerability 28, 93, 163n6
 organizing for workable lives 116, 119, 120, 121–122, 123, 124, 125, 128, 129, 130, 131, 134, 137, 139, 141
 on politics 121–123
'ascribed global vulnerabilities' 45–46
Ashcroft, Karen Lee 164n11
Ashley, Susan 88, 109, 162n16, 162n18
assembly 10, 11, 33, 68, 117, 121, 123–124, 131, 134
Athanasiou, Athena 12, 74, 95, 108
Auden, W.H. 151n10
autonomy 15, 18–19, 20, 31, 43, 44–45, 46, 57, 118–119, 142

B

Bahr, Mohammed 16–17
Bakhtin, M. 146
Barad, Karan 157n15
'bare life' 43–44
Barillas, Laure 33, 154n26, 154n27
Battersby, Christine 153n18
Bauman, Zygmunt 5, 164n16

176

INDEX

Beauvoir, Simone 152n7
Berardi, Franco 55, 155n2
Berger, John 95
Berlant, Lauren 149
Bernini, Lorenzo 153n18
Black Lives Matter 52, 91–92
borderization 2, 5, 6, 7, 12, 15, 22, 26, 37, 50, 51, 56–57, 59–60, 61, 62, 71, 86, 95, 117, 129, 130, 140
Boubil, E. 93
Braidotti, Rosi 150n6
breathing (existing) 4, 8, 11, 14, 49–50, 68–69, 117–118, 142
  and organizations 60–61
  phenomenological perspectives on 50, 51–54
  and radical vulnerability 60–68
  and recognition 49–50, 51–52, 53, 54, 55, 56–69
    'full' recognition 65, 127, 144–145
    reflexive forms of recognition 50, 64, 65–68, 127–128, 137, 143, 145
    reified forms of recognition 50, 63, 65, 69, 144
  respiratory poverty and precarity 8, 14, 49, 52, 118
  social inequalities in 50–51
  social organization of 49, 50–55, 69
  sociological perspectives on 50, 53–54
Brouwer, D. 77, 83, 84
Burnham, Clint 160n23
Butler, Judith 2, 5–6, 7, 12, 13, 23, 26, 27–31, 35, 93, 101, 117, 151n7, 157n15
  appearing (enacting) 10, 15, 90, 91, 92, 95, 96, 103, 105, 106–107, 108, 111, 112, 113
  and Arendt 5, 10, 19, 28, 72, 92, 94, 103, 105, 106–107, 108, 111, 119, 120, 121, 123, 124, 125, 128, 134, 137, 139, 141, 149, 153n16, 154n27
  breathing (existing) 50, 56, 57, 60, 62–63, 64, 137–138
  Force of Nonviolence, The 5, 6, 17, 37–42, 52, 57–58, 61, 71, 75–76, 78, 90, 106–107, 110, 113, 115, 117, 119, 122, 123, 128–129, 133, 142, 154n26, 154n30, 156n12
  grieving (enduring) 9, 37, 56, 69, 70–72, 75, 77–78, 80, 81–82, 86, 87, 88–89
    loss 72–74
  and Hegel 5, 29–30, 31, 34, 38, 40, 57–58, 61, 62–63, 64, 67, 72, 73, 74, 78, 81–82, 101, 105, 112, 126, 135, 136, 141–142, 143, 151n14, 157n13, 159n19, 159n20
  on the 'human condition' 27, 31, 77, 80, 124, 140
  on intelligibility 41, 62, 64, 93, 94, 144, 159n20

  on intersubjectivity 13, 33, 34, 35, 37, 74, 138, 141
  and Levinas 31, 89, 94
  on liveability/unliveability 17, 31–32, 33–34, 35–36, 116, 154n29
  on nonviolence 36–42, 128–129
  on organizing for workable lives 115, 117, 119, 120, 121, 123–124, 125, 126–127, 128–129, 131, 133, 134–143, 144, 145–146
  Precarious Life 12–13, 23, 27, 55, 72–74, 75, 88–89
  on precarity 19, 23, 27
Byers, Catriona 76–77, 85
Byron, Paul 131

C

care 18, 22–26
  care deficit 15, 69, 117, 129
  'carewashing' 129
  'caring consciousness' 26
  promiscuous care 129, 132, 143
  'taking care' 34
The Care Collective 23, 24, 36, 125, 134, 140, 143
The Care Manifesto 129–131, 132, 133, 141
'catching up' 148–149
Cavarero, Adriana 6, 7, 15, 22, 23, 43, 57, 70–71, 78, 93, 117, 123, 148, 151n7
  appearing (enacting) 90, 91, 92, 98, 100, 103, 104, 105–106, 107, 111
  and Arendt 19, 20, 21, 22, 70–71, 79, 80–81, 91, 92, 103, 104–106, 108, 111, 119, 120–122, 123, 124–125, 134, 149, 159n16, 159n18, 163n5, 163n6, 164n9, 164n10
  breathing (existing) 57
  grieving (enduring) 70–71, 79–81, 82, 83, 86
  'human condition', the 19, 20, 71, 80
  on inclination 18–22, 27, 28–29, 37, 38, 143
  and Levinas 6, 19, 21–22
  on narrative 79–81, 82, 83, 86, 105–106
  on organizing for workable lives 117, 119, 120–121, 122–123, 124–125, 133, 134, 143
  on surging democracy 120–121, 122, 164n10
Celikates, Robin 127
Charpentier, Arto 33, 154n26, 154n27
Chattri Indian war memorial, Brighton, UK 88, 109, 162n16
chrononormativity 39
civil in/attention 101–102
climate crisis 25, 50, 52, 69, 133
  see also air pollution
co-appearance 104, 105, 106, 110, 116–117, 122, 130, 133, 134, 137, 143
Collage Femicides, France 107–108, 109

177

colonialism 39, 56, 88, 151n8, 162n17
commemoration *see* grieving (enduring)
'contingent' vulnerabilities 45
corruption 146
Cortambert, Lucie 146–147
COVID-19 pandemic 11–12, 57, 87, 133–134, 138–139, 140
  and breathing 50, 52, 57, 58–59
  grievability 76
  Hart Island interments 77, 85
  health and social care workers 25–26, 65, 144, 157n14
Crimp, Douglas 131
critical race studies 43
critical social theory 18
critical vitalism 32–34, 36
Cutcher, L. 68

D

Dale, Karen 146–147, 161n7
Dartington, Tim 24
death
  and vulnerability 71
  see also grieving (enduring)
demonstration 106
de-narrativization 78–79
de-realization 60, 74, 76, 78, 89, 94, 95, 109
desire, and loss 70
'destructive inclination' 7
Devenney, Mark 2, 153n19
disability
  and breathing 57
  critical disability studies 43, 66
  disability activism 11, 24–25, 39, 44–46, 63–64
  and passing 102
  and staring 95, 98
disinclination 2, 7, 156n11
dispossession 72–74, 76, 157n7
  dispossessed people 11, 64, 75
Dutton, James 156n3

E

effacement 94
Ehrenreich, Barbara 25
ek-statis 13, 19, 30, 72, 93, 157n3
Elizabeth II, Queen 160n23
employee recognition schemes 64–75, 144
enacting *see* appearing (enacting)
enduring *see* grieving (enduring)
entrelac (interlacing) 138, 139, 140
Etzioni, Amitai 150n5
European Parliament 87
existential vulnerability 2, 72, 93, 141
existing *see* breathing (existing)

F

Fanon, Franz 41, 61, 66, 95, 145, 156n12
Fassin, Didier 154n27

feminism 6, 11, 15, 18, 119–120
feminist writing 15, 103
  on ethics and relationality 9, 11, 18, 42–43, 46, 48, 66, 72
  on gendered power relations 95
  on solidarity 46–47, 51, 66
  and vulnerability 2–3, 4–5, 6, 15, 17, 18, 29, 42, 67, 93, 114
Fineman, Martha 2
Floyd, George 91–92
Forti, Simona 164n12
Fotaki, Marianna 5, 46–47, 132, 147, 164n16
Foucault, Michel 41, 74, 95, 161n7
Freud, Sigmund 6, 23, 57, 73
Fromm, Eric 23

G

Garland-Thompson, Rosemarie 96–99, 100, 101, 102, 113
Gaza, Israel's war on 16–17
gender
  and breathing 52
  gender-based violence 119–120
Gerrard, Jessica 161n10
Gilroy, Paul 133
Gilson, E. 42
Goffman, Erving 101, 162n12
Górska, Magdalena 49, 52–53
grieving (enduring) 4, 8–9, 11, 14, 37, 56, 69, 70–72, 75, 77–78, 80, 81–82, 86, 87, 88–89, 117–118, 142
  and/as organization 71, 75–78
  and loss 72–74
  narration and memorialization 78–88
Guaraldo, Olivia 152n9
Guenther, Lisa 86, 87
Gullette, Margaret 25

H

Hancock, Philip 64–75, 144, 164n14
Harding, Anahita 163n19
Harding, Nancy 157n15
Hart Island, New York 76–78
  HIP (Hart Island Project) 82–87, 88, 162n18
Hegel, G.W.F. 29, 37, 67, 143, 154n22, 155n35, 157n5, 165n18
  and Butler 5, 29–30, 31, 34, 38, 40, 57–58, 61, 62–63, 64, 67, 72, 73, 74, 78, 81, 82, 101, 112, 126, 135, 136, 141–142, 143, 151n14, 157n13, 159n19, 159n20
Hindmarsh, J. 156n6
homeless people 146–147, 161n10, 162n15
Honig, Bonnie 28, 153n17, 153n18
Honneth, A. 32, 60, 61, 63, 65, 135, 136, 143, 144, 154n22, 159n20
hooks, bell 112–113
'horrorism' 91

INDEX

Howard, Neil 58–59, 61, 62
Howson, Peter 156n11
'human condition', the 2, 3, 6, 13, 23, 46, 48, 49, 60, 68, 110, 113
  Arendt on 1–4, 10, 43, 44, 69, 71, 73, 91, 122, 124, 138, 139, 151n11
  Butler on 27, 29, 31, 77, 80, 124, 140
  Cavarero on 19, 20, 71, 80
human rights legislation 150n4
Hunt, Melinda 82
  see also Hart Island, New York

I

identity struggles 15
Ikäheimo, Heikki 29
inclination 18–22, 37, 143
  and maternalism 21, 27, 28–29, 38
India
  COVID-19 pandemic 76
  influenza deaths, 1918 162n17
indigenous people
  recognition and rights 11, 43, 64
  United States 25
industrial air pollution 8, 50, 52, 53, 55, 156n7
influencers 10
  see also social media
Ingold, T. 61, 68
'inherent vulnerability' 3, 4, 45, 72
intelligibility 41, 94, 97
  Butler on 41, 62, 64, 93, 94, 144, 159n20
  cultural 60, 81, 157n7
  non-intelligibility 64, 143
interdependence 1, 2, 4, 6, 7, 11–12, 13, 14, 15, 20, 23, 31, 32, 35–36, 39, 46, 50, 51, 56, 60, 69, 71, 77–78, 81, 87, 99, 101, 114, 116, 117, 118, 119, 122, 131, 132, 138, 139, 140, 141–142
  mutual 5–6, 15, 20, 30, 34, 38, 42, 44, 45, 54, 58, 62, 65, 66, 68, 70, 72, 73, 88, 96, 103, 117, 121, 123, 125, 126, 128, 129, 134, 144, 145
International Women's Strike against gender-based violence 120
intersubjectivity 13, 33, 34, 35, 37, 74, 138, 141
invulnerability, myth of 1, 22, 29
Israel, war on Gaza 16–17

J

Jagannathan, S. 76
Jay, Martin 90
Johannson, J. 3
Jokela-Pansini, M. 53

K

Kaasila-Pakanen, A.-L. 42
Karpf, Anne 25
Keene, Michael 77
Kenny, Kate 145–146

Kittay, Eva Feder 155n36
Klein, Naomi 162n18
Kottman, P. 79
Kracauer, Siegfried 100

L

labour 124–125
Lapper, Alison 109–110, *111*, 144
Lasch, Christopher 162n11
Leopold, Kristina 126
Levi, Primo 150n2
Levinas, E. 130, 146, 154n24, 163n3
  and Butler 31, 89, 94
  and Cavarero 6, 19, 21–22, 31
  and Segal 23, 31
LGBTQIA+ communities 66, 86, 108, 120, 131, 158n10
Liebe Perla (film) 161n9
lifeworld 139
Lloyd, Moya 73–74
looking 9–10, 11, 14, 90, 92, 99–101, 102–103, 108, 113
  'look of recognition' 112–113
  see also appearing (enacting)
Lora-Wainright, Anna 55
Lorde, Audre 90

M

MacIntyre, Alistair 155n36
Mackenzie, C. 2, 3–4, 118–119, 150n4
Mahalingam, R. 79
'male gaze' 95
Mandalaki, Emmanouela 147
Margolles, Teresa 110, *112*
Mbembe, Achille 48, 66–67, 68, 95, 116, 145, 150n3, 151n2, 153n10
  necropolitics and borderization 5, 6, 7, 12, 22, 26, 37, 50, 51, 56–57, 59–60, 61, 62, 71, 86, 95, 117, 130
Merleau-Ponty, M. 8, 41, 51, 52, 67, 69, 115, 138, 139, 140, 141, 156n12
MeToo movement 52
migrant people 5, 43, 75, 87, 164n16
'Mil Veces Un Instante' (A Thousand Times in an Instant) (Margolles) 110, *112*
Militz, E. 53
'more than human' world 18
Moro, Valentina 22, 26, 36, 39–40, 91–92, 119–120, 125
Morris, C. 77, 83, 84
mourning *see* grieving (enduring)
Mulvey, Laura 95
Murphy, Robert 102
Musk, Elon 145
mutual interdependence 5–6, 15, 20, 30, 34, 38, 42, 44, 45, 54, 58, 62, 65, 66, 68, 70, 72, 73, 88, 96, 103, 117, 121, 123, 125, 126, 128, 129, 134, 144, 145

mutual recognition 7, 10, 22, 23, 24, 27, 30, 42, 46, 50, 51, 54, 60, 68–69, 78, 81–82, 92, 93, 102, 103, 107, 114, 116–117, 119, 120, 122, 125, 127, 131, 134, 143, 145, 146–147

N

nakedness 21, 22, 28
Nancy, Jean-Luc 162n13
narcissism 10, 100, 162n11
narration, grieving and commemoration 78–82
  HIP (Hart Island Project) 82–87, 88
nascent vulnerability 28, 93, 163n6
natality 19, 20, 73, 121
Nava, Mica 133
necropolitics 6, 12, 50, 51, 56, 59–60, 130
Ni Una Menos 119–120
non-intelligibility 64, 143
non-violence 36–42, 58, 106, 128–129
normality, tyranny of 98–99

O

ocularcentrism 9, 10, 90, 92, 93–94, 98, 99, 101, 102, 109
  see also appearing (enacting)
Olympic Games, Paris 2024 162n15
ontological vulnerability 29, 30, 48
ontology, and natality 20–21
organization 2, 11–15, 16–18, 115–119, 150n5
  labour and workability 124–125
  nonviolence, care and solidarity 128–134
  and radical vulnerability 141–147
  and recognition 117–118, 119, 122, 125, 126–139, 140, 142–145, 147, 148
  and relationality 119–124, 134–139
  for workable lives 115–149
Oxley, R. 54–55

P

Parker, Martin 133–134
particularistic vulnerability 26, 39–40, 42–43, 47
"passing" 102
paternalism 34, 40, 43–44, 45, 47, 58, 64, 65, 67, 68, 116, 118, 119, 126, 127, 145
'pathogenic vulnerabilities' 4, 119
Pelicot, Gisèle 107–108, 109
Pérezts, M. 55
performativity
  and gender 30–31
  of vulnerability 26
Pianezzi, Daniela 151n1, 153n15, 156n10
Pilnick, A. 156n6
Polis, the 103
political vulnerability 29–30
precarity, and loss 72–74
Priestley, J. B. 16

Q

Quinn, Marc 109–110, *111*

R

race, and breathing 52, 53
racism 41
  and staring 41, 61, 66, 95, 156n12
radical happiness 116, 149, 162n16, 165n21
radical vulnerability 2, 4, 11–15, 20, 25–26, 47, 116, 121, 125, 141–147
  and breathing 60–68
  organization for 141–147
Rai, R. 76
rationalization 98
Raudon, Sally 76, 77, 83, 158n11, 160n21
recitation 60, 64, 81, 127, 143
recognition 2–8, 9, 10–12, 14, 15, 17–18, 26, 33–34, 35, 36, 42–43, 46, 48, 126–128
  and appearing (enacting) 90, 92, 93, 94–95, 96, 97, 98, 99, 101–103, 105–106, 107, 109, 110, 112, 113, 114
  and breathing (existing) 49–50, 51–52, 53, 54, 55, 56–69
  'full' (affirmative) recognition 65, 127, 144–145
  reflexive forms of recognition 50, 64, 65–68, 127–128, 137, 143, 145
  reified forms of recognition 50, 63, 65, 69, 144
  and grieving (enduring) 70, 71, 72, 73, 74, 75–76, 78–79, 80–82, 84, 85–86, 87, 88, 89
  'moments' of 59, 62, 112, 131, 133, 149
  mutual 7, 10, 22, 23, 24, 27, 30, 42, 46, 50, 51, 54, 60, 68–69, 78, 81–82, 92, 93, 102, 103, 107, 114, 116–117, 119, 120, 122, 125, 127, 131, 134, 143, 145, 146–147
  organizing for 117–118, 119, 122, 125, 126–139, 140, 142–145, 147, 148
recognition-based solidarity 10, 11, 26, 31, 47, 128–134
  rhetorical/minimal form of 127
  and vulnerability 27–31
recognizability 13, 29–30, 40, 41, 50, 62–63, 64, 65–66, 67, 69, 74, 75, 93, 94, 96, 126, 127, 128, 135–136, 141, 142, 144, 145, 156n12, 157n5, 157n13, 159n17, 159n20
rectitude 18, 19, 20, 29, 38, 57, 152n8, 156n9
Rees, Abby 86, 87
refugees 75
  see also migrant people
relational ontology 6, 7, 15, 19, 21, 22, 23, 34
relationality 6–7
  and care 22
  ethics of 2, 15, 18, 37, 40, 47, 92, 106, 116, 141

INDEX

and organization 134–139
and vulnerability 119–124
respiration *see* breathing
Ricoeur, Paul 78
Russell, A. 54–55

S

Sartre, Jean-Paul 95–96, 97
Scheibmayr, Isabella 12
Scully, Jackie Leach 44–46
Segal, Lynne 6, 15, 36, 59, 82, 90, 116, 134, 138, 143, 147, 149, 162n16, 165n21
  on care 23–26
selfie culture 10, 100
self-mastery 15, 22
self-reliance 6, 24, 27, 44, 45, 58, 99
sexual categorization 152n8
sexual violence
  Gisèle Pelicot 107–108, 109
Shepherd, D. 151n7
Shildrick, Margrit 24
situational vulnerability 3–4, 48
skin 21, 22
Sloterdijk, Peter 53, 61, 156n3
Smith, Barbara Ellen 156n7
Smolović Jones, S. 66
social class, and breathing 52, 53
social death 86
social justice 5–6, 11, 15, 25, 26, 31, 47, 56, 113, 116, 117
social media 49, 100, 120, 129, 140, 146
social movements 119–120
social vulnerability 13, 30, 70
solidarity 18, 20, 23, 42, 46–47, 51–52, 66, 117, 118, 119, 125, 128, 137, 141, 145, 148, 149
  politics of 2, 26, 47, 92, 116
  post-recognition 64, 143
  recognition-based 10, 11, 26, 31, 47, 128–134
  spaces of/for 103–113
Srinivas, Nidhi 162n17
Stahl, Titus 154n21, 165n18
Standing, Guy 155n34
staring 4, 9–10, 11, 14, 90, 92, 94–98, 99, 100–101, 102–103, 108, 113
  see also appearing (enacting)
stigma 162n12
  Hart Island interments 77
surging democracy 120–121, 122, 164n10

T

'taking care' 34, 123
'taking place' 95, 108
TallBear, Kim 25
Tennyson, A. 70, 73
trans people 11, 43, 63–64, 102
  care models 131

Turkey 108
Tronto, Joan 22–23, 36, 116, 153n11
Trump, Donald 145, 146
Turkey, trans rights 108
Turner, B.S. 150n4

U

UNCAC (United Nations Convention Against Corruption) 146
United Nations, Breathe Life campaign 52
universalistic vulnerability 26, 39, 42–43, 47
'unliveable' life 18, 31–33, 35–36, 77–78, 126, 136
'uprightness' 6, 18–19, 20, 21
  Butler on 27–29

V

Vachhani, Sheena 147
Varman, Rohit 162n17
verticality 6, 18–19, 20, 21, 26, 27–29, 32, 38
vulnerability 12, 16–18, 47–48
  and care 18, 22–26
  ethics and politics of 42–47
  of non-violence 36–42
  and inclination 18–22
  labour and workability 124–125
  and liveability 17, 31–34
  and loss 72–74
  performativity of 26
  and recognition 27–31, 125, 126–128
  and relationality 119–124
  stigmatisation and abjection of 22
vulneraphobia 22, 25, 98, 142
vulnus ('wound', Latin) 2, 20, 22

W

Wall Kimmerer, Robin 54, 64
Weber, Max 98
whistleblower activism 145–146
Whistleblowing International Network 146
Wickström. A. 3
Williams, Tennessee 90
Woolf, Virginia 20
work 143
  and labour 124–125
workability 9, 11, 14, 124–125, 136, 149, 164n13
  organizing for workable lives 11–15, 115–149
Worms, Frédéric 32–34, 35–46, 116, 133, 154n29

Y

Young, Iris Marion 68

Z

Zochrot 162n18

www.ingramcontent.com/pod-product-compliance
Lightning Source LLC
Chambersburg PA
CBHW051548020426
42333CB00016B/2156